Christmas

Contents

GET SOCIAL WITH US!

 **LIKE US**
facebook.com/tasteofhome

 **PIN US**
pinterest.com/taste_of_home

 FOLLOW US
@tasteofhome

TWEET US
twitter.com/tasteofhome

To find a recipe
tasteofhome.com

To submit a recipe
tasteofhome.com/submit

**To find out about other
Taste of Home products**
shop.tasteofhome.com

Taste of Home

© 2023 RDA Enthusiast Brands, LLC.
1610 N. 2nd St., Suite 102, Milwaukee WI
53212-3906

All rights reserved. Taste of Home
is a registered trademark of
RDA Enthusiast Brands, LLC.

International Standard Book Number:
D 978-1-62145-964-4
U 978-1-62145-965-1
International Standard Serial Number: 1948-8386
Component Number:
D 119600112H
U 119600114H

INSTANT POT is a trademark of Double Insight Inc.
This publication has not been authorized, sponsored
or otherwise approved by Double Insight Inc.

Chief Content Officer, Home & Garden:
Jeanne Sidner
Content Director: Mark Hagen
Creative Director: Raeann Thompson
Senior Editor: Christine Rukavena
Editor: Hazel Wheaton
Senior Art Director: Courtney Lovetere
Art Director: Maggie Conners
Designer: Carrie Peterson
Deputy Editor, Copy Desk: Dulcie Shoener
Food Editor: Rashanda Cobbins

Cover:
Photographer: Dan Roberts
Food Stylist: Josh Rink
Set Stylist: Emiko Franzen

Pictured on front cover:
Super Holiday Cupcakes, p. 117

Pictured on back cover:
Overnight Reindeer Rolls, p. 133; Snowflake
Tomato Soup, p. 133; Cranberry-Stuffed Beef
Tenderloin, p. 27; Cran-Raspberry Pie, p. 190

Holly illustration:
Shutterstock/Leigh Prather

Printed in U.S.A.
1 3 5 7 9 10 8 6 4 2

MAKE YOUR CELEBRATIONS THE BEST EVER WITH *TASTE OF HOME CHRISTMAS*

1. SPIRITS OF THE SEASON
Raise a glass to Christmas and the New Year! Dazzling cocktails and sophisticated party foods let you toast the holidays in style.

2. HOP ABOARD THE HOLIDAY EXPRESS
Entertaining is easy with these recipes that combine convenience and elegance, from quick-prep dishes to make-ahead marvels.

3. BREAKFAST AT THE CABIN
When you want to evoke the feel of a rustic getaway far from the hustle and bustle, these dishes make for a hearty breakfast spread.

4. HOLIDAY FEASTS
Three complete menus—featuring prime rib, rack of lamb and turkey—make planning your grand feast a snap.

5. SEASONAL SIDE DISH CASSEROLES
Casseroles come together quickly and can be made in advance, so they fit perfectly into a busy holiday cooking schedule.

6. BOXING DAY LUNCHEON
Embrace the leftovers! Boxing Day is the day after Christmas—use these recipes to make second-day delicacies that are all first-rate.

7. CHRISTMAS CAKES
Decadent desserts, sweet snacks for house guests or perfect contributions to potlucks—there's a cake for every occasion here.

8. SEASONAL GET-TOGETHERS
Plan a holiday party for kids or a festive Mexico-themed celebration, or assemble a gorgeous charcuterie board.

3

4

5

9. BUON NATALE
Dip into the rich and inviting culture—and cuisine!—of Italy to create a holiday with a distinctive and unforgettable flavor.

10. CHOCOLATE COOKIES
Mixed into a rich dough, used as tempting filling or drizzled on top, chocolate has no match in making indulgent, delicious treats.

11. FOR THE LOVE OF RUM
Whether you're creating a cozy fireside feel or evoking a tropical escape, there's a place for rum throughout the holiday menu.

12. NIGHT OF PIES
Pies can be large or small, sweet or savory—and are always welcome. So why not celebrate with a menu full of pies?

13. MERRY BIRTHDAY!
December-birthday babies can get overlooked in the holiday rush. Here are recipes to help celebrate every part of their special day.

14. CHRISTMAS SNACK EXCHANGE
These tempting nibbles are perfect as party fare or as gifts—and with a snack exchange party, they can be both!

15. CHRISTMAS IN AN INSTANT POT®
During the busiest cooking season, this ultra convenient gadget cuts down on cooking time and frees up oven space.

15

16. HOLIDAY PLANNER
This handy guide will help you keep your preparations on track, preserve your memories of the season—and prepare for next year!

6

7

10

9

8

SPIRITS OF
THE SEASON

**Let's raise a glass to Christmas and the New Year!
These dazzling cocktails and sophisticated party foods
will help you and your guests toast the holidays in style.**

CHERRY CHEESECAKE CUPS

These delectable cups are always my home-baked contribution to our church's annual Christmas party. The holidays inspired the cheery garnish of cherries, and I often add mint leaves for even more seasonal color.
—*Leanne Beagley, Rochester, NY*

Prep: 20 min. • **Bake:** 35 min. + cooling
Makes: about 2 dozen

- 3 pkg. (8 oz. each) cream cheese, softened
- 1½ cups sugar, divided
- 1½ tsp. vanilla extract, divided
- 5 large eggs
- 1 cup sour cream
- 1½ cups cherry pie filling
  Mint leaves, optional

1. Preheat oven to 300°. In a large bowl, beat cream cheese, 1 cup sugar and 1 tsp. vanilla until smooth. Add eggs, 1 at a time, beating well after each addition.
2. Spoon into about 24 foil-lined muffin cups. Bake for 25-30 minutes or until a toothpick inserted in the center comes out clean. Cool for 5 minutes.
3. Combine sour cream and remaining ½ cup sugar and ½ tsp. vanilla until smooth. Spoon onto cups. Return to oven for 6-8 minutes or until set. Cool for 10 minutes before removing from pans to wire racks to cool completely.
4. Top with pie filling; garnish with mint if desired. Store in the refrigerator.
1 CHEESECAKE CUP: 202 cal., 13g fat (8g sat. fat), 82mg chol., 105mg sod., 18g carb. (17g sugars, 0 fiber), 4g pro.

ORANGE PISTACHIO COOKIES

I had never tried pistachios until I visited a friend who served me these cookies. I was in love! I made the recipe my own, and now my family can't get enough of them.
—*Lorraine Caland, Shuniah, ON*

Prep: 20 min. + chilling
Bake: 10 min./batch + cooling
Makes: about 4½ dozen

- ¾ cup butter, softened
- 1 cup sugar
- 1 large egg, room temperature
- 1 Tbsp. grated orange zest
- 1 tsp. vanilla extract
- 2 cups all-purpose flour
- ¼ cup cornstarch
- ½ cup pistachios, toasted and finely chopped

ICING
- 2¼ cups confectioners' sugar
- ¼ cup orange juice
- 1 Tbsp. butter, melted
  Additional pistachios, toasted and finely chopped, optional

1. In a large bowl, cream butter and sugar until light and fluffy, 5-7 minutes. Beat in egg, orange zest and vanilla. In another bowl, whisk flour and cornstarch; gradually beat into the creamed mixture.
2. Divide dough in half. Shape each portion roughly into a 7-in. roll along the long end of a 14x8-in. sheet of waxed paper. Tightly roll waxed paper over dough, using the waxed paper to mold the dough into a smooth roll. Place waxed paper-wrapped roll in an airtight container; freeze 30 minutes or until firm, or refrigerate overnight.
3. Preheat oven to 350°. Set out dough at room temperature until the surface is soft. Sprinkle pistachios on a rimmed baking sheet. Unwrap and roll each roll of dough in pistachios. Cut dough crosswise into ¼-in. slices. Place slices ½ in. apart on parchment-lined baking sheets. Bake 6-8 minutes or until bottoms are light brown. Cool slightly on pan, then remove to wire racks to cool completely.
4. In a small bowl, combine confectioners' sugar, orange juice and butter until smooth. Spread over cookies. If desired, sprinkle with additional pistachios. Let stand until set.
NOTE: To toast nuts, bake in a shallow pan in a 350° oven for 5-10 minutes or cook in a skillet over low heat until lightly browned, stirring occasionally.
1 COOKIE: 83 cal., 3g fat (2g sat. fat), 10mg chol., 27mg sod., 13g carb. (9g sugars, 0 fiber), 1g pro.

DIABLO MARGARITA

This spicy margarita is a favorite among my friends!
They rave about it whenever I serve it at any occasion.
—*Lisa Tripp, Los Gatos, CA*

Takes: 5 min. • **Makes:** 1 serving

- 1 lime wedge, optional
- Smoked salt, optional
- Ice cubes
- ½ Anaheim pepper with seeds, roughly chopped
- 2 oz. tequila
- 3 Tbsp. fresh lime juice
- ¾ oz. maple syrup

1. If desired, moisten rim of a cocktail glass with lime wedge; place salt on a plate and dip rim in salt. Fill glass with ice.
2. In an empty shaker, muddle pepper. Fill shaker three-fourths full with ice. Add remaining ingredients; cover and shake until condensation forms on the outside of shaker, 10-15 seconds. Strain into prepared glass.

1 SERVING: 228 cal., 0 fat (0 sat. fat), 0 chol., 10mg sod., 26g carb. (20g sugars, 1g fiber), 1g pro.

HOLIDAY HELPER

Smoked salt is exactly what it sounds like—salt that has been smoked to create a rich, smoky flavor. If you can't find it in your grocery store, check specialty food shops or online. If you have a home smoker, you can make your own, starting with coarse kosher or sea salt.

POMEGRANATE MACADAMIA CHEESE BALL

Cheese balls are a common sight during the holidays, but this one earns points for being posh. It's creamy, sweet, spicy and studded with pecans and pomegranate seeds. We scoop it up with pita chips, but it can also be served with chutney, jam or high-quality crackers.
—*Nancy Heishman, Las Vegas, NV*

Prep: 25 min. + chilling • **Makes:** 4½ cups

- 2 pkg. (8 oz. each) cream cheese, softened
- 2 cups shredded smoked white cheddar cheese
- ½ cup crumbled goat cheese
- 2 garlic cloves, minced
- ½ tsp. salt
- ½ tsp. cayenne pepper
- ¼ cup dried cranberries, minced
- 2 Tbsp. white wine
- 1 can (8 oz.) crushed pineapple, drained and patted dry
- 1 cup finely chopped macadamia nuts, divided
- 4 Tbsp. minced fresh chives, divided
- 1 cup pomegranate seeds
- Baked pita chips or assorted crackers

1. Beat the first 6 ingredients until blended. Beat in cranberries and wine. Stir in pineapple, ½ cup macadamia nuts and 3 Tbsp. chives. Refrigerate, covered, for 30 minutes.
2. In a shallow bowl, toss pomegranate seeds and remaining ½ cup chopped nuts. Shape cheese mixture into a ball; roll in seed mixture. Wrap and refrigerate 1 hour or overnight.
3. Unwrap ball; roll in the remaining 1 Tbsp. chives. Serve with pita chips.

2 TBSP.: 117 cal., 10g fat (5g sat. fat), 22mg chol., 141mg sod., 4g carb. (3g sugars, 1g fiber), 3g pro.

CINNAMON ROLL MACARONS

These macarons are a fall and winter staple for me. Inspired by the classic cinnamon roll, they are a treat for a cold or snowy day. These can be eaten as a party dessert or just an indulgent snack. Other fillings would taste great with this recipe—custard, mousse, ganache or other buttercream.
—*Elizabeth Ding, El Cerrito, CA*

Prep: 45 min. • **Bake:** 10 min./batch
Makes: 5 dozen

- 4 large egg whites
- 1½ cups almond flour
- 1¼ cups confectioners' sugar
- ½ tsp. ground cinnamon
- ¾ cup sugar

FILLING

- 4 oz. cream cheese, softened
- 3 Tbsp. butter, softened
- 1 tsp. vanilla extract
- 1½ cups confectioners' sugar
  Additional ground cinnamon

1. Place egg whites in a small bowl; let stand at room temperature for 30 minutes. Sift almond flour, 1¼ cups confectioners' sugar and cinnamon together twice.
2. Preheat oven to 325°. Beat egg whites on medium speed until soft peaks form. Gradually add sugar, 1 Tbsp. at a time, beating on high until stiff peaks form. Fold in almond flour mixture.
3. With a pastry bag, pipe 1-in.-diameter cookies 2 in. apart onto parchment-lined baking sheets. Bake until lightly browned and firm to the touch, 9-12 minutes. Keeping cookies on the parchment, transfer to wire racks; cool completely.
4. For filling, in a small bowl, beat cream cheese and butter until creamy. Beat in vanilla. Gradually beat in confectioners' sugar until fluffy. Refrigerate until the mixture firms to a spreading consistency, about 10 minutes.
5. Spread about ¼ tsp. filling onto the bottom of each of half of the cookies; top with the remaining cookies. Sprinkle with additional cinnamon. Store in airtight containers in the refrigerator.
1 COOKIE: 60 cal., 3g fat (1g sat. fat), 3mg chol., 15mg sod., 9g carb. (8g sugars, 0 fiber), 1g pro.

CRANBERRY ENDIVE APPETIZERS

You can pack a lot of flavor into an elegant appetizer just by using the right combination of ingredients. I created this blue cheese filling for a holiday gathering and everyone loved it.
—*Margee Berry, White Salmon, WA*

Takes: 20 min. • **Makes:** 2 dozen

- 4 oz. cream cheese, softened
- 2 Tbsp. apple jelly
- ⅓ cup crumbled blue cheese
- ¼ cup dried cranberries, chopped
- 24 leaves Belgian endive
- ¼ cup chopped pecans, toasted

In a large bowl, beat cream cheese and jelly until smooth. Stir in blue cheese and cranberries. Spoon 1-2 heaping teaspoonfuls onto each endive leaf. Sprinkle with pecans.
1 APPETIZER: 40 cal., 3g fat (1g sat. fat), 7mg chol., 41mg sod., 3g carb. (2g sugars, 0 fiber), 1g pro.

APPLE CIDER SMASH

A smash is a fruity and chilled cocktail—very refreshing! This sparkling apple creation is a delicious cocktail for the fall and winter holidays.
—*Moffat Frazier, New York, NY*

Takes: 20 min. • **Makes:** 16 servings

- 2 cups finely chopped Gala or other red apples (about 2 small)
- 2 cups finely chopped Granny Smith apples (about 2 small)
- 2½ cups bourbon
- ⅔ cup apple brandy
- 4 tsp. lemon juice
  Ice cubes
- 5⅓ cups chilled sparkling apple cider

1. In a bowl, toss apples to combine. In a small pitcher, mix bourbon, brandy and lemon juice.
2. To serve, fill each of 16 rocks glasses halfway with ice. To each, add ¼ cup apple mixture and 3 Tbsp. bourbon mixture; top with ⅓ cup cider.
¾ CUP: 152 cal., 0 fat (0 sat. fat), 0 chol., 3mg sod., 13g carb. (11g sugars, 1g fiber), 0 pro.

LAVENDER & OLIVE FOCACCIA

Lavender imparts a delicate flavor to this homemade focaccia. It reminds me of my trips to Italy, and eating it brings back the relaxed vacation mood.
—*Sherry Haddox, Austin, TX*

Prep: 30 min. + rising • **Bake:** 25 min.
Makes: 2 loaves (8 wedges each)

- 1 pkg. (¼ oz.) active dry yeast
- 1⅔ cups warm water (110° to 115°), divided
- 1 Tbsp. honey
- 6 Tbsp. olive oil, divided
- 2 tsp. salt
- 4 to 5 cups all-purpose flour
- 15 Greek olives, chopped
- 1 Tbsp. dried lavender flowers
- 1 garlic clove, minced
- 1 tsp. kosher salt

1. In a large bowl, dissolve yeast in ½ cup warm water. Stir in the honey; let stand for 5 minutes. Add 4 Tbsp. oil, salt and remaining warm water. Add 2 cups flour; beat until smooth. Stir in enough of the remaining flour to form a soft dough.
2. Turn dough onto a lightly floured surface; knead until smooth and elastic, 6-8 minutes. Place in a large greased bowl, turning once to grease top. Cover and let rise in a warm place until doubled, about 1 hour.
3. Punch dough down; divide in half. Cover and let rest for 10 minutes. Shape each portion into a 9-in. circle. Place on greased baking sheets. Cover and let rise until doubled, about 30 minutes.
4. Using the end of a wooden spoon handle, make several ¼-in. indentations in each loaf. Combine the olives, lavender, garlic and remaining 2 Tbsp. oil; brush over loaves. Sprinkle with kosher salt.
5. Bake at 375° for 25-30 minutes or until golden brown. Remove from pans to wire racks. Serve warm.
NOTE: Look for dried lavender flowers in spice shops. If using lavender from the garden, make sure it hasn't been treated with chemicals.
1 WEDGE: 174 cal., 6g fat (1g sat. fat), 0 chol., 471mg sod., 26g carb. (2g sugars, 1g fiber), 3g pro.

POM-BERRY MARTINI

This festive cocktail is so easy to make during the holiday season. It gets everyone in a merry party mood!
—*Renee Page, Rochelle, IL*

Takes: 15 min. • **Makes:** 2 servings

- Ice cubes
- 3 oz. vodka
- 3 oz. pomegranate juice
- 1½ oz. cranberry juice
- 1 oz. grenadine syrup
- 2 Tbsp. fresh lime juice
- Lime slices, optional

Fill a shaker three-fourths full with ice; add all remaining ingredients. Cover and shake until condensation forms on outside of shaker, 10-15 seconds. Strain into chilled martini glasses. If desired, garnish with lime slice.

1 SERVING: 167 cal., 0 fat (0 sat. fat), 0 chol., 9mg sod., 18g carb. (17g sugars, 1g fiber), 0 pro.

HOLIDAY HELPER

If you don't have a cocktail shaker, the quickest and most effective substitution is a Mason jar. The lid and screw-on ring create a leakproof seal that will keep the contents safely inside while shaking. Plus, the flat lid can be positioned off-center against the top of the jar to hold back the ice while you're pouring.

CRAB & CHEESE SPIRALS

I came across a similar cheese roll recipe and started trying different combinations to come up with these spirals. They're very popular during the holidays, and I just can't seem to make enough of them!
—*Lisa Harke, Old Monroe, MO*

Prep: 20 min. • **Bake:** 15 min. • **Makes:** 2½ dozen

- 2 pkg. (8 oz. each) cream cheese, softened
- 2 cups chopped imitation crabmeat
- 1 can (4¼ oz.) chopped ripe olives
- ¼ cup minced chives
- 3 tubes (8 oz. each) refrigerated crescent rolls
- ¾ cup shredded part-skim mozzarella cheese
- ¾ cup shredded Parmesan cheese

1. Preheat oven to 375°. In a small bowl, beat cream cheese, crab, olives and chives. Unroll 1 tube of crescent dough into 1 long rectangle; seal seams and perforations.
2. Spread with 1 cup crab mixture; sprinkle with ¼ cup of each cheese. Roll up jelly-roll style, starting with a long side; pinch seam to seal.
3. Using a serrated knife, cut into 10 slices; place cut side down on a greased baking sheet. Repeat with remaining crescent dough, crab mixture and cheeses.
4. Bake 14-16 minutes or until golden brown. Serve warm.
1 APPETIZER: 173 cal., 12g fat (5g sat. fat), 21mg chol., 368mg sod., 11g carb. (2g sugars, 0 fiber), 5g pro.

BACON-PECAN STUFFED MUSHROOMS

During the remodeling of my kitchen, I lost the recipe for these mushrooms. Luckily, I'd shared it so many times I had no trouble finding someone to give it back to me!
—*Beverly Pierce, Indianola, MS*

Takes: 30 min. • **Makes:** 1 dozen

- 4 Tbsp. butter, divided
- 2 Tbsp. canola oil
- 12 large fresh mushrooms (about 1 lb.), stems removed
- ¼ tsp. salt
- 2 Tbsp. finely chopped onion
- 1 cup soft bread crumbs
- 6 bacon strips, cooked and crumbled
- 2 Tbsp. chopped pecans
- 2 Tbsp. sherry or beef broth
- 2 Tbsp. sour cream
- 2 Tbsp. minced fresh chives

1. Preheat broiler. In a large skillet, heat 2 Tbsp. butter and the oil over medium-high heat. Add mushroom caps; cook for 2 minutes on each side. Sprinkle with salt. Remove with tongs; drain on paper towels, stem side down.
2. In same pan, heat remaining 2 Tbsp. butter over medium-high heat. Add onion; cook and stir until tender. Remove from heat; stir in remaining ingredients. Spoon into mushroom caps.
3. Place on a broiler pan. Broil 5 in. from heat 2-3 minutes or until filling is browned.
NOTE: To make soft bread crumbs, tear bread into pieces and place in a food processor or blender. Cover and pulse until crumbs form. One slice of bread yields ½-¾ cup crumbs.
1 STUFFED MUSHROOM: 184 cal., 16g fat (6g sat. fat), 25mg chol., 277mg sod., 7g carb. (2g sugars, 1g fiber), 5g pro.

BUDGET-FRIENDLY CHAMPAGNE ALTERNATIVES

A bottle of bubbly is an iconic marker of special occasions and always a solid choice for a sophisticated holiday party. However, your budget may not allow for a premium Champagne. Don't despair!

By definition, Champagne is French ... because it comes from the Champagne region in France. All other sparkling wines must go by other names—and many will have lower price tags.

If you're looking for non-French Champagne-style wine, check the label for the words "methode Champenoise" or "methode traditionnelle." This indicates the wine was made using the same double-fermentation method used to make Champagne. Spanish cavas as well as many California sparkling wines fall under this category.

Other sparkling wines use a faster, single-fermentation method. Italian Proseccos and lambruscos both use this "tank" method and deliver a fresh, drinkable wine that will not break your budget.

BISCOCHITO MARTINI

This sweetly delightful cocktail tastes as if you were taking a big bite of a fresh homemade cookie—without the crunch. Make sure you shake the martini well.
—*Letitia Montoya, Santa Fe, NM*

Takes: 5 min. • **Makes:** 1 serving

    Optional: Honey and biscochito
    cookie crumbs
    Ice cubes
1½ oz. vanilla vodka
1½ oz. RumChata liqueur
1 oz. anise liqueur

1. If desired, place honey on a plate and crushed cookies on second plate. Holding chilled glass upside down, dip the rim into honey, then into crushed cookie crumbs.

2. Fill a shaker three-fourths full with ice. Add vodka and liqueurs; cover and shake until condensation forms on outside of shaker, 10-15 seconds. Strain into prepared glass.

1 SERVING: 347 cal., 17g fat (10g sat. fat), 61mg chol., 17mg sod., 6g carb. (0 sugars, 0 fiber), 1g pro.

HOLIDAY HELPER ✳☆★

A shortbread-like cookie with a dose of anise, orange and cinnamon, the biscochito is the state cookie of New Mexico. Depending on where you live, they can be difficult to find—unless you make your own! If you can't find biscochitos in your neck of the woods, you can substitute another cookie to dip the rim in, such as a shortbread, snickerdoodle or crunchy vanilla wafer.

ASIAGO BEEF TART

I love simple recipes that are fancy enough for guests. To get a velvety texture in this tart, I use creme fraiche, but sour cream works, too.
—*Veronica Callaghan, Glastonbury, CT*

Prep: 25 min. • **Bake:** 15 min.
Makes: 16 servings

- 1 sheet refrigerated pie crust
- ¾ lb. lean ground beef (90% lean)
- 1 shallot, finely chopped
- 2 large eggs
- ¾ cup sour cream
- ½ tsp. salt
- ¼ tsp. pepper
- ¾ cup shredded part-skim mozzarella cheese
- ⅔ cup shredded Asiago cheese
- ⅓ cup oil-packed sun-dried tomatoes, coarsely chopped
- ¼ cup coarsely chopped fresh basil
- 1 tsp. minced fresh rosemary or ¼ tsp. dried rosemary, crushed

TOPPINGS
- 2 Tbsp. pine nuts, toasted
  Thinly sliced fresh basil, optional

1. Preheat oven to 400°. On a clean work surface, unroll crust; roll to a 12-in. circle. Press crust onto bottom and up sides of an ungreased 11-in. tart pan with removable bottom. Refrigerate crust while preparing filling.
2. In a large skillet, cook beef and shallot over medium heat until beef is no longer pink, 5-7 minutes, breaking up beef into crumbles. Remove from heat.
3. In a small bowl, whisk eggs, sour cream, salt and pepper until blended. Stir in cheeses, sun-dried tomatoes, chopped basil and rosemary. Stir into beef mixture; pour into the tart shell.
4. Bake on a lower oven rack until the crust is golden brown and filling is set, 15-20 minutes. Just before serving, add pine nuts and, if desired, sliced basil.
NOTE: To toast nuts, cook in a skillet over low heat until lightly browned, stirring occasionally.
1 PIECE: 172 cal., 11g fat (5g sat. fat), 54mg chol., 202mg sod., 9g carb. (1g sugars, 0 fiber), 9g pro.

SEAFOOD CAKES WITH HERB SAUCE

Living near the ocean, I have a wide variety of seafood available. This recipe uses salmon and scallops, but shrimp, crab, lobster or any firm whitefish (halibut or cod) would work as well.
—*Elizabeth Truesdell, Petaluma, CA*

Prep: 65 min. • **Bake:** 5 min./batch
Makes: 40 appetizers (½ cup sauce)

- ¾ cup mayonnaise
- 4½ tsp. dill pickle relish
- 1 Tbsp. minced chives
- 1 Tbsp. minced fresh parsley
- 2 tsp. tomato paste
- 1 tsp. grated lemon zest
- ⅛ tsp. salt
- ⅛ tsp. pepper

SEAFOOD CAKES
- 1¼ cups panko bread crumbs
- 1 medium sweet red pepper, finely chopped
- 1 medium sweet yellow pepper, finely chopped
- ⅓ cup finely chopped onion
- 1 large egg, lightly beaten
- 2 Tbsp. minced fresh parsley
- 2 tsp. minced chives
- 1 lb. bay scallops, coarsely chopped
- ½ lb. salmon fillet, skin removed and coarsely chopped
- ⅔ cup butter, cubed
  Additional finely chopped sweet red and yellow peppers and minced chives

1. Preheat oven to 400°. Combine the first 8 ingredients; set aside ¼ cup. Chill the remaining sauce until serving.
2. In a large bowl, combine panko bread crumbs, peppers, onion, egg, parsley, chives and the ¼ cup sauce. Gently fold in scallops and salmon.
3. With floured hands, shape mixture by 2 tablespoonfuls into ½-in.-thick patties. In a large skillet over medium heat, cook patties in butter in batches until golden brown, 2-3 minutes on each side. Transfer to ungreased baking sheets.
4. Bake until golden brown, 5-6 minutes. Serve with sauce. Garnish with additional peppers and chives.
1 SEAFOOD CAKE WITH ABOUT ½ TSP. SAUCE: 88 cal., 7g fat (3g sat. fat), 21mg chol., 86mg sod., 2g carb. (1g sugars, 0 fiber), 3g pro.

FIRECRACKER SHRIMP WITH CRANPOTLE DIPPING SAUCE

Bacon-wrapped shrimp are always a big hit at my parties. I like to serve mine with a little bit of heat and tang. This recipe is simple to make, so it's an amazing—and convenient—appetizer.
—*Suzanne Forsberg, Manteca, CA*

Prep: 30 min. • **Grill:** 10 min.
Makes: 20 appetizers (1 cup sauce)

- ½ cup whole-berry cranberry sauce
- ¼ cup canola oil
- 3 Tbsp. lemon juice
- 1 tsp. Dijon mustard
- 2 chipotle peppers in adobo sauce, chopped
- 1 garlic clove, minced
- ½ tsp. crushed red pepper flakes
- ¼ tsp. cayenne pepper
- 10 bacon strips
- 20 uncooked jumbo shrimp, peeled and deveined (tails on)

1. For sauce, place first 8 ingredients in a blender; cover and blend until smooth, about 30 seconds. Transfer to a small bowl; cover and refrigerate until serving.
2. Cut each bacon strip in half widthwise. In a large skillet, cook the bacon over medium heat until partially cooked but not crisp. Remove to paper towels to drain. Wrap a piece of bacon around each shrimp; thread onto metal or soaked wooden skewers.
3. Grill, covered, on a lightly oiled grill rack over medium heat or broil 4 in. from the heat until shrimp turn pink and bacon is crisp, 3-5 minutes on each side. Serve with dipping sauce.
NOTE: Chipotle is a smoked and dried jalapeno pepper originating in the area surrounding Mexico City. Often found canned in a chili sauce in the United States, chipotles are medium to hot in heat levels and are used in a variety of Mexican and American dishes that require a hot, spicy flavor.
1 WRAPPED SHRIMP WITH 2¼ TSP. SAUCE: 110 cal., 8g fat (2g sat. fat), 39mg chol., 142mg sod., 3g carb. (2g sugars, 0 fiber), 5g pro.

CRAN-APPLE PRALINE GINGERBREAD

Start with a spice-rich batter baked atop apples and cranberries in a caramel sauce, then invert for a beautiful topsy-turvy dessert. The old-time holiday taste will delight family and friends!
—*Jeanne Holt, St. Paul, MN*

Prep: 25 min. • **Bake:** 30 min. + cooling
Makes: 8 servings

- ⅔ cup fat-free caramel ice cream topping
- 2 medium tart apples, peeled and thinly sliced
- ⅔ cup fresh or frozen cranberries
- ¼ cup butter, softened
- ¼ cup sugar
- 1 large egg
- 6 Tbsp. molasses
- ¼ cup unsweetened applesauce
- 1½ cups all-purpose flour
- ¾ tsp. baking soda
- ½ tsp. ground ginger
- ½ tsp. apple pie spice
- ¼ tsp. salt
- ¼ cup hot water

YOGURT CREAM
- ¾ cup reduced-fat whipped topping
- ½ cup fat-free vanilla yogurt

1. Preheat oven to 350°. Coat a 9-in. round baking pan with cooking spray. Pour caramel topping into pan and tilt to coat bottom evenly. Arrange apples and cranberries in a single layer over the caramel.
2. In a large bowl, beat the butter and sugar until crumbly, about 2 minutes. Add egg; mix well. Beat in molasses and applesauce (mixture may appear curdled). Combine the flour, baking soda, ginger, pie spice and salt; add to the butter mixture just until moistened. Stir in hot water.
3. Pour over fruit; smooth top. Bake for 30-35 minutes or until a toothpick inserted in the center comes out clean. Cool for 10 minutes before inverting onto a serving plate.
4. Combine whipped topping and yogurt; serve with gingerbread.
1 PIECE WITH 2 TBSP. CREAM: 289 cal., 7g fat (5g sat. fat), 42mg chol., 284mg sod., 53g carb. (28g sugars, 2g fiber), 4g pro.

ROASTED GRAPE CROSTINI

A trip to Spain introduced me to its culinary treasures, like Manchego cheese and sherry. This appetizer always impresses folks who've never tasted roasted grapes. They're amazing!
—*Janice Elder, Charlotte, NC*

Prep: 35 min. • **Broil:** 5 min. • **Makes:** 2 dozen

- 3 cups seedless red or green grapes, halved lengthwise
- 2 Tbsp. sherry vinegar or rice vinegar
- 2 Tbsp. olive oil
- ½ tsp. salt
- ¼ tsp. freshly ground pepper
- 1 tsp. grated orange zest
- 24 slices French bread baguette (cut diagonally ½ in. thick)
- ½ cup shaved Manchego or Romano cheese
  Thinly sliced fresh basil leaves

1. Preheat oven to 400°. Toss the first 5 ingredients; spread in a greased 15x10x1-in. pan. Roast until grapes are lightly browned and softened, 30-35 minutes. Stir in orange zest.
2. Preheat broiler. Arrange bread slices on an ungreased baking sheet. Broil 3-4 in. from heat until lightly browned, 1-2 minutes per side. Top with warm grape mixture; sprinkle with cheese and basil.

1 APPETIZER: 52 cal., 2g fat (1g sat. fat), 2mg chol., 110mg sod., 8g carb. (3g sugars, 0 fiber), 1g pro. **DIABETIC EXCHANGES:** ½ starch, ½ fat.

MINI SAUSAGE BUNDLES

These savory hors d'oeuvres cut the fat as well as cleanup by eliminating the need for a deep fryer.
—*Taste of Home Test Kitchen*

Prep: 25 min. • **Bake:** 10 min. • **Makes:** 1 dozen

- ½ lb. turkey Italian sausage links, casings removed
- 1 small onion, finely chopped
- ¼ cup finely chopped sweet red pepper
- 1 garlic clove, minced
- ½ cup shredded cheddar cheese
- 12 sheets phyllo dough (14x9-in. size)
  Cooking spray
- 12 whole chives, optional

1. Preheat oven to 425°. In a large skillet, cook and crumble sausage with onion, red pepper and garlic over medium-high heat until no longer pink, 4-6 minutes. Stir in cheese; let cool slightly.
2. Place 1 sheet of phyllo dough on a work surface; spritz with cooking spray. Layer with 2 additional phyllo sheets, spritzing each layer. (Keep remaining phyllo covered with a damp towel to prevent it from drying out.) Cut phyllo crosswise into 3 strips (about 4½ in. wide).
3. Place 1 rounded Tbsp. sausage mixture near the end of each strip. Fold end of strip over filling, then fold in sides and roll up. Place on an ungreased baking sheet, seam side down. Repeat with remaining phyllo and filling.
4. Bake until lightly browned, 8-10 minutes. If desired, tie bundles with chives. Serve warm.

1 APPETIZER: 74 cal., 3g fat (1g sat. fat), 12mg chol., 154mg sod., 7g carb. (1g sugars, 0 fiber), 4g pro. **DIABETIC EXCHANGES:** 1 lean meat, ½ starch.

SWEET & SPICY ASIAN CHICKEN PETITES

Using crescent roll dough and two types of chili sauce, I came up with these irresistible chicken bites. Freeze a batch to reheat when you have drop-in guests.
—*Jeanette Nelson, Bridgeport, WV*

Prep: 25 min. • **Bake:** 10 min.
Makes: 16 appetizers

- 4 tsp. olive oil, divided
- ⅓ cup finely chopped sweet red pepper
- 3 green onions, finely chopped
- 2 garlic cloves, minced
- 1 cup finely chopped cooked chicken breast
- 2 Tbsp. island teriyaki sauce
- 1 Tbsp. white grapefruit juice or water
- 1 Tbsp. sesame oil
- 1 tsp. Sriracha chili sauce
- 1 tube (8 oz.) refrigerated crescent rolls
- 2 tsp. sesame seeds
  Sweet chili sauce

1. Preheat oven to 375°. In a large skillet, heat 2 tsp. olive oil over medium-high heat. Add red pepper, green onions and garlic; cook and stir until vegetables are tender, 3-5 minutes. Stir in chicken, teriyaki sauce, grapefruit juice, sesame oil and chili sauce. Remove from heat; cool slightly.
2. Unroll crescent dough into 1 long rectangle; press perforations to seal. Roll dough into a 12-in. square; cut into sixteen 3-in. squares. Place 1 Tbsp. chicken mixture in the center of each square. Bring edges of dough over filling, pinching seams to seal; shape into a ball.
3. Place balls on ungreased baking sheets, seam side down. Brush tops with the remaining 2 tsp. olive oil; sprinkle with sesame seeds. Bake until golden brown, 10-12 minutes. Serve warm with sweet chili sauce.
FREEZE OPTION: Freeze cooled appetizers in an airtight container. To use, reheat desired number of appetizers on a baking sheet in a preheated 375° oven until heated through.
1 APPETIZER: 97 cal., 5g fat (1g sat. fat), 7mg chol., 199mg sod., 8g carb. (2g sugars, 0 fiber), 4g pro.

BAKED FIGS

Here's a nice change from the traditional savory party offerings. To keep the flavorful figs warm during your party, serve them in a chafing dish.
—*Deirdre Cox, Kansas City, MO*

Prep: 15 min. • **Bake:** 45 min.
Makes: about 1½ dozen

- ¾ lb. dried figs
- ¾ cup orange juice
- ¼ cup orange liqueur
- ⅛ tsp. ground cloves
- ¼ cup sugar
  Optional: Whipped cream, grated orange zest and orange wedges

1. Preheat oven to 325°. Prick holes in figs with a fork; place in a greased 8-in. square baking dish. In a small bowl, combine orange juice, liqueur and cloves. Sprinkle sugar over figs; pour juice mixture over the top.
2. Bake, uncovered, 45-55 minutes or until tender, basting occasionally with juice mixture. Serve warm; if desired, top with whipped cream, orange zest and orange wedges.
1 SERVING: 71 cal., 0 fat (0 sat. fat), 0 chol., 2mg sod., 17g carb. (13g sugars, 2g fiber), 1g pro.

HOLIDAY HELPER

The two most common varieties of figs are Mission figs (also called Black Mission figs) and the green-gold Smyrna figs. (Turkish Smyrnas are the same variety as Calimyrna, which are grown in California.) We used the smaller, firmer Mission figs with their more delicate seeds for this recipe, but Smyrnas would work as well.

HOP ABOARD THE HOLIDAY EXPRESS

Entertaining at the holidays doesn't have to be time-consuming.
From easy-prep dishes to make-ahead marvels, these recipes blend
convenience and elegance—allowing you to create a spread
that looks like you spent hours in the kitchen.

PARMESAN BUTTERNUT SQUASH

Butternut squash sprinkled with Parmesan and bread crumbs makes a superb side dish we love to share. Using the microwave cuts down on long roasting time.
—*Jacqueline O'Callaghan, Troy, MI*

Takes: 25 min. • **Makes:** 8 servings

- 1   medium butternut squash (about 3 lbs.), peeled and cut into 1-in. cubes
- 2   Tbsp. water
- ½   cup panko bread crumbs
- ½   cup grated Parmesan cheese
- ¼   tsp. salt
- ⅛   tsp. pepper

1. Place squash and water in a large microwave-safe bowl. Microwave, covered, on high until tender, 15-17 minutes; drain.
2. Preheat broiler. Transfer squash to a greased 15x10x1-in. baking pan. Toss bread crumbs with cheese, salt and pepper; sprinkle over squash. Broil 3-4 in. from heat until topping is golden brown, 1-2 minutes.
¾ CUP: 112 cal., 2g fat (1g sat. fat), 4mg chol., 168mg sod., 23g carb. (5g sugars, 6g fiber), 4g pro. **DIABETIC EXCHANGES:** 1½ starch.

EASY MINI CARAMEL APPLE CHEESECAKES

Cheesecake is the ultimate comfort food, but a big, rich slice can be too much. These muffin-size cheesecakes topped with apples and creamy caramel dazzle the senses without overwhelming them.
—*Brandie Cranshaw, Rapid City, SD*

Prep: 30 min. • **Bake:** 15 min. + cooling
Makes: 1 dozen

- 1   cup graham cracker crumbs
- 2   Tbsp. sugar
- ¼   tsp. ground cinnamon
- 3   Tbsp. butter, melted

CHEESECAKE
- 2   pkg. (8 oz. each) cream cheese, softened
- ½   cup sugar
- 1   tsp. vanilla extract
- 2   large eggs, room temperature, lightly beaten

TOPPING
- 1   large apple, peeled and finely chopped
- 1   Tbsp. butter
- 1   Tbsp. sugar
- ¼   tsp. ground cinnamon
     Dash ground cloves
- ½   cup butterscotch-caramel ice cream topping

1. Preheat oven to 350°. Line 12 muffin cups with paper liners.
2. In a small bowl, mix cracker crumbs, sugar and cinnamon; stir in melted butter. Spoon 1 rounded Tbsp. crumb mixture into each muffin cup; press down with a narrow glass or a spoon.
3. In a large bowl, beat cream cheese and sugar until smooth. Beat in vanilla. Add eggs; beat on low speed just until blended. Pour over crusts.
4. Bake 15-18 minutes or until the centers are set (do not overbake). Cool in pan on a wire rack for 30 minutes.
5. Right before serving, in a small skillet, cook and stir the chopped apple, butter, sugar, cinnamon and cloves over medium heat until tender, 4-5 minutes; stir in the butterscotch-caramel topping. Spoon over cheesecakes. Refrigerate leftovers.
1 MINI CHEESECAKE WITH ABOUT 1 TBSP. TOPPING: 307 cal., 19g fat (10g sat. fat), 84mg chol., 244mg sod., 31g carb. (23g sugars, 0 fiber), 4g pro.

HOLIDAY HELPER

You can change up the topping for these mini cheesecakes; a homemade berry compote or a premade pie filling would work well.

DIJON-MARINATED COCKTAIL SHRIMP

I like to prepare the shrimp for this recipe a day ahead and store them in an airtight container in the refrigerator. Then all you have to do is serve the dish when you're ready!
—*Sarah Conaway, Lynchburg, VA*

Prep: 15 min. + marinating • **Makes:** 3½ dozen

- ½ cup olive oil
- ¼ cup tarragon vinegar
- ¼ cup Dijon mustard
- 1 tsp. salt
- 1 tsp. crushed red pepper flakes
- ¼ tsp. pepper
- 1½ lbs. peeled and deveined cooked shrimp (26-30 per lb.)
- 2 green onions, chopped
- ¼ cup minced fresh parsley
  Optional: Seafood cocktail sauce, lemon wedges, minced fresh tarragon and additional minced fresh parsley

1. In a bowl or shallow dish, whisk together first 6 ingredients. Add shrimp, green onions, parsley and marinade; turn to coat. Cover and refrigerate 2 hours or overnight.
2. To serve, remove shrimp from marinade; discard marinade. If desired, serve with cocktail sauce and lemon wedges, and sprinkle with minced fresh tarragon and additional minced fresh parsley.
1 SHRIMP: 32 cal., 2g fat (0 sat. fat), 25mg chol., 78mg sod., 0 carb. (0 sugars, 0 fiber), 3g pro.

MOLDED CRANBERRY NUT SALAD

We try lots of cranberry recipes, and this one is always requested for family get-togethers at Thanksgiving and Christmas. It has also been a favorite dish at every church potluck I've taken it to!
—*Eleanor Arthur, Seattle, WA*

Prep: 20 min. + chilling • **Makes:** 10-12 servings

- 1 envelope unflavored gelatin
- 1½ cups cold water, divided
- 4 cups (16 oz.) fresh or frozen cranberries
- 1½ cups sugar
- 1½ cups dry red wine or cranberry juice
- 1 pkg. (6 oz.) lemon gelatin
- 1½ cups diced celery
- ¾ cup chopped walnuts
- 1 cup sour cream
- ¾ cup mayonnaise
  Celery leaves, optional

1. Soften unflavored gelatin in ½ cup cold water; set aside. In a 3-qt. saucepan, combine cranberries, sugar and wine; heat the mixture to boiling, stirring occasionally. Reduce heat and simmer 5 minutes, stirring frequently. Remove from heat. Add lemon gelatin and softened unflavored gelatin; stir until dissolved. Stir in remaining 1 cup cold water. Chill until mixture is partially set. Fold in celery and walnuts. Pour into greased 8-cup mold; cover and chill until set.
2. Meanwhile, for dressing, combine the sour cream and mayonnaise; refrigerate until ready to serve. To serve, unmold gelatin and top each serving with dollop of dressing. Garnish with celery leaves if desired.
½ CUP: 377 cal., 19g fat (4g sat. fat), 18mg chol., 134mg sod., 44g carb. (40g sugars, 2g fiber), 5g pro.

BROWNED BUTTER CHESS PIE

This simple pie is so smooth and velvety, it will warm your heart. It's a timeless recipe with southern roots.
—*Michael Cohen, Los Angeles, CA*

Prep: 20 min. + chilling
Bake: 40 min. + chilling
Makes: 8 servings

        Dough for single-crust pie
 ½   cup butter, cubed
 3   large eggs, room temperature
 1½ cups packed dark brown sugar
 ¼   cup whole milk
 4   tsp. white vinegar
 1   Tbsp. cornmeal
 1¼ tsp. vanilla extract
 ½   tsp. ground cinnamon
     Vanilla ice cream, optional

1. Preheat oven to 400°. On a lightly floured surface, roll dough to a ⅛-in.-thick circle; transfer to a 9-in. pie plate. Trim crust to ½ in. beyond rim of plate; flute edge. Refrigerate 30 minutes.
2. Line unpricked crust with a double thickness of heavy-duty foil. Fill with dried beans, uncooked rice or pie weights; bake 8 minutes. Remove foil and weights; bake 5 minutes longer. Cool on a wire rack. Reduce oven setting to 350°.
3. In a small heavy saucepan, cook and stir butter over medium heat until golden brown, 5-7 minutes; remove from heat.
4. Beat the eggs for 3 minutes. Gradually add brown sugar; beat until the mixture becomes thick, about 2 minutes. Beat in the milk, vinegar, cornmeal, vanilla, cinnamon and the browned butter. Pour into crust. Cover edge with foil.
5. Bake until a knife inserted near the center comes out clean, 40-45 minutes. Cool on a wire rack. Cover and refrigerate until cold, 3 hours. If desired, serve with ice cream. Refrigerate leftovers.
DOUGH FOR SINGLE-CRUST PIE: Combine 1¼ cups all-purpose flour and ¼ tsp. salt; cut in ½ cup cold butter until crumbly. Gradually add 3-5 Tbsp. ice water, tossing with a fork until dough holds together when pressed. Shape into a disk; wrap and refrigerate 1 hour.
1 PIECE: 469 cal., 25g fat (15g sat. fat), 131mg chol., 288mg sod., 57g carb. (41g sugars, 1g fiber), 5g pro.

CRANBERRY-STUFFED BEEF TENDERLOIN

Fresh cranberries and cranberry juice lend a satisfying sweet-tart taste to beef tenderloin. Serving plated dishes to your guests makes for a pretty presentation.
—*Carolyn Cope, Allston, MD*

Prep: 25 min. • **Bake:** 40 min.
Makes: 12 servings (1 cup sauce)

 1   cup fresh or frozen cranberries, thawed
 ¼   cup dry red wine or beef broth
 2   shallots, chopped
 1   Tbsp. butter
 1   beef tenderloin roast (4 lbs.)
 ¼   tsp. salt
 ¼   tsp. pepper
CRANBERRY WINE SAUCE
 2   shallots, chopped
 2   Tbsp. butter, divided
 ¾   cup cranberry juice
 ¾   cup dry red wine or beef broth
 ½   cup beef broth
 ½   tsp. minced fresh thyme

1. Preheat oven to 425°. In a large saucepan, combine the cranberries, wine, shallots and butter. Cook over medium heat until berries pop, about 15 minutes.
2. Cut a lengthwise slit down the center of the tenderloin to within ½ in. of bottom. Open tenderloin so it lies flat. On each half, make another lengthwise slit down the center to within ½ in. of bottom; open roast and cover with plastic wrap. Flatten to ½-in. thickness. Remove plastic.
3. Sprinkle beef with salt and pepper; spread cranberry mixture over meat. Roll up jelly-roll style, starting with a long side. Tie tenderloin at 2-in. intervals with kitchen string. Place on a rack in a shallow roasting pan.
4. Bake 40-50 minutes or until meat reaches desired doneness (for medium-rare, a thermometer should read 135°; medium, 140°; medium-well, 145°). Let stand for 10 minutes before slicing.
5. Meanwhile, for the sauce, saute shallots in 1 Tbsp. butter until tender. Add the juice, wine, broth and thyme. Bring to a boil; cook until liquid is reduced by half, about 20 minutes. Remove from the heat; stir in remaining 1 Tbsp. butter. Serve sauce with beef. If desired, garnish beef with additional fresh thyme sprigs.
4 OZ. COOKED BEEF WITH ABOUT 1 TBSP. SAUCE: 271 cal., 12g fat (5g sat. fat), 74mg chol., 109mg sod., 5g carb. (3g sugars, 1g fiber), 33g pro.

QUICK CRANBERRY CHIP COOKIES

I received these delightful cookies for Christmas a few years ago, and I just couldn't stay away from them! The tart cranberries blend beautifully with the semisweet chocolate and sweet vanilla chips.
—Jo Ann McCarthy, Canton, MA

Prep: 25 min. • **Bake:** 10 min./batch
Makes: 6 dozen

- ½ cup butter, softened
- ½ cup shortening
- ¾ cup sugar
- ¾ cup packed brown sugar
- 2 large eggs, room temperature
- 1 tsp. vanilla extract
- 2¼ cups all-purpose flour
- 1 tsp. baking soda
- ½ tsp. salt
- 1 cup semisweet chocolate chips
- 1 cup white baking chips
- 1 cup dried cranberries
- 1 cup chopped pecans

1. Preheat oven to 375°. In a large bowl, cream butter, shortening and sugars until light and fluffy, 5-7 minutes. Add eggs, 1 at a time, beating well after each addition. Beat in vanilla. Combine the flour, baking soda and salt; gradually add to the creamed mixture and mix well. Stir in the chips, cranberries and pecans.
2. Drop by tablespoonfuls 2 in. apart onto ungreased baking sheets. Bake until golden brown, 9-11 minutes. Cool on pans for 2 minutes before removing to wire racks to cool completely.

1 COOKIE: 97 cal., 5g fat (2g sat. fat), 10mg chol., 48mg sod., 12g carb. (8g sugars, 0 fiber), 1g pro.

CHOCOLATE NUT COOKIES: Omit the semisweet chocolate chips, cranberries and pecans. Substitute 1 tsp. almond extract for the vanilla. Decrease flour to 2 cups. Mix in ¼ cup baking cocoa to flour mixture. Stir in 1 cup chopped almonds with the white baking chips. Proceed as recipe directs.

CHOCOLATE-BUTTERSCOTCH CHIP COOKIES: Omit white baking chips, cranberries and pecans. Increase vanilla extract to 2 tsp. Increase semisweet chocolate chips to 2 cups and add 1 cup butterscotch chips. Proceed as recipe directs.

EASY SCALLOPED POTATOES

We all loved my mom's rich scalloped potatoes. I tweaked her original recipe to keep all the flavor but cut the fat. The cheese blend is the clincher. It's all about experimenting.
—Diane Bramlett, Stockton, CA

Prep: 30 min. • **Bake:** 20 min.
Makes: 12 servings

- 3 lbs. Yukon Gold potatoes (about 11 medium), peeled and thinly sliced
- ¼ cup water
- ¼ cup butter, cubed
- 1 large sweet onion, chopped
- 4 garlic cloves, chopped
- ¼ cup all-purpose flour
- 1 tsp. salt
- 1 tsp. pepper
- ⅛ tsp. cayenne pepper
- 2 cups chicken broth
- ⅓ cup half-and-half cream
- 1 cup shredded Gruyere or Swiss cheese
- 1 cup shredded Monterey Jack or cheddar cheese
  Minced fresh chives, optional

1. Preheat oven to 400°. Place potatoes and water in a large microwave-safe bowl; microwave, covered, on high until almost tender, 12-14 minutes.
2. In a 6-qt. stockpot, heat butter over medium-high heat; saute onion and garlic until tender, 5-7 minutes. Stir in flour and seasonings until blended; gradually stir in broth and cream. Bring to a boil, stirring occasionally; cook and stir until slightly thickened, 2-3 minutes. Stir in cheeses until melted.
3. Drain potatoes; add to sauce, stirring gently. Transfer to a greased 13x9-in. baking dish. Bake, uncovered, until lightly browned, about 20 minutes. If desired, sprinkle with chives.

½ CUP: 245 cal., 11g fat (7g sat. fat), 33mg chol., 526mg sod., 29g carb. (4g sugars, 2g fiber), 8g pro.

SPATCHCOCKED HERB-ROASTED TURKEY

This moist and tender turkey cooks up with even browning and crispy skin in half the time of a traditional turkey.
—*Matthew Hass, Ellison Bay, WI*

Prep: 15 min. + chilling • **Bake:** 1¼ hours + standing
Makes: 16 servings

- 1 turkey (12 to 14 lbs.)
- 3 Tbsp. kosher salt
- 2 tsp. coarsely ground pepper
- 1 Tbsp. minced fresh rosemary
- 1 Tbsp. minced fresh thyme
- 1 Tbsp. minced fresh sage

1. Place turkey, breast side down and tail end facing you, on a work surface. Using kitchen shears, cut along each side of the backbone; remove and save for making gravy. Turn turkey over so breast side is up; flatten by pressing down firmly on the breastbone until it cracks. Twist and tuck wings under to secure them in place.
2. Mix the remaining ingredients; rub onto all sides of turkey. Transfer turkey to a rack in a foil-lined rimmed baking pan. Refrigerate, uncovered, overnight.
3. Preheat oven to 450°. Remove turkey from refrigerator while oven heats. Roast until a thermometer inserted in thickest part of thigh reads 170°-175°, 1¼-1½ hours. Remove roasted turkey from oven; let stand 15 minutes before carving.
7 OZ. COOKED TURKEY: 399 cal., 18g fat (5g sat. fat), 184mg chol., 1210mg sod., 0 carb. (0 sugars, 0 fiber), 54g pro.

BOUQ-YAY!

A smart tape trick takes the fuss out of floral arranging. A stunning display is just moments away!

1. With ¼-in. clear tape, create 3-4 rows (depending on the width of your vase) horizontally and vertically to make a grid.
2. Place a few trimmed stems in each hole of the grid, then conceal the tape by adding a shorter layer of flowers or foliage around the edge of the vase.

CRANBERRY WHITE SANGRIA

I tinkered with the ingredients in this sangria until it was perfect. It's also good with peach, apple or cherry wine and a dash of vodka.
—*Patti Leake, Columbia, MO*

Prep: 15 min. + chilling
Makes: 24 servings

- 1 large Granny Smith apple, halved and thinly sliced
- ½ cup fresh or frozen cranberries
- ½ cup whiskey
- ¼ cup sugar
- ¼ cup lemon juice
- ¼ cup lime juice
- 2 bottles (750 milliliters each) sweet white wine
- 1 bottle (750 milliliters) cranberry wine or 3¼ cups cranberry juice
  Ice cubes
- 6 cups cold pineapple soda

1. In a large pitcher, combine the first 6 ingredients; let stand 30 minutes. Stir in wines. Cover and refrigerate until cold, about 30 minutes.
2. To serve, fill each glass halfway with ice; add ½ cup wine mixture. Top each with ¼ cup pineapple soda.
¾ CUP: 131 cal., 0 fat (0 sat. fat), 0 chol., 12mg sod., 14g carb. (4g sugars, 0 fiber), 0 pro.

HOLIDAY HELPER ✳☆★

To save time on party day, make the wine mixture in the morning or the night before, then just add the soda when you're serving.

BUTTERNUT-GOUDA POT STICKERS

My family can't get enough butternut squash. I had some left over, so I used pot sticker wrappers and chopped veggies to create fun little appetizers. They can be made in advance, so they're perfect for entertaining.
—*Carla Mendres, Winnipeg, MB*

Prep: 45 min. • **Cook:** 15 min.
Makes: about 4 dozen

- 1 small butternut squash (about 2½ lbs.)
- 1 Tbsp. butter
- 1 small sweet red pepper, finely chopped
- 1 small onion, finely chopped
- 2 cups shredded Gouda cheese
- ½ tsp. salt
- ½ tsp. minced fresh thyme or ⅛ tsp. dried thyme
- ½ tsp. pepper
- 1 pkg. (10 oz.) pot sticker or gyoza wrappers
- 3 Tbsp. canola oil, divided
- ¾ cup water, divided

1. Halve squash lengthwise; discard seeds. Place squash, cut side down, in a microwave-safe dish; add ½ in. of water. Microwave, covered, on high until soft, 15-20 minutes; cool slightly. Scoop out squash flesh and mash it.
2. In a skillet, heat butter over medium heat; saute chopped pepper and onion until tender, 4-6 minutes. Add to squash; stir in cheese, salt, thyme and pepper.
3. Place 1 Tbsp. filling on 1 wrapper (keep remaining wrappers covered with a damp towel). Moisten edge of wrapper with water; fold over to enclose filling, pleating front side to form a pouch. Stand pot sticker on work surface to flatten bottom, curving ends slightly. Repeat with remaining filling and wrappers.
4. In a large nonstick skillet, heat 1 Tbsp. oil over medium heat. Place a third of the pot stickers into pan; cook until bottoms are lightly browned, 1-2 minutes. Add ¼ cup water to pan (water may spatter). Cook, covered, until filling is heated through, 3-4 minutes. Uncover; cook until bottoms are crisp and water has evaporated, 1-2 minutes. Repeat twice.
FREEZE OPTION: Cover and freeze uncooked pot stickers on lightly floured baking sheets until firm. Transfer to airtight freezer containers; return to freezer. To use, cook pot stickers as directed, increasing time as necessary to heat through.
1 POT STICKER: 55 cal., 3g fat (1g sat. fat), 7mg chol., 84mg sod., 7g carb. (1g sugars, 1g fiber), 2g pro.

ROSEMARY PORK WITH CHERRY-PISTACHIO TOPPING

Thirty years ago, my new mother-in-law asked me to do something with a large frozen pork loin for a Christmas Eve buffet. I assembled some fragrant ingredients and this is the result. Both the pork and the topping are prepared the day before, so it's easy to fit into party preparations.
—*Sheila Brown, Canton, MI*

Prep: 35 min. + chilling
Bake: 15 min. + cooling
Makes: 12 servings

- 2 pork tenderloins (1 lb. each)
- 1 Tbsp. olive oil
- 1 tsp. salt
- ½ tsp. pepper
- 3 garlic cloves, thinly sliced
- 2 fresh rosemary sprigs

TOPPING
- 2 Tbsp. olive oil
- ¾ cup dried cherries
- ¾ cup shelled pistachios
- 3 garlic cloves, thinly sliced
- 1½ tsp. minced fresh rosemary
  Horseradish mayonnaise or honey mustard
  Croissants, optional

1. Preheat oven to 425°. Rub pork with oil; sprinkle with salt and pepper. Cut slits in pork and insert garlic. Place on a rack in a shallow roasting pan; top with rosemary sprigs. Bake until a thermometer reads 145°, 12-15 minutes. Remove roast from oven; tent with foil. Cool completely; discard rosemary. Refrigerate, covered, overnight.
2. Meanwhile, for topping, heat oil in a large skillet over medium heat. Add cherries, pistachios, garlic and rosemary. Cook and stir until cherries soften and pistachios turn bright green, 4-5 minutes; cool slightly. Transfer to a food processor; pulse until coarsely chopped. Refrigerate, covered, overnight.
3. Thinly slice pork. Serve with pistachio topping and horseradish mayonnaise or honey mustard. If desired, serve on croissants.
1 SERVING: 197 cal., 10g fat (2g sat. fat), 42mg chol., 261mg sod., 11g carb. (7g sugars, 1g fiber), 17g pro.

MINI CHEESE BALLS

These mini cheese balls are the perfect quick appetizer for any party. Roll them in toasted sesame seeds, fresh rosemary or paprika to add even more flavor.
—*Judy Spivey, Ennice, NC*

Prep: 30 min. + chilling
Makes: 36 cheese balls

- 1 pkg. (8 oz.) cream cheese, softened
- 2 cups shredded sharp cheddar cheese
  Optional toppings: Toasted sesame seeds, minced fresh rosemary and paprika
  Optional garnishes: Halved rye crisps and rolled tortilla chips

In a large bowl, combine cheeses. Shape into 36 balls; roll in toppings as desired. Refrigerate, covered, for 8 hours or overnight. If desired, press a rye crisp or rolled tortilla chip into the top of each cheese ball just before serving.
1 CHEESE BALL: 47 cal., 4g fat (2g sat. fat), 13mg chol., 61mg sod., 1g carb. (0 sugars, 0 fiber), 2g pro.

EXTRA QUICK YEAST ROLLS

Making homemade rolls usually takes a lot of ingredients and time, but this recipe makes it so simple. The rolls come together quickly and freeze well too.
—*Eleanor Paine, Junction City, OR*

Prep: 20 min. + rising • **Bake:** 10 min.
Makes: 2 dozen

- 1 pkg. (¼ oz.) quick-rise yeast
- 1 Tbsp. sugar
- ¾ cup warm water (110° to 115°)
- 2½ cups biscuit/baking mix

1. Dissolve yeast and sugar in the warm water. Stir in biscuit mix and turn dough onto a lightly floured surface. Knead until smooth and elastic, about 5 minutes.
2. Divide and shape dough into 24 small balls. Place on a greased baking sheet. Cover and let rise in a warm place until doubled, about 30 minutes.
3. Bake at 400° until golden brown, 10-15 minutes.
1 ROLL: 54 cal., 2g fat (1g sat. fat), 0 chol., 158mg sod., 8g carb. (1g sugars, 0 fiber), 1g pro.

ROASTED SWEET POTATO & APPLE SOUP

Savory with a touch of sweetness, this soup is sure to keep the winter chill away. Serve it as a first course or pair it with a grilled sandwich for lunch or a light dinner.
—*Lisa Kalmbach, Papillion, NE*

Prep: 20 min. • **Bake:** 40 min.
Makes: 4 servings

 2 medium sweet potatoes, peeled and cubed
 1 large onion, cut into 1-in. pieces
 1 large Gala or other apple, peeled and cubed
 3 garlic cloves
 2 Tbsp. olive oil
 3 cups vegetable or chicken broth
 ¾ tsp. salt
 ¼ tsp. pepper
    Optional: Reduced-fat sour cream and minced fresh chives

1. Preheat oven to 400°. Place sweet potatoes, onion, apple and garlic cloves in a greased 15x10x1-in. baking pan; drizzle with oil and toss to coat. Roast until very tender, 40-45 minutes, stirring occasionally.
2. Cool slightly. Process in batches in a blender with the broth until smooth. Transfer to a large saucepan. Stir in salt and pepper; heat through, stirring occasionally. If desired, serve with sour cream and top with minced chives.
1¼ CUPS: 206 cal., 7g fat (1g sat. fat), 0 chol., 954mg sod., 34g carb. (16g sugars, 4g fiber), 3g pro

HOLIDAY HELPER

To save time on cleanup, you can process the vegetables with the broth right in the saucepan, using an immersion blender. This is a nice, thick soup; if you prefer it a little thinner, add more broth until it's the consistency you desire.

ROASTED PEAR SALAD

Oven-roasted pears star in this salad with crispy greens, dried cranberries and hazelnuts. The creamy dressing, sweetened with a touch of honey, adds even more pear flavor.
—*Taste of Home Test Kitchen*

Prep: 15 min. • **Bake:** 15 min. + cooling
Makes: 4 servings

 2 medium pears, halved and cored
 4 tsp. olive oil, divided
 2 Tbsp. cider vinegar
 1 tsp. water
 1 tsp. honey
 ¼ tsp. salt
 ⅛ tsp. white pepper
 1 pkg. (10 oz.) mixed baby salad greens
 1 cup watercress sprigs
 ¼ cup chopped hazelnuts, toasted
 ¼ cup dried cranberries

1. Preheat oven to 400°. In a small bowl, toss pears with 1 tsp. oil. Place in a 5x10x1-in. baking pan coated with cooking spray. Bake 10 minutes. Turn pears over; bake until golden and tender, 5-7 minutes longer.
2. When roasted pears are cool enough to handle, peel them and thinly slice 2 pear halves lengthwise; set aside. Place the remaining pear halves in a blender. Add the vinegar, water, honey, salt and white pepper; cover and process until smooth. While processing, gradually add the remaining 3 tsp. oil in a steady stream.
3. In a large bowl, toss the salad greens, watercress, hazelnuts and cranberries. Arrange reserved pear slices on top; drizzle with dressing.
1 SERVING: 174 cal., 9g fat (1g sat. fat), 0 chol., 178mg sod., 24g carb. (0 sugars, 5g fiber), 3g pro.

EASY NO-BAKE CANDIED FRUIT COOKIES

Family and friends always want me to make these for Christmas, so I make lots of them. They're easy to handle and store.
—*Nan Bush, Morganton, NC*

Prep: 25 min. + chilling • **Makes:** 5 dozen

- 1 pkg. (10 to 12 oz.) vanilla wafers, crushed
- 2 cups chopped pecans or walnuts
- 1 can (14 oz.) sweetened condensed milk
- 1 cup chopped candied pineapple
- 1 cup red and green candied cherries, chopped
- ¼ cup confectioners' sugar

1. In a large bowl, mix first 5 ingredients until blended. Divide the mixture into 3 portions. Shape each portion into a 10x2-in. rectangle. Roll each rectangle in confectioners' sugar to coat. Wrap; refrigerate 2 hours or until firm.
2. Unwrap logs and cut crosswise into ½-in. slices. Store in airtight containers in the refrigerator.
1 COOKIE: 86 cal., 4g fat (1g sat. fat), 3mg chol., 33mg sod., 12g carb. (9g sugars, 0 fiber), 1g pro.

HOLIDAY HELPER ✳☆★

To shape the dough into a neat rectangle, first shape it into a roll, then wrap the roll in waxed paper. Place on a flat surface and roll over lightly with a rolling pin; rotate the dough and roll over it again. Repeat until you have the shape you want.

PARTY CHEESE BREAD

You can't go wrong with this recipe. The cheesy, buttery loaf looks fantastic and is so simple to make—people just flock to it. The taste is positively sinful, much better than usual garlic bread.
—*Karen Grant, Tulare, CA*

Prep: 25 min. • **Bake:** 30 min.
Makes: 16 servings

- 1 round loaf sourdough bread (1 lb.)
- 1 lb. Monterey Jack cheese, sliced
- ½ cup butter, melted
- 2 Tbsp. lemon juice
- 2 Tbsp. Dijon mustard
- 1½ tsp. garlic powder
- ½ tsp. onion powder
- ½ tsp. celery salt
  Minced fresh chives, optional

1. Preheat oven to 350°. Cut bread into 1-in. slices to within ½ in. of bottom of loaf. Repeat cuts in opposite direction. Insert cheese in cuts.
2. Mix all remaining ingredients except chives; drizzle over bread. Wrap loaf in foil; place on a baking sheet.
3. Bake 20 minutes. Unwrap; bake until cheese is melted, about 10 minutes longer. If desired, sprinkle with chives.
1 SERVING: 237 cal., 15g fat (9g sat. fat), 41mg chol., 468mg sod., 15g carb. (2g sugars, 1g fiber), 10g pro.

TIMESAVER

You can assemble your bread ahead of time, wrap it in foil and keep it in the refrigerator until ready to bake. This is helpful if you're taking it to a party—you can bake it at your destination if your host has oven room. Sprinkle chives after baking.

CRANBERRY CREME BRULEE

Love traditional creme brulee? Dress it up for the Christmas season with ruby red cranberries in a sweet-tart sauce. This is a convenient dessert because the filled ramekins can wait in the fridge until you're ready; caramelize the tops right before serving.
—Taste of Home *Test Kitchen*

Prep: 35 min. + chilling
Bake: 35 min. + chilling
Makes: 8 servings

- 1 pkg. (12 oz.) fresh or frozen cranberries
- 1 cup sugar
- ¼ cup water
- ⅛ tsp. salt

CUSTARD
- 2½ cups heavy whipping cream, divided
- 10 large egg yolks
- ⅔ cup sugar
- 1 tsp. vanilla extract
- 8 tsp. superfine sugar

1. Preheat oven to 325°. In a large saucepan, combine the cranberries, sugar, water and salt. Cook mixture over medium heat until the berries pop, 12-15 minutes, stirring frequently. Remove from heat. Spoon 2 Tbsp. sauce into each of eight 6-oz. broiler-safe ramekins or custard cups; refrigerate 10 minutes. Cover and refrigerate remaining sauce until serving.

2. For custard, in a small saucepan, heat 1 cup cream over medium heat until bubbles form around sides of the pan; remove from heat. In a large bowl, whisk egg yolks and sugar until smooth. Slowly stir in the hot cream. Stir in the vanilla and remaining 1½ cups cream.
3. Place prepared ramekins in a baking pan large enough to hold them without touching. Spoon custard mixture over cranberry sauce. Place pan on oven rack; add 1 in. very hot water to the pan. Bake until set, 35-40 minutes (centers will still be soft). Immediately remove ramekins from water bath to a wire rack; cool for 10 minutes. Refrigerate at least 8 hours or until cold.
4. For caramelized topping, gently blot surface of custard with a paper towel to remove any moisture. Sprinkle tops with superfine sugar. Using a kitchen torch, hold flame 2 in. above custard surface and move it slowly until the superfine sugar is evenly caramelized.
5. Serve custards with the remaining cranberry sauce.
NOTE: To caramelize topping in a broiler, place ramekins on a baking sheet; let stand at room temperature 15 minutes. Preheat broiler. Gently blot surface of custard with a paper towel to remove any moisture. Sprinkle tops with superfine sugar. Broil 3-4 in. from heat 1-2 minutes or until sugar is caramelized.
1 SERVING: 530 cal., 34g fat (19g sat. fat), 368mg chol., 75mg sod., 54g carb. (50g sugars, 2g fiber), 5g pro.

HOT MUSHROOM SPREAD

I've made this creamy, hearty mushroom appetizer for years—and it's a big hit every time.
—Barbara Pletzke, Herndon, VA

Takes: 25 min. • **Makes:** 1½ cups

- 2 Tbsp. butter
- ½ lb. sliced fresh mushrooms, chopped
- 1 shallot, finely chopped
- 1 garlic clove, minced
- 1 pkg. (8 oz.) cream cheese, softened
- 4 tsp. minced fresh oregano or 1 tsp. dried oregano
- 2 tsp. Worcestershire sauce
- 1½ tsp. lemon juice
- ¼ tsp. salt
- ¼ tsp. pepper
  French bread baguette slices, toasted if desired

In a large skillet, heat butter over medium-high heat. Add mushrooms and shallot; cook and stir until tender, 3-4 minutes. Add garlic; cook 1 minute longer. Reduce heat to low; stir in the cream cheese, oregano, Worcestershire sauce, lemon juice, salt and pepper until blended and heated through. Serve with baguette slices and, if desired, top with additional fresh oregano.
¼ CUP: 184 cal., 17g fat (10g sat. fat), 48mg chol., 269mg sod., 5g carb. (3g sugars, 0 fiber), 4g pro.

BREAKFAST AT THE CABIN

Whether you're spending the holiday in the woods or just want to evoke the feel of a rustic family getaway far from the hustle and bustle, these dishes make for a hearty breakfast spread.

FESTIVE CRANBERRY FRUIT SALAD

This fruit salad is a tradition on my Christmas table. It goes together quickly, which is a plus on such a busy day.
—*Rousheen Arel Wolf, Delta Junction, AK*

Takes: 25 min. • **Makes:** 14 servings

- 1 pkg. (12 oz.) fresh or frozen cranberries
- ¾ cup water
- ½ cup sugar
- 5 medium apples, diced
- 2 medium firm bananas, sliced
- 1½ cups fresh or frozen blueberries, thawed
- 1 can (11 oz.) mandarin oranges, undrained
- 1 cup fresh or frozen raspberries, thawed
- ¾ cup fresh strawberries, halved

1. In a large saucepan, combine the cranberries, water and sugar. Cook and stir over medium heat until berries pop, about 15 minutes. Remove from the heat; cool slightly.
2. In a large bowl, combine the remaining ingredients. Add the cranberry mixture; stir gently. Refrigerate until serving.
¾ CUP: 105 cal., 0 fat (0 sat. fat), 0 chol., 2mg sod., 27g carb. (21g sugars, 4g fiber), 1g pro.

MUSHROOM-HERB STUFFED FRENCH TOAST

This recipe transforms French toast into a savory delight with mushrooms and cheese. Its ooey-gooey texture is irresistible!
—*Lisa Huff, Wilton, CT*

Prep: 25 min. • **Cook:** 5 min./batch
Makes: 8 servings

- 1 lb. thinly sliced baby portobello mushrooms
- 4 Tbsp. butter plus 2 Tbsp. melted butter, divided
- 1 pkg. (8 oz.) reduced-fat cream cheese
- 2 cups shredded Gruyere or Swiss cheese, divided
- 4 Tbsp. minced chives, divided
- 1 Tbsp. minced fresh tarragon or 1 tsp. dried tarragon
- 1 garlic clove, minced
- ⅛ tsp. salt
- ⅛ tsp. pepper
- 16 slices Texas toast
- 4 large eggs, room temperature
- 2 cups 2% milk

1. In a large skillet, saute mushrooms in 1 Tbsp. butter until tender; set aside.
2. In a small bowl, beat cream cheese, 1 cup Gruyere cheese, 2 Tbsp. chives, tarragon, garlic, salt and pepper until blended. Spread over the bread slices. Spoon mushrooms over half the slices; place remaining bread slices over top, spread side down.
3. In a shallow bowl, whisk the eggs, milk and 2 Tbsp. melted butter. Dip both sides of the sandwiches into the egg mixture.
4. In a large skillet, toast sandwiches in remaining 3 Tbsp. butter in batches until golden brown, 2-3 minutes on each side. Sprinkle with remaining 1 cup Gruyere cheese and 2 Tbsp. chives.
NOTE: Baby portobello mushrooms are also known as cremini mushrooms. They can be used instead of white mushrooms for a flavor boost in many recipes.
1 SERVING: 531 cal., 30g fat (17g sat. fat), 185mg chol., 757mg sod., 41g carb. (8g sugars, 2g fiber), 24g pro.

MINI ITALIAN FRITTATAS

I created this recipe when my friends and I planned a picnic breakfast. I wanted an egg meal that was portable and easy to make. The result was this crowd-pleasing frittata!
—*Jess Apfe, Berkeley, CA*

Prep: 20 min. • **Bake:** 20 min.
Makes: 1 dozen

- ½ cup boiling water
- ¼ cup sun-dried tomatoes (not packed in oil)
- ¾ cup shredded part-skim mozzarella cheese, divided
- ½ cup chopped fresh spinach
- ⅓ cup water-packed artichoke hearts, rinsed, drained and chopped
- ⅓ cup chopped roasted sweet red peppers
- ¼ cup grated Parmesan cheese
- ¼ cup ricotta cheese
- 2 Tbsp. minced fresh basil
- 1 Tbsp. prepared pesto
- 2 tsp. Italian seasoning
- ¼ tsp. garlic powder
- 8 large eggs, room temperature
- ½ tsp. pepper
- ¼ tsp. salt

1. Preheat oven to 350°. Pour boiling water over tomatoes in a small bowl; let stand 5 minutes. Drain and chop the tomatoes.

2. In a small bowl, combine ½ cup mozzarella cheese, spinach, artichoke hearts, red peppers, Parmesan cheese, ricotta cheese, basil, pesto, Italian seasoning, garlic powder and tomatoes. In a large bowl, whisk eggs, pepper and salt until blended; stir in the cheese mixture.

3. Fill 12 greased or foil-lined muffin cups three-fourths full. Sprinkle with remaining ¼ cup mozzarella cheese. Bake until set, 18-22 minutes. Cool for 5 minutes before removing from pan. Serve warm, with additional pesto if desired.

1 MINI FRITTATA: 95 cal., 6g fat (3g sat. fat), 149mg chol., 233mg sod., 2g carb. (1g sugars, 0 fiber), 8g pro. **DIABETIC EXCHANGES:** 1 lean meat, 1 fat.

APPLE-CRANBERRY GRAINS

I made some changes to my diet in order to lose weight. My kids are skeptical when it comes to healthy food, but they adore these wholesome grains.
—*Sherisse Dawe, Black Diamond, AB*

Prep: 10 min. • **Cook:** 4 hours
Makes: 16 servings

- 2 medium apples, peeled and chopped
- 1 cup sugar
- 1 cup fresh cranberries
- ½ cup wheat berries
- ½ cup quinoa, rinsed
- ½ cup oat bran
- ½ cup medium pearl barley
- ½ cup chopped walnuts
- ½ cup packed brown sugar
- 1½ to 2 tsp. ground cinnamon
- 6 cups water
  Optional: Milk, sliced apples, dried cranberries and chopped walnuts

In a 4- or 5-qt. slow cooker, combine the first 11 ingredients. Cook, covered, on low until grains are tender, 4-5 hours. Serve with toppings as desired.

¾ CUP: 180 cal., 3g fat (0 sat. fat), 0 chol., 3mg sod., 37g carb. (22g sugars, 4g fiber), 3g pro.

HOLIDAY HELPER

Wheat berries are unprocessed whole grain wheat. Crunchy and high in fiber, they can be used much like other whole grains. Some recipes call for soaking wheat berries; this shortens cooking time but is not necessary. If you like, you can toast wheat berries prior to use to increase their flavor.

POTATO & SAUSAGE STUFFED PEPPERS WITH COUNTRY GRAVY

This is absolutely a brunch favorite! When I'm cooking these for vegetarians, I use soy sausage, but the result is still savory and incredible.
—*Deanna Wolfe, Muskegon, MI*

Prep: 40 min. • **Bake:** 30 min.
Makes: 6 servings

- 1 lb. bulk pork sausage
- 2 Tbsp. butter
- 1 lb. potatoes (about 2 medium), peeled and finely chopped
- 1 large onion, finely chopped
- ¼ tsp. paprika
- 3 garlic cloves, minced
- ½ tsp. salt
- ¼ tsp. pepper
- 6 large sweet yellow, orange or red peppers

GRAVY
- 2 Tbsp. butter
- 2 Tbsp. all-purpose flour
- ½ tsp. garlic powder
- ½ tsp. paprika
- ¼ tsp. salt
- ¼ tsp. pepper
- 1½ cups 2% milk

1. Preheat oven to 350°. In a large skillet, cook sausage over medium heat until no longer pink, 5-7 minutes, breaking into crumbles; drain.
2. In the same pan, heat butter over medium heat. Add potatoes, onion and paprika; cook and stir until the potatoes are just tender, 8-10 minutes. Add garlic; cook 1 minute longer. Stir in sausage, salt and pepper.
3. Cut tops from peppers, reserving the tops; remove seeds and ribs. In a 6-qt. stockpot, cook peppers in boiling water until crisp-tender, 4-6 minutes; drain and rinse in cold water.
4. Place peppers in a greased 13x9-in. baking dish. Fill with potato mixture; replace tops. Bake, covered, until peppers are tender, 30-35 minutes.
5. Meanwhile, for the gravy, in a large saucepan, melt butter over medium heat. Stir in flour and seasonings until smooth; gradually whisk in milk. Bring to a boil, stirring constantly; cook and stir until thickened, 1-2 minutes. Serve with stuffed peppers.

1 STUFFED PEPPER WITH ABOUT 3 TBSP. GRAVY: 400 cal., 26g fat (11g sat. fat), 66mg chol., 851mg sod., 31g carb. (5g sugars, 3g fiber), 14g pro.

WILD MUSHROOM & BACON PIE

Rustic flavors of roasted garlic and mushrooms make this savory pie a perfect option for a brunch or weeknight dinner. A mixture of mushrooms gives the pie depth of flavor—so feel free to use your favorites!
—*Barbara Estabrook, Appleton, WI*

Prep: 25 min. • **Bake:** 30 min. + standing
Makes: 8 servings

- 3 garlic cloves, peeled
- 1 tsp. canola oil
- 1 sheet refrigerated pie crust
- 4 bacon strips, cut into ½-in. pieces
- 1 lb. sliced assorted fresh mushrooms
- ¼ cup finely chopped sweet onion
- 3 large eggs, room temperature
- 1 pkg. (8 oz.) cream cheese, softened
- ½ tsp. salt
- ¼ tsp. pepper
- 1 cup shredded sharp cheddar cheese
- 2 Tbsp. grated Parmesan cheese
- ⅛ tsp. paprika

1. Preheat oven to 425°. Place garlic on a double thickness of heavy-duty foil; drizzle with oil. Wrap foil around garlic. Bake until softened, 15-20 minutes. Cool. Reduce oven setting to 375°. Unroll crust into a 9-in. pie plate; flute edge.
2. In a large skillet, cook bacon over medium heat until crisp, 3-5 minutes. Remove to paper towels with a slotted spoon; drain, reserving 2 tsp. drippings. Saute mushrooms and onion in drippings until tender, about 3 minutes; set aside.
3. In a large bowl, whisk eggs until foamy; add the cream cheese and whisk until blended. Stir in salt, pepper and the mushroom mixture. Squeeze softened garlic into mixture and mix well.
4. Sprinkle cheddar cheese over crust; top with bacon. Pour egg mixture over the top. Sprinkle with Parmesan cheese and paprika.
5. Bake until a knife inserted in the center comes out clean, 30-35 minutes. Let stand for 15 minutes before cutting.

1 PIECE: 468 cal., 35g fat (19g sat. fat), 181mg chol., 719mg sod., 24g carb. (3g sugars, 1g fiber), 16g pro.

SWEET POTATO WAFFLES WITH NUT TOPPING

Ready in just minutes, these tender waffles have a wonderfully sweet and crunchy topping. What a mouthwatering way to get your family out of bed in the morning!
—*Christine Keating, Norwalk, CA*

Prep: 20 min. • **Cook:** 5 min./batch
Makes: 12 waffles

- 2 cups biscuit/baking mix
- 2 Tbsp. brown sugar
- ½ tsp. ground cinnamon
- ¼ tsp. ground ginger
- ¼ tsp. ground nutmeg
- 1 large egg
- 1⅓ cups 2% milk
- 1 cup canned sweet potatoes, mashed
- 2 Tbsp. canola oil
- 1 tsp. vanilla extract

TOPPING
- 1 Tbsp. butter
- ½ cup chopped pecans
- ½ cup chopped walnuts
- 2 Tbsp. brown sugar
- 1 Tbsp. water
- ⅛ tsp. ground cinnamon
  Dash salt
  Dash ground nutmeg
  Maple syrup

1. In a large bowl, combine biscuit mix, brown sugar and spices. In another bowl, whisk the egg, milk, sweet potatoes, oil and vanilla. Stir into the dry ingredients just until combined.
2. Bake in a preheated waffle iron according to manufacturer's directions until golden brown.
3. Meanwhile, in a small skillet, melt butter over medium heat. Add pecans and walnuts. Cook and stir for 2 minutes. Add the brown sugar, water, cinnamon, salt and nutmeg. Cook and stir until sugar is dissolved. Serve waffles with topping and syrup.
2 WAFFLES: 457 cal., 28g fat (5g sat. fat), 44mg chol., 598mg sod., 46g carb. (17g sugars, 3g fiber), 9g pro.

SMOKED BLUEFISH SPREAD

Growing up on Block Island, Rhode Island, we'd surf-cast off the shores for bluefish. Its strong flavor makes it an excellent candidate for smoking so that it could be used throughout the year. Smoked fillets make a wonderfully creamy spread to serve with crackers.
—*Pamela Gelsomini, Wrentham, MA*

Prep: 15 min. + chilling • **Makes:** 3 cups

- 1 lb. smoked bluefish fillets or flaked smoked trout
- 1 pkg. (8 oz.) cream cheese, softened
- ¾ cup finely chopped red onion
- ¼ cup snipped fresh dill
- ¼ cup lemon juice
- ¼ cup sour cream
- 3 Tbsp. capers, drained
- 2 Tbsp. prepared horseradish
- 2 Tbsp. grated lemon zest
  Assorted crackers, fresh vegetables and lemon wedges

1. Scrape fish from skin if needed. Place fish in a food processor; pulse until finely chopped. Combine cream cheese, red onion, dill, lemon juice, sour cream, capers, horseradish and zest; gently stir in fish. Refrigerate, covered, until serving.
2. Serve with crackers, vegetables and lemon wedges. If desired, top with additional red onion and dill.
2 TBSP.: 64 cal., 5g fat (2g sat. fat), 14mg chol., 209mg sod., 2g carb. (1g sugars, 0 fiber), 4g pro.

HOLIDAY HELPER

If you can't find smoked bluefish or smoked trout, this spread is just as delicious when made with smoked mackerel, smoked salmon or smoked tuna. It's also great when used as a bagel spread!

OLD-FASHIONED BUTTERMILK DOUGHNUTS

Guests will have a touch of nostalgia when they bite into one of these old-fashioned doughnuts. Accents of nutmeg and cinnamon, along with a subtle burst of lemon, make them hard to resist.
—June Jones, Harveyville, KS

Prep: 20 min. • **Cook:** 5 min./batch
Makes: 2½ dozen

- 2   cups mashed potatoes (without added milk and butter)
- 2   large eggs, room temperature
- 1¼ cups sugar
- ⅔   cup buttermilk
- ¼   cup butter, melted
- 1   Tbsp. grated lemon zest
- 4   cups all-purpose flour
- 3   tsp. baking powder
- 2   tsp. salt
- 2   tsp. ground nutmeg
- ¼   tsp. baking soda
      Oil for deep-fat frying

TOPPING
- ½   cup sugar
- 1½ tsp. ground cinnamon

1. In a large bowl, beat the potatoes, eggs, sugar, buttermilk, butter and lemon zest until blended. In a second bowl, combine the flour, baking powder, salt, nutmeg and baking soda; gradually beat into the potato mixture and mix well.
2. Turn dough onto a lightly floured surface; roll to ½-in. thickness. Cut with a floured 2½-in. doughnut cutter. In a deep cast-iron or electric skillet, heat oil to 375°. Fry doughnuts and doughnut holes, a few at a time, until golden brown on both sides. Drain on paper towels.
3. Combine sugar and cinnamon; roll warm doughnuts in mixture.
1 DOUGHNUT WITH 1 DOUGHNUT HOLE: 184 cal., 7g fat (2g sat. fat), 18mg chol., 232mg sod., 27g carb. (12g sugars, 1g fiber), 3g pro.

HOLIDAY HELPER ✳☆★

If you're out of buttermilk, you do have options! Regular milk with white vinegar or lemon juice is the most common, or you can use plain yogurt. Plain Greek yogurt or sour cream will also do but should be thinned with milk or water until it's the consistency of buttermilk.

BUTTERMILK-BEER PANCAKES

A friend of mine shared these pancakes with me when I was in college. His dad had made them for as long as he could remember. I love them because they are so light and fluffy!
—Carrie Auldridge, Hudson Oaks, TX

Prep: 10 min. • **Cook:** 5 min./batch
Makes: 36 pancakes

- 5   cups all-purpose flour
- 2   Tbsp. sugar
- 2   tsp. salt
- 2   tsp. baking soda
- 4   large eggs, room temperature
- 4   cups buttermilk
- ¼   cup canola oil
- 1   bottle (12 oz.) beer

1. In a large bowl, whisk flour, sugar, salt and baking soda. In a second bowl, whisk eggs, buttermilk and oil until blended. Add to dry ingredients, stirring just until moistened. Stir in beer.
2. Lightly grease a griddle; heat over medium heat. Pour batter by ¼ cupfuls. Cook until bubbles on top begin to pop and bottoms are golden brown. Turn; cook until second side is golden brown.
3 PANCAKES: 308 cal., 7g fat (1g sat. fat), 65mg chol., 784mg sod., 47g carb. (7g sugars, 1g fiber), 10g pro.

BRING THE OUTDOORS INSIDE

To add a rustic look (and a lovely aroma!) to your holiday place settings, simply wrap fresh rosemary sprigs around each linen napkin. Carefully insert the cutlery.

TURKEY & MUSHROOM SPICY SCOTCH EGGS

I grew up in Scotland, where greasy Scotch eggs were often sold alongside pies in bakeries. I decided to make my own version with less grease and more taste—and the air fryer helped me achieve that goal. You can omit the mushrooms if preferred and try adding other finely chopped vegetables. Also, different herbs or curry powder could be used instead of the taco seasoning.
—*Fiona Green, Keller, TX*

Prep: 30 min. • **Cook:** 10 min./batch
Makes: 6 servings

- 1   lb. ground turkey
- ½   cup shredded part-skim mozzarella cheese
- ½   cup finely chopped fresh mushrooms
- ¼   cup oil-packed sun-dried tomatoes, chopped
- 1   jalapeno pepper, seeded and minced
- 2   tsp. taco seasoning
- ½   tsp. garlic powder
- 6   hard-boiled large eggs
- ⅓   cup all-purpose flour
- 1   large egg, beaten
- 1   cup seasoned bread crumbs
- ¼   cup olive oil
      Spicy dipping sauce

1. Preheat air fryer to 400°. In a large bowl, mix the first 7 ingredients lightly but thoroughly. Divide the mixture into 6 portions; flatten. Shape each portion around a peeled hard-boiled egg.
2. Place flour, beaten egg and bread crumbs in separate shallow bowls. Dip eggs in flour to coat all sides; shake off excess. Dip into beaten egg, then into crumbs, patting to help coating adhere. Brush with oil.
3. In batches, place eggs in greased air fryer; brush with oil. Cook until golden brown and the turkey is no longer pink, 10-12 minutes. Serve with sauce.
1 EGG: 364 cal., 23g fat (6g sat. fat), 271mg chol., 402mg sod., 11g carb. (2g sugars, 1g fiber), 26g pro.

CAST-IRON APPLE NUTMEG COFFEE CAKE

In an effort to practice my baking, I used up the last bit of the morning coffee to make a coffee cake—literally. It is super moist and crumbly and tastes as if you dunked your cake right into a cup of hot joe. If you want some crunch, add pecans to the apples.
—*Darla Andrews, Boerne, TX*

Prep: 25 min. • **Bake:** 20 min. + cooling
Makes: 8 servings

- 3   Tbsp. butter, cubed
- 2   cups chopped peeled Gala apples
- ½   cup packed brown sugar, divided
- ¼   cup brewed coffee
- ⅔   cup canola oil
- ½   cup sugar
- 1   large egg plus 1 large egg white, room temperature
- 2   tsp. vanilla extract
- 1½ cups all-purpose flour
- 2   tsp. ground cinnamon
- ½   tsp. salt
- ½   tsp. baking soda
- ¼   tsp. ground nutmeg

DRIZZLE
- ⅓   cup brewed coffee
- ¼   cup heavy whipping cream
- 1½ cups confectioners' sugar

1. Preheat oven to 375°. In a 10-in. cast-iron or other ovenproof skillet, melt butter over low heat. Add apples and ¼ cup brown sugar. Cook and stir until crisp-tender, about 5 minutes. Stir in coffee; remove from heat.
2. In a large bowl, beat oil, sugar, egg, egg white, vanilla and the remaining ¼ cup brown sugar until well blended. In another bowl, whisk flour, cinnamon, salt, baking soda and nutmeg; gradually beat into the oil mixture. Gently spread over the apple mixture.
3. Bake until a toothpick inserted in center comes out clean, 18-22 minutes. Cool on a wire rack 10 minutes.
4. Meanwhile, for drizzle, in a small saucepan, bring coffee and cream to a boil; cook until liquid is reduced to ¼ cup, 10-12 minutes. Remove from heat; stir in confectioners' sugar. Let stand 10 minutes. Drizzle over cake.
1 PIECE: 532 cal., 27g fat (6g sat. fat), 43mg chol., 284mg sod., 71g carb. (51g sugars, 1g fiber), 4g pro.

HOLIDAY HELPER
To make this an indulgent dessert, serve with ice cream and then top with the coffee drizzle.

CAMPFIRE PANCAKES WITH PEANUT MAPLE SYRUP

My family loves eating s'mores around the campfire when we vacation at the lake. Campfire pancakes are my tribute to those happy times.

—*Cheryl Snavely, Hagerstown, MD*

Takes: 20 min.
Makes: 8 pancakes (¼ cup syrup)

- 1 pkg. (6½ oz.) chocolate chip muffin mix
- ⅔ cup 2% milk
- 1 large egg, room temperature, lightly beaten
- ½ cup miniature marshmallows
- ¼ cup butterscotch chips
- ¼ cup maple syrup
- 1 Tbsp. chunky peanut butter

1. In a large bowl, combine muffin mix, milk and egg; stir just until moistened. Fold in marshmallows and chips.
2. Lightly grease a griddle; heat over medium heat. Pour batter by ¼ cupfuls onto griddle. Cook until bubbles on top begin to pop and bottoms are golden brown. Turn; cook until second side is golden brown.
3. Meanwhile, microwave maple syrup and peanut butter in 10- to 20-second intervals until heated through. Serve with pancakes.

2 PANCAKES WITH 1 TBSP. SYRUP MIXTURE: 407 cal., 13g fat (7g sat. fat), 50mg chol., 386mg sod., 63g carb. (43g sugars, 2g fiber), 8g pro.

TWISTED EGGS BENEDICT SALAD

Salad for breakfast? Absolutely. You can prepare everything but the dressing and the eggs and chill it overnight; in the morning, dress the salad and poach the eggs.

—*Noelle Myers, Grand Forks, ND*

Prep: 20 min. • **Cook:** 20 min.
Makes: 8 servings

- 4 Tbsp. olive oil, divided
- 1½ lbs. fresh asparagus, trimmed and chopped
- 1⅓ cups chopped fennel bulb
- 8 oz. diced deli ham or Canadian bacon
- 6 cups baby kale salad blend (about 4 oz.)
- 1 cup chopped roasted sweet red peppers
- 3 Tbsp. chopped green onion tops
- 3 Tbsp. Dijon mustard
- 2 Tbsp. cider vinegar
- ¼ tsp. salt
- ¼ tsp. pepper
- 2 qt. water
- 8 large eggs

1. In a large nonstick skillet, heat 1 Tbsp. olive oil over medium heat. Add the asparagus, fennel and ham; saute until vegetables are crisp-tender, about 8 minutes. Cool 3 minutes.
2. Toss vegetable mixture with salad blend, peppers and green onions. Whisk together mustard, vinegar, salt, pepper and the remaining oil until smooth.
3. In a large saucepan, bring water to a boil; reduce heat to a gentle simmer. Break eggs, 1 at a time, into a small bowl; slip eggs into water. Poach, uncovered, until whites are completely set and yolks begin to thicken, 3-5 minutes.
4. Meanwhile, toss salad with dressing. Divide salad among 8 plates. Using a slotted spoon, remove eggs from water; place 1 on top of each salad.

1 CUP SALAD WITH 1 EGG: 199 cal., 13g fat (3g sat. fat), 200mg chol., 710mg sod., 5g carb. (3g sugars, 2g fiber), 14g pro. **DIABETIC EXCHANGES:** 2 lean meat, 2 fat, 1 vegetable.

BRIE & SAUSAGE BRUNCH BAKE

I've made this brunch bake for holidays as well as for a weekend at a friend's cabin, and I always get requests for the recipe. It has make-ahead convenience, reheats well and tastes great even the next day.
—*Becky Hicks, Forest Lake, MN*

Prep: 30 min. + chilling
Bake: 50 min. + standing
Makes: 12 servings

1   lb. bulk Italian sausage
1   small onion, chopped
8   cups cubed day-old sourdough bread
½   cup chopped roasted
      sweet red peppers
½   lb. Brie cheese, rind removed, cubed
⅔   cup grated Parmesan cheese
2   Tbsp. minced fresh basil
      or 2 tsp. dried basil
8   large eggs, room temperature
2   cups heavy whipping cream
1   Tbsp. Dijon mustard
1   tsp. pepper
½   tsp. salt
¾   cup shredded part-skim
      mozzarella cheese
3   green onions, sliced

1. In a large skillet, cook sausage and onion over medium heat until meat is no longer pink, 5-7 minutes, breaking into crumbles; drain.
2. Place bread cubes in a greased 13x9-in. baking dish. Layer with sausage mixture, red peppers, Brie and Parmesan cheeses, and basil. In a large bowl, whisk eggs, cream, mustard, pepper and salt; pour over top. Cover and refrigerate overnight.
3. Remove dish from the refrigerator 30 minutes before baking. Preheat oven to 350°. Bake, uncovered, until a knife inserted in the center comes out clean, 45-50 minutes.
4. Sprinkle with mozzarella cheese. Bake until cheese is melted, 4-6 minutes longer. Let stand for 10 minutes before cutting. Sprinkle with green onions.

1 PIECE: 451 cal., 34g fat (18g sat. fat), 217mg chol., 843mg sod., 16g carb. (3g sugars, 1g fiber), 19g pro.

HOLIDAY HELPER

This recipe as written serves 12; however, it's easy to cut it in half and bake it in an 8-in. square pan if you're serving a smaller guest list.

MASON MARVELS

Using simple jars, create a beautiful system for decoration and organization. These make a lovely homemade gift—either empty or already filled with carefully selected goodies. If you want to use the jars as closed containers for candy or other edible treats, paint lids as well as the rings in Step 4.

WHAT YOU'LL NEED
- 32-oz. wide-mouth Mason jars with rings
- Cream chalk paint
- Fine-grit sandpaper
- Spray sealant
- Oil-rubbed bronze spray paint

INSTRUCTIONS
1. Paint the outside of Mason jars with cream chalk paint; let them dry.
2. For a distressed look, use sandpaper to gently scrape away some of the paint.
3. Seal with spray sealant (make sure you're in a well-ventilated area).
4. Add metallic flair by spray-painting the rings with the oil-rubbed bronze spray paint; let them dry.
5. Screw on the rings and fill the jars with gifts.

HOLIDAY FEASTS

Three carefully constructed menus—created around rack of lamb, a traditional turkey and a beef ribeye roast—take the work out of planning the perfect Christmas feast. An added section of a la carte items gives you lots of choices to create your own menu too!

PRIME RIB FEAST

SEASONED RIBEYE ROAST

This is an especially savory way to prepare a boneless beef roast. Gravy made from the drippings is exceptional.
—*Evelyn Gebhardt, Kasilof, AK*

Prep: 10 min. • **Bake:** 1½ hours + standing
Makes: 8 servings

- 1½ tsp. lemon-pepper seasoning
- 1½ tsp. paprika
- ¾ tsp. garlic salt
- ½ tsp. dried rosemary, crushed
- ¼ tsp. cayenne pepper
- 1 beef ribeye roast (3 to 4 lbs.)

1. Preheat oven to 350°. Mix seasonings. Place roast on a rack in a roasting pan, fat side up; rub with seasonings.
2. Roast, uncovered, until meat reaches desired doneness (for medium-rare, a thermometer should read 135°; medium, 140°), 1½-2 hours. Remove from oven; tent with foil. Let stand for 10 minutes before slicing.
4 OZ. COOKED BEEF: 372 cal., 27g fat (11g sat. fat), 100mg chol., 321mg sod., 0 carb. (0 sugars, 0 fiber), 30g pro.

HOLIDAY HELPER

You have a choice of boneless or bone-in when it comes to a ribeye roast; which you pick is up to you. Boneless roasts are quicker to cook and easier to carve; bone-in roasts get a boost of flavor from the bone. If you do opt for a bone-in roast, allow more cooking time; start checking the internal temperature at the 2-hour mark.

When shopping for your roast, look for good marbling and a fat cap. Boneless roasts will often come already tied; if yours is not, you may want to make sure you have some cotton butcher's twine on hand and tie your own. This isn't mandatory, but tying the roast into as consistent a shape as possible (with the twine spaced about every 2 in.) ensures more even cooking throughout the roast.

GRUYERE MASHED POTATOES

Gruyere cheese and chives take mashed potatoes to a whole new level this holiday season! Don't have chives? Just use extra green onion instead.
—*Preci D'Silva, Dubai, UAE*

Takes: 25 min. • **Makes:** 8 servings

- 2 lbs. potatoes, peeled and cubed
- ½ cup sour cream
- ⅓ cup 2% milk, warmed
- 1 garlic clove, minced
- ¼ cup butter, cubed
- ¼ cup shredded Gruyere or Swiss cheese
- ¼ cup minced fresh chives
- 2 green onions, chopped
- ½ tsp. garlic salt
- ¼ tsp. pepper

1. Place potatoes in a 6-qt. stockpot; add water to cover. Bring to a boil. Reduce heat; simmer, uncovered, until potatoes are tender, 10-15 minutes.
2. Drain; return to pot. Mash potatoes, gradually adding sour cream, milk and garlic. Stir in the remaining ingredients.
¾ CUP: 169 cal., 10g fat (6g sat. fat), 23mg chol., 206mg sod., 17g carb. (2g sugars, 1g fiber), 3g pro.

CHRISTMAS TORTELLINI & SPINACH SOUP

I made this soup for the first time in the summer, but when I saw its bright red and green colors, my first thought was that it would make a perfect first course for Christmas dinner.
—*Marietta Slater, Justin, TX*

Takes: 25 min. • **Makes:** 6 servings

- 2 cans (14½ oz. each) vegetable broth
- 1 pkg. (9 oz.) refrigerated cheese tortellini or tortellini of your choice
- 1 can (15 oz.) cannellini beans, rinsed and drained
- 1 can (14½ oz.) Italian diced tomatoes, undrained
- ¼ tsp. salt
- ⅛ tsp. pepper
- 3 cups fresh baby spinach
- 3 Tbsp. minced fresh basil
- ¼ cup shredded Asiago cheese

1. In a large saucepan, bring broth to a boil. Add tortellini; reduce heat. Simmer, uncovered, for 5 minutes.
2. Stir in the beans, tomatoes, salt and pepper; return to a simmer. Cook until tortellini are tender, 4-5 minutes longer.
3. Stir in spinach and basil; cook until the spinach is wilted. Top individual servings with shredded cheese.
1 CUP: 239 cal., 5g fat (3g sat. fat), 23mg chol., 1135mg sod., 38g carb. (7g sugars, 5g fiber), 11g pro.

CREAMY CELERY ROOT & PEARL ONIONS

I have made creamed onions for several recent holiday dinners and wanted to change the recipe, so I decided to add celery root. It's perfect with the onions, and the creamy sauce is addicting!
—*Tina Mirilovich, Johnstown, PA*

Prep: 15 min. • **Cook:** 20 min.
Makes: 8 servings

- 1 large celery root (about 1½ lbs.), peeled and cubed
- 3 Tbsp. butter
- 1 pkg. (14.4 oz.) pearl onions, thawed
- ¾ cup chicken broth
- 1 tsp. sugar
- ½ tsp. salt
- 1½ cups heavy whipping cream
- 2 Tbsp. minced fresh parsley
- ½ tsp. pepper

1. Place celery root in a 6-qt. stockpot; add water to cover. Bring to a boil. Reduce heat; simmer, uncovered, until tender, 4-6 minutes. Drain; set aside.
2. In a large skillet or Dutch oven, heat butter over medium heat. Add pearl onions, broth, sugar and salt. Cook, stirring often, until the onions begin to brown, 12-15 minutes.
3. Add celery root and cream; simmer until slightly thickened, 3-5 minutes. Stir in parsley and pepper.
⅔ CUP: 250 cal., 21g fat (13g sat. fat), 63mg chol., 379mg sod., 14g carb. (6g sugars, 3g fiber), 3g pro.

HOLIDAY HELPER

Celery root, also known as celeriac, is the bulb of a special variety of celery specifically grown for its root. Choose a relatively small, firm root; avoid any with soft spots. To use, cut off the base and top, and peel it with a vegetable peeler. Once peeled, the root will discolor fairly quickly, so if you're not using it immediately, place it in water with a little lemon juice to keep it from turning brown.

ROASTED BRUSSELS SPROUTS WITH CRANBERRIES & ALMONDS

If Brussels sprouts usually taste bitter to you, roast them for a gentle sweetness that goes with cranberries and almonds. This side dish won us over.
—Claudia Lamascolo, Melbourne, FL

Prep: 10 min. • **Bake:** 30 min.
Makes: 8 servings

- 3 lbs. fresh Brussels sprouts, trimmed and halved
- ¼ cup olive oil
- ¾ tsp. salt
- ¼ tsp. garlic powder
- ¼ tsp. pepper
- 1 cup balsamic vinegar
- ½ cup sugar
- 1 cup dried cranberries
- ½ cup sliced almonds, toasted

1. Preheat oven to 400°. In a large bowl, toss Brussels sprouts with oil, salt, garlic powder and pepper. Transfer to a greased 15x10x1-in. baking pan. Roast until tender, 30-35 minutes, stirring occasionally.
2. In a small saucepan, combine vinegar and sugar; bring to a boil, stirring to dissolve the sugar. Reduce heat; simmer uncovered until syrupy, 15-20 minutes, stirring occasionally.
3. To serve, place Brussels sprouts in a serving dish; drizzle with glaze and toss to coat. Sprinkle with cranberries and almonds.
NOTE: To toast nuts, bake in a shallow pan in a 350°; oven for 5-10 minutes or cook in a skillet over low heat until lightly browned, stirring occasionally.
¾ CUP: 284 cal., 10g fat (1g sat. fat), 0 chol., 260mg sod., 48g carb. (34g sugars, 7g fiber), 6g pro.

HERB FOCACCIA ROLLS

Yeast rolls speckled with fresh thyme and rosemary are a breeze to make without kneading and long wait times. Break out the good butter for these adorable rolls.
—Linda Schend, Kenosha, WI

Prep: 15 min. + rising • **Bake:** 20 min.
Makes: 1½ dozen

- 3 cups all-purpose flour
- 1 pkg. (¼ oz.) quick-rise yeast
- 2 Tbsp. minced fresh thyme, divided
- 2 Tbsp. minced fresh rosemary, divided
- 1 Tbsp. sugar
- 1½ tsp. kosher salt, divided
- 1½ cups warm water (120° to 130°)
- 6 Tbsp. extra-virgin olive oil, divided

1. Combine flour, yeast, 1 Tbsp. thyme, 1 Tbsp. rosemary, sugar and 1 tsp. salt. Add water and 2 Tbsp. oil; beat 1 minute (dough will be very sticky).
2. Divide dough among 18 greased muffin cups. Let rise in a warm place until doubled, about 30 minutes.
3. Preheat oven to 375°. In a small saucepan over medium-low heat, stir together remaining fresh herbs, salt and olive oil just until herbs are fragrant and oil is hot, about 1½ minutes. Remove from heat; cool.
4. Gently spoon the cooled herb mixture over each roll. Bake until golden brown, 20-25 minutes.
1 ROLL: 120 cal., 5g fat (1g sat. fat), 0 chol., 161mg sod., 17g carb. (1g sugars, 1g fiber), 2g pro.
STANDARD FOCACCIA: Spread dough into a greased 13x9-in. pan. Let rise in a warm place until doubled, about 30 minutes. Top with herb mixture; bake at 375° until golden brown, 25-30 minutes.

ROOM TO RISE

The unproofed dough will fill the muffin cups about halfway then will rise to the top edge of the cup or slightly below. The dough will not rise much farther during baking.

SALTED BUTTERSCOTCH CHEESECAKE

Salted butterscotch is everywhere—candy, ice cream and this cheesecake! Silky smooth cheesecake is dressed with a dreamy butterscotch sauce that really stands out next to the salty pretzel crust.
—Taste of Home *Test Kitchen*

Prep: 40 min. • **Bake:** 55 min. + chilling
Makes: 12 servings

1¼ cups finely crushed pretzels
½ cup butter, melted
¼ cup sugar

FILLING
1 can (14 oz.) sweetened condensed milk
¾ cup 2% milk
1 pkg. (3.4 oz.) instant butterscotch pudding mix
3 pkg. (8 oz. each) cream cheese, softened
1 tsp. vanilla extract
3 large eggs, room temperature, lightly beaten

BUTTERSCOTCH SAUCE
¼ cup butter, cubed
1 cup packed dark brown sugar
¾ cup heavy whipping cream
3 tsp. vanilla extract
½ tsp. salt

TOPPING
1 carton (8 oz.) Mascarpone cheese, softened
Sea salt

1. Preheat oven to 350°. Place a greased 9-in. springform pan on a double thickness of heavy-duty foil (about 18 in. square). Securely wrap foil around pan.
2. In a small bowl, combine the pretzels, butter and sugar. Press onto the bottom of prepared pan. Place pan on a baking sheet. Bake 10 minutes; cool on a wire rack. Reduce oven setting to 325°.
3. In a small bowl, whisk the condensed milk, milk and pudding mix for 2 minutes. Let stand until soft-set, 2 minutes.
4. In a large bowl, beat cream cheese until smooth. Beat in pudding mixture and vanilla. Add eggs; beat on low speed just until combined. Pour over crust.
5. Place springform pan in a large baking pan; add 1 in. hot water to the larger pan. Bake until center is almost set and top appears dull, 55-65 minutes.

6. Remove springform pan from water bath. Cool on a wire rack for 10 minutes. Carefully run a knife around edge of pan to loosen; cool 1 hour longer.
7. For the sauce, in a small saucepan, melt butter. Stir in brown sugar and cream. Bring to a boil, stirring constantly. Remove from the heat; stir in vanilla and salt.
8. For the topping, in a small bowl, combine Mascarpone cheese and ⅓ cup sauce until smooth. Spread over cooled cheesecake; refrigerate overnight. Cover and refrigerate the remaining sauce.
9. Remove sides of pan. Just before serving, sprinkle cheesecake with sea salt; drizzle with butterscotch sauce.
1 PIECE WITH 4½ TSP. SAUCE: 714 cal., 50g fat (30g sat. fat), 202mg chol., 698mg sod., 58g carb. (47g sugars, 0 fiber), 12g pro.

HOLIDAY HELPER

Cheesecake is a decadent, showstopping treat—embrace it! Use regular cream cheese and other dairy products unless the recipe specifically calls for reduced-fat alternatives.

Make sure the eggs and cream cheese are room temperature; this will prevent lumps.

To prevent cracks, grease the pan, even if it's nonstick; use a water bath to increase humidity in the oven; and open the oven door as little as possible, especially during the first 30 minutes of bake time.

Cheesecake cuts best when it's cold but tastes best at room temperature. So cut the cake, then let the slices stand for 15 minutes before serving.

LAMB FEAST

HERB-CRUSTED RACK OF LAMB WITH MUSHROOM SAUCE

With this easy, surefire recipe, you don't have to be afraid to make an elegant rack of lamb for a holiday dinner!
—Mary Kay LaBrie, Clermont, FL

Prep: 25 min. • **Bake:** 15 min.
Makes: 4 servings (1 cup sauce)

- 2 frenched racks of lamb (1½ lbs. each)
- 1 Tbsp. steak seasoning
- 4½ tsp. olive oil
- 1 Tbsp. Dijon mustard
- ⅓ cup panko bread crumbs
- 1 Tbsp. minced fresh thyme or 1 tsp. dried thyme
- 1 Tbsp. minced fresh mint or 1 tsp. dried mint
- 1 tsp. Worcestershire sauce
- ½ tsp. dried rosemary, crushed

MUSHROOM SAUCE
- ¾ lb. sliced fresh mushrooms
- 2 Tbsp. olive oil
- ¼ cup butter, divided
- 4 garlic cloves, minced
- ½ cup dry red wine or beef broth
- ¼ cup beef broth
- ½ tsp. honey
- 2 Tbsp. minced chives, optional

1. Preheat oven to 375°. Sprinkle lamb with steak seasoning. Heat oil in a large skillet over medium-high heat; brown lamb, 2 minutes on each side. Brush with mustard.
2. In a small bowl, combine panko, thyme, mint, Worcestershire sauce and rosemary; press onto lamb. Transfer to a greased 15x10-in. baking pan. Bake, uncovered, until meat reaches desired doneness (for medium-rare, a thermometer should read 135°; medium, 140°; medium-well, 145°), 15-20 minutes.
3. Meanwhile, in the same skillet, saute mushrooms in olive oil and 2 Tbsp. butter until tender, 3-5 minutes. Add garlic; cook 1 minute longer. Stir in wine. Bring to a boil; cook until liquid is reduced by half. Remove from heat. Stir in broth, honey, remaining butter and, if desired, chives.
4. Remove lamb from oven; loosely cover with foil and let stand 5 minutes before slicing. Serve with sauce.
½ RACK WITH ¼ CUP SAUCE: 532 cal., 39g fat (14g sat. fat), 130mg chol., 861mg sod., 10g carb. (2g sugars, 1g fiber), 33g pro.

FRENCHING LAMB

"Frenching" a rib or a chop means removing the fat, sinew and meat from the slender end of the bone before cooking.

Why do it? For one simple reason: appearance. Frenched (aka french-trimmed) meat has a cleaner look and makes more elegant presentations possible. A rack of lamb may be brought to the table with the chops standing on their sides, bones crossed in the center like a woven basket. A crown roast of pork is arrayed in a circle, the center filled with dressing.

In previous eras, the bone ends would be covered with paper bonnets called chop frills, which date back to the 1800s. Some butchers supply them on request; you can also find them in kitchen supply stores.

It might seem a waste to cut away meat, but the small bit of edible meat at the slender end of the bone tends to overcook before the rest of the chop is done, so the sacrifice is small.

LEMON-SCENTED BROCCOLINI

Even the most finicky eaters will eagerly eat this vegetable seasoned with lemon pepper, lemon peel and lemon juice. If you prefer, use broccoli instead.
—Kim Champion, Phoenix, AZ

Takes: 30 min. • **Makes:** 12 servings

- 2½ lbs. Broccolini or broccoli spears
- 6 Tbsp. butter
- 1 Tbsp. plus 1½ tsp. lemon juice
- 1 Tbsp. lemon-pepper seasoning
- 1 tsp. grated lemon zest
- ¼ tsp. salt

1. In a large saucepan, bring 4 cups water to a boil. Add Broccolini; cook, uncovered, until just tender, 5-7 minutes. Drain and immediately place Broccolini in ice water. Drain and pat dry.
2. In a large skillet, melt butter. Stir in the lemon juice, lemon pepper, lemon zest and salt. Add Broccolini; toss until heated through.
1 SERVING: 90 cal., 6g fat (4g sat. fat), 15mg chol., 232mg sod., 7g carb. (2g sugars, 1g fiber), 3g pro. **DIABETIC EXCHANGES:** 1 vegetable, 1 fat.
ZESTY BROCCOLINI: Cook Broccolini as directed. Saute 3 minced garlic cloves and 1 tsp. grated fresh ginger in ¼ cup olive oil for 1 minute. Add Broccolini and ¼ tsp. crushed pepper flakes; saute for 1-2 minutes or until heated through.

SPICED PEARL COUSCOUS WITH PINE NUTS

This side dish is ideal for entertaining, as you can prepare the topping ahead of time and the couscous takes only a few minutes. Add a cup of drained and rinsed garbanzo beans or chickpeas to boost the protein in this dish!
—*Cindy Beberman, Orland Park, IL*

Takes: 30 min. • **Makes:** 4 servings

- 2 Tbsp. olive oil
- 1¾ cups finely chopped sweet onion
- 1½ cups uncooked pearl (Israeli) couscous
- 1¾ cups water
- ¾ tsp. salt
- ½ tsp. ground cinnamon
- ½ tsp. curry powder
- ¼ tsp. ground cumin
- ¼ tsp. ground coriander
- ⅓ cup dried currants
- ¼ cup minced fresh cilantro
- 2 Tbsp. finely chopped mint leaves
- 2 tsp. grated lemon zest
- ⅓ cup pine nuts, toasted
    Lemon wedges, optional

1. In a large saucepan, heat oil over medium heat. Add onions; cook and stir until tender, 6-8 minutes. Add couscous; cook and stir until couscous is lightly browned, 2-3 minutes.
2. Add water, salt, cinnamon, curry powder, cumin and coriander; bring to a boil. Reduce heat; simmer covered until liquid is absorbed and couscous is tender, 7-10 minutes. Stir in currants, cilantro, mint and lemon zest; let stand 5 minutes. Fluff with a fork. Sprinkle with toasted pine nuts. If desired, serve with lemon wedges.
1 CUP: 414 cal., 15g fat (2g sat. fat), 0 chol., 449mg sod., 63g carb. (12g sugars, 3g fiber), 10g pro.

HOLIDAY HELPER

Like regular couscous, pearl couscous is made of semolina flour, but it comes in larger balls and has a soft, chewy texture. If cooked too long, it can get mushy, so test it at the low end of the cooking range. Once it's al dente, drain it instead of waiting for all the liquid to absorb.

ROSEMARY-GARLIC DINNER ROLLS

These rolls are so soft and have such wonderful flavor. What a nice touch to bring to both holiday dinners and family meals.
—*Linda Crawford, Milwaukee, WI*

Prep: 15 min. + rising • **Bake:** 15 min.
Makes: 16 rolls

- 1 cup water (70° to 80°)
- 2 Tbsp. butter, softened
- 1 large egg, room temperature, lightly beaten
- 3 Tbsp. sugar
- 1 Tbsp. dried rosemary, crushed
- 2 tsp. dried minced garlic
- 1 tsp. salt
- 3¼ cups bread flour
- 1 pkg. (¼ oz.) active dry yeast
    Large egg, beaten, optional

1. In bread machine pan, place first 9 ingredients in order suggested by manufacturer. Select dough setting (check dough after 5 minutes of mixing; add 1-2 Tbsp. water or flour if needed).
2. When cycle is completed, turn dough onto a lightly floured surface. Divide into 16 portions; shape into balls. Arrange 8 balls in each of 2 greased 9-in. round baking pans. Cover and let dough rise until doubled in size, about 30 minutes. Preheat oven to 375°.
3. If desired, brush rolls with beaten egg; bake until golden brown, 12-15 minutes. Remove from pans to wire racks.
1 ROLL: 111 cal., 2g fat (1g sat. fat), 17mg chol., 162mg sod., 21g carb. (2g sugars, 1g fiber), 4g pro.

PARMESAN, WALNUT & ARUGULA BASKETS

Want to impress your guests? Serve up salad in crispy Parmesan baskets and just watch the reaction!
—*Anna Maria Wharton, Staten Island, NY*

Takes: 30 min. • **Makes:** 6 servings

- 1 cup plus 2 Tbsp. shredded Parmesan cheese
- 2 Tbsp. finely chopped walnuts

SALAD
- 4 cups fresh arugula or spring mix salad greens
- ½ cup green grapes, halved
- 2 Tbsp. chopped walnuts
- 2 Tbsp. olive oil
- 1 Tbsp. raspberry vinegar
- ¼ tsp. salt
- ⅛ tsp. pepper

1. Heat a small nonstick skillet over medium-high heat. Sprinkle 3 Tbsp. cheese and 1 tsp. walnuts over the bottom of the skillet. Cook until edges are golden brown and cheese is bubbly, 1-2 minutes. Remove from the heat; let stand for 30 seconds.
2. Using a spatula, carefully remove cheese mixture and immediately drape over an inverted glass with a 2-in.-diameter bottom; let cool completely. Repeat with the remaining cheese and walnuts, forming 5 more baskets.
3. In a large bowl, combine arugula, grapes and walnuts. Whisk oil, vinegar, salt and pepper; pour over the arugula mixture and toss to coat. Place ½ cup salad in each basket.
1 SERVING: 147 cal., 12g fat (3g sat. fat), 11mg chol., 357mg sod., 4g carb. (3g sugars, 1g fiber), 7g pro.

EARL GREY PANNA COTTA

Panna cotta is a simple dessert that others will think is fancy. Earl Grey tea is one of my favorite flavors, so combining the two seemed like a no-brainer. This recipe is flexible enough that you can make it with other flavors, including green tea (add matcha powder for a stronger flavor) and chai. Or you can omit the tea and serve it as vanilla, either using 2 teaspoons vanilla extract or 1 vanilla bean. For a richer panna cotta, use a mix of 2 cups heavy cream and 1 cup milk instead of the half-and-half.
—*Judith Chow, Saugus, MA*

Prep: 25 min. + chilling • **Makes:** 6 servings

- 1 envelope unflavored gelatin
- 3 cups half-and-half cream
- ¼ cup sugar
  Dash salt
- 2 Earl Grey tea bags
  Fresh berries, optional

1. In a small saucepan, sprinkle gelatin over half-and-half; let stand 1 minute. Stir in sugar and salt. Heat and stir over low heat until gelatin and sugar are completely dissolved. Remove from heat. Add tea bags; steep, covered, 10-15 minutes according to taste. Discard tea bags.
2. Pour into six 4-oz. ramekins or custard cups coated with cooking spray. Refrigerate, covered, until set, about 5 hours. Unmold panna cotta onto plates. Garnish with fresh berries if desired.
1 PANNA COTTA: 196 cal., 12g fat (8g sat. fat), 60mg chol., 87mg sod., 12g carb. (12g sugars, 0 fiber), 5g pro.

FAVORITE WILD RICE SOUP

I'm crazy about homemade soup during the fall and winter months. This wild rice soup is one of my favorite cool-weather experiments.
—*Deborah Williams, Peoria, AZ*

Prep: 10 min. • **Cook:** 50 min.
Makes: 6 servings

2   cups water
⅓   cup uncooked wild rice
¾   tsp. salt, divided
¼   cup butter, cubed
1   medium onion, finely chopped
2   celery ribs, finely chopped
¼   cup all-purpose flour
¼   tsp. freshly ground pepper
5   cups 2% milk
1   tsp. chicken bouillon granules

1. In a small saucepan, bring water to a boil. Stir in wild rice and ¼ tsp. salt. Reduce heat; simmer, covered, until kernels are puffed open, 40-45 minutes.

2. In a large heavy saucepan, heat butter over medium heat; saute onion and celery until tender, 5-7 minutes. Stir in flour, pepper and remaining ½ tsp. salt until blended; gradually stir in the milk and bouillon. Bring to a boil, stirring constantly; cook and stir until thickened, 2-3 minutes.

3. Drain the rice; add to soup. Cook, uncovered, over medium heat for 5 minutes, stirring occasionally.
1 CUP: 231 cal., 12g fat (7g sat. fat), 37mg chol., 604mg sod., 23g carb. (11g sugars, 1g fiber), 9g pro.

HOLIDAY HELPER

Unlike long grain rice, wild rice doesn't always absorb all the water; you may need to drain excess cooking liquid before adding the rice to the soup.

HOW TO SET A FORMAL TABLE

BASIC SETTING
Set the plate in the center, with the fork to the left and the knife and spoon to the right. The water glass goes above the knife, and a napkin is placed under the fork or on the plate.

FORMAL DINNER
Start with a basic setting. Depending on your menu, add:
- Salad fork to the left of the dinner fork. Small plate (for salad or bread) above the forks with a butter spreader across the plate.
- Soup bowl on the plate; soupspoon to the right.
- Cup and saucer to the right of the water glass, above the spoons, with the cup's handle angled to the right.
- Wine glasses to the left of the coffee cup.
- Dessert spoon to the right of the knife. You can also bring them to the table before the dessert course.
- If desired, place a charger under the dinner plate.

✳ ☆ ★
TURKEY FEAST

HONEY-GLAZED TURKEY

Even during the holidays, my husband wouldn't eat turkey—until I tried this recipe. Now he loves it! The sweet and spicy turkey glaze gives the bird a wonderful flavor.
—*Mary Smolka, Spring Grove, IL*

Prep: 25 min. • **Bake:** 3¾ hours
Makes: 20 servings (8 cups stuffing)

1 turkey (14 to 16 lbs.)
GLAZE
½ cup honey
½ cup Dijon mustard
1½ tsp. dried rosemary, crushed
1 tsp. onion powder
½ tsp. salt
¼ tsp. garlic powder
¼ tsp. pepper
STUFFING
½ cup butter, cubed
2 cups chopped onion
1½ cups chopped celery
12 cups unseasoned stuffing
cubes or dry bread cubes
1 Tbsp. poultry seasoning
2 tsp. chicken bouillon granules
1 tsp. pepper
1 tsp. dried rosemary, crushed
1 tsp. lemon-pepper seasoning
¾ tsp. salt
3¼ to 3¾ cups boiling water

1. Preheat oven to 325°. Place turkey on a rack in a shallow roasting pan, breast side up. Tuck wings under turkey; tie drumsticks together. Bake for 2 hours.
2. In a small bowl, mix glaze ingredients; brush over turkey. Bake 1¾-2¼ hours longer or until a thermometer inserted in thickest part of thigh reads 170°-175°. Baste occasionally with pan drippings. (Cover loosely with foil if turkey browns too quickly.)
3. For stuffing, in a Dutch oven, heat the butter over medium-high heat. Add onion and celery; cook and stir until tender. Add stuffing cubes and seasonings; toss to combine. Stir in enough boiling water to reach desired moistness; transfer to a greased 13x9-in. baking dish. Bake, covered, for 1 hour. Uncover; bake until lightly browned, 10-15 minutes longer.

4. Remove turkey from oven; cover loosely with foil and let stand 15 minutes before carving. If desired, skim fat and thicken pan drippings for gravy. Serve with turkey and stuffing.
7 OZ. COOKED TURKEY WITH ABOUT ⅓ CUP STUFFING: 464 cal., 14g fat (6g sat. fat), 133mg chol., 794mg sod., 32g carb. (9g sugars, 2g fiber), 51g pro.

HOLIDAY HELPER ✳☆★

An easy way to thicken or thin a glaze is to apply heat. If the glaze is too thick, place it in a saucepan over low heat, stirring until it is of a thinner consistency that will be easier to brush onto the turkey. If the glaze is too thin, heat the mixture over medium-low heat until it gently bubbles and evaporates a bit, stirring constantly (so it does not burn) until the liquid has reduced a little and reaches the desired thickness.

WHY PAT THE TURKEY DRY?

Since a dry turkey is every cook's holiday nightmare, it might seem wrong to remove moisture before cooking. But moisture on the surface of the turkey (and in the cavity) is actually counterproductive. It will prevent the turkey from forming a nice crisp skin, and it's that crisp skin that helps keep the bird's natural moisture inside the meat.

PROSCIUTTO & PEAS

This distinctive side dish has a delicious, slightly salty flavor. Even people who hate peas will like this one!
—*Ann Sheehy, Lawrence, MA*

Takes: 20 min. • **Makes:** 4 servings

1 Tbsp. olive oil
4 to 8 thin slices prosciutto, julienned
½ cup sliced fresh shiitake mushrooms
2 cups frozen peas, thawed
1 small onion, chopped

1. In a large cast-iron or other heavy skillet, heat oil over medium heat. Add prosciutto; cook until crisp, stirring occasionally. Remove with a slotted spoon; drain on paper towels.
2. Cook and stir mushrooms, peas and onion in drippings until tender, 5-7 minutes. Sprinkle with prosciutto.
¾ CUP: 122 cal., 5g fat (1g sat. fat), 13mg chol., 349mg sod., 11g carb. (4g sugars, 4g fiber), 8g pro.

SWEET POTATO PONE

Sweet potatoes are among my favorite vegetables, and this recipe is my absolute favorite way to prepare them. Not only is it an eagerly anticipated side dish for holiday dinner with family and friends each year, but also I make it to dress up ordinary meals. You can almost serve it as a dessert!
—*Kristine Chayes, Smithtown, NY*

Prep: 15 min. • **Bake:** 55 min. + standing
Makes: 12 servings

- 2½ lbs. large sweet potatoes (about 4 large), peeled and shredded
- ½ cup sugar
- ½ cup light corn syrup
- ½ cup butter, melted
- 1 Tbsp. grated orange zest
- ¾ cup all-purpose flour
- 1 tsp. ground nutmeg
- 1 tsp. ground cinnamon

1. Preheat oven to 350°. In a large bowl, combine sweet potatoes, sugar, corn syrup, butter and orange zest. In a second bowl, combine flour, nutmeg and cinnamon. Add to the sweet potato mixture; mix well.
2. Transfer to a greased 13x9-in. baking dish. Bake until the sweet potatoes are bubbly and golden brown, 55-60 minutes. Let stand 10 minutes before serving.
1 SERVING: 270 cal., 8g fat (5g sat. fat), 20mg chol., 80mg sod., 49g carb. (29g sugars, 3g fiber), 3g pro.

BUTTER-DIPPED BISCUIT SQUARES

These are the easiest and best biscuits I've ever made. They're light and buttery, and they go well with virtually any meal.
—*Rebekah DeWitt, Star City, AR*

Prep: 10 min. • **Bake:** 20 min. + cooling
Makes: 9 servings

- 4 cups self-rising flour
- 2 Tbsp. sugar
- 2 cups 2% milk
- ½ cup butter, melted

1. Preheat oven to 450°. In a large bowl, combine flour and sugar; stir in milk just until moistened. Pour half the butter into a 9x9-in. baking dish. Spoon batter into dish. Gently spread batter evenly in dish using a spatula. Score top of batter into 9 pieces. Drizzle with remaining butter.
2. Bake until the top is lightly browned, 20-25 minutes. Cool in pan on a wire rack for 10 minutes before cutting into pieces. Serve warm.
1 PIECE: 325 cal., 12g fat (7g sat. fat), 31mg chol., 769mg sod., 47g carb. (6g sugars, 2g fiber), 7g pro.

HOLIDAY HELPER

If you don't have self-rising flour on hand, you can make your own. For each cup of self-rising flour called for, place 1½ tsp. baking powder and ½ tsp. salt in a measuring cup, then add all-purpose flour to measure 1 cup.

If you have trouble spreading the batter, try spritzing your spatula with a bit of cooking spray—or oil your hands and use your fingers to push it into place.

CRANBERRY PINEAPPLE SALAD

Impress dinner guests with this delightfully different take on traditional cranberry sauce. The nuts add a tasty crunch.
—*Dorothy Angley, Carver, MA*

Prep: 15 min. + chilling • **Makes:** 12 servings

1¾ cups boiling water
2 pkg. (3 oz. each) raspberry gelatin
1 can (14 oz.) jellied cranberry sauce
1 can (8 oz.) crushed pineapple, undrained
¾ cup orange juice
1 Tbsp. lemon juice
½ cup chopped walnuts
   Lettuce leaves, optional
   Miracle Whip, optional

1. Add boiling water to gelatin; stir until dissolved, about 2 minutes. Stir in cranberry sauce. Add pineapple, orange juice and lemon juice. Refrigerate until thickened, about 30 minutes. Stir in nuts. Pour into an 11x7-in. dish. Refrigerate until set.
2. Cut into 12 squares. If desired, serve each with a lettuce leaf and a dollop of Miracle Whip.
1 PIECE: 149 cal., 3g fat (0 sat. fat), 0 chol., 49mg sod., 30g carb. (25g sugars, 1g fiber), 2g pro.

HOLIDAY HELPER

You can use whole-berry cranberry sauce for this recipe, if you prefer—either canned or homemade. It is not recommended that you use fresh pineapple in this recipe, as the gelatin will not set. If you do prefer to use fresh pineapple, either boil it or steam it for a few minutes before adding it. An alternative method would be to add it to the boiling water before adding the gelatin.

HOLIDAY STUFFED MUSHROOMS

I've been making this recipe for years. It's easy to multiply the recipe and it's very forgiving! Make them ahead of time and then pop them into the oven just before serving. Sometimes I get white blue cheese with cranberries in the specialty cheese section of my grocery store. If you can't find it, the recipe is just as good with a mild blue cheese or feta and chopped dried cranberries.
—*Shannon Copley, Upper Arlington, OH*

Takes: 30 min. • **Makes:** 10 mushrooms

3 bacon strips, cooked crisp and crumbled
2 Tbsp. minced shallots
2 Tbsp. crumbled blue cheese
1 Tbsp. grated Parmesan cheese
1 Tbsp. dried cranberries, finely chopped
¼ tsp. pepper
½ lb. whole baby portobello mushrooms, stems removed
2 Tbsp. shredded cheddar cheese

Preheat oven to 350°. Combine the first 6 ingredients; spoon into the mushroom caps. Sprinkle with shredded cheddar. Bake on a foil-lined baking pan until cheese is melted and mushrooms are tender, 15-20 minutes.
1 STUFFED MUSHROOM: 43 cal., 3g fat (1g sat.fat), 7mg chol., 103mg sod., 2g carb. (2g sugars, 0 fiber), 3g pro.

2. Preheat oven to 425°. On a lightly floured surface, roll larger portion of dough to a ⅛-in.-thick circle; transfer to a 9-in. deep-dish pie plate. Trim crust to ½ in. beyond edge of pie plate. Refrigerate until ready to fill.

3. Roll the smaller portion of dough to ⅛-in. thickness. Cut with a small floured shaped cookie cutter; place some cutouts 1 in. apart on a baking sheet, reserving the unbaked cutouts for decorative edge if desired. Bake until golden brown, 8-10 minutes.

4. Meanwhile, beat together the filling ingredients until blended; transfer to the prepared crust. Flute the edge or decorate with unbaked cutouts, brushing off flour before pressing them lightly onto edge. Bake on a lower oven rack 10 minutes. Cover edge loosely with foil. Reduce oven setting to 350°. Bake until a knife inserted near the center comes out clean, 45-50 minutes.

5. Cool on a wire rack; serve or refrigerate within 2 hours. Top with baked pumpkin cutouts before serving.

NOTE: This recipe was tested with commercially prepared apple butter.

1 PIECE: 647 cal., 28g fat (12g sat. fat), 112mg chol., 277mg sod., 89g carb. (47g sugars, 4g fiber), 9g pro.

AUTUMN HARVEST PUMPKIN PIE

This is the best holiday pie I've ever tasted. In place of the pumpkin-shaped cutouts, you could make whatever shape you like for a Christmasy or other theme.
—*Stan Strom, Gilbert, AZ*

Prep: 30 min. + chilling
Bake: 55 min. + cooling
Makes: 8 servings

2 cups all-purpose flour
1 cup cake flour
2 Tbsp. sugar
½ tsp. salt
½ cup cold unsalted butter, cubed
½ cup butter-flavored shortening
1 large egg
⅓ cup cold water
1 Tbsp. cider vinegar

FILLING
2½ cups canned pumpkin (about 19 oz.)
1¼ cups packed light brown sugar
¾ cup half-and-half cream
2 large eggs
¼ cup apple butter
2 Tbsp. orange juice
2 Tbsp. maple syrup
2 tsp. ground cinnamon
2 tsp. pumpkin pie spice
¼ tsp. salt

1. In a large bowl, mix first 4 ingredients; cut in the butter and shortening until crumbly. Whisk together egg, water and vinegar; gradually add to flour mixture, tossing with a fork until the dough holds together when pressed. Divide dough in half so that 1 portion is slightly larger than the other; shape each into a disk. Wrap; refrigerate 1 hour or overnight.

FRESH VS. CANNED PUMPKIN

You can use cook your own pumpkin to make fresh puree from scratch, but there is no shame in using canned pumpkin—it is easier to use and more budget-friendly. Also, because of the varying water content in individual pumpkins, canned will generally produce more consistent results.

MORE CHOICES FOR CHRISTMAS MENUS

Swap in recipes from this section for individual feast courses to suit your family's taste ... or create a whole new menu, from appetizer to dessert!

ROASTED PEPPERS ON GOAT CHEESE

I love all these flavors and my friends do too! I serve this at any party, barbecue or potluck and it's gone before I can set it down. The pepper and onion mix for this recipe can made a day or two in advance, making it a convenient party option.
—*McKenzie Muscat, Poway, CA*

Takes: 30 min. • **Makes:** 20 servings

- 1   each medium green, sweet red and yellow peppers
- 1   log (11 oz.) fresh goat cheese
- 1   large sweet onion, thinly sliced
- ¼   cup olive oil
- 6   garlic cloves, minced
- 4½   tsp. chopped seeded jalapeno pepper
- 1   tsp. paprika
- 1   tsp. pepper
- ½   tsp. salt
- 3   Tbsp. minced fresh parsley
      Sliced French bread baguette

1. Broil peppers 4 in. from the heat until skins blister, about 5 minutes. With tongs, rotate peppers a quarter turn. Broil and rotate until all sides are blistered and blackened. Immediately place peppers in a large bowl; cover and let stand for 20 minutes. Preheat oven to 350°.

2. Peel off and discard charred skins; remove stems and seeds. Thinly slice peppers. Place cheese in a greased 2-qt. baking dish. Bake just until heated through, 8-10 minutes.

3. Meanwhile, in a large skillet, saute onion in oil until tender. Add the garlic, jalapeno, paprika, pepper and salt; cook 2 minutes longer. Stir in peppers and parsley. Spoon over cheese. Serve with baguette slices.

NOTE: Wear disposable gloves when cutting hot peppers; the oils can burn exposed skin. Avoid touching your face.

ABOUT ½ OZ. CHEESE WITH 7 TSP. PEPPER MIXTURE: 62 cal., 5g fat (2g sat. fat), 10mg chol., 124mg sod., 3g carb. (1g sugars, 1g fiber), 2g pro.

PEAR BROWN BETTY WITH CHINESE FIVE-SPICE

Each fall in the Pacific Northwest, we celebrate the pear and apple harvests. I always make a classic American dish— the brown betty, using pears but adding a new twist, the cinnamon flavors of Chinese five-spice powder. You can use apples instead of the pears, or try a combination of both.
—*David Ross, Spokane Valley, WA*

Prep: 20 min. • **Bake:** 65 min.
Makes: 8 servings

- 6   large ripe Bartlett pears, peeled and chopped
- 1   cup packed dark brown sugar
- ½   tsp. Chinese five-spice powder
- 2   cups soft bread crumbs
- 10   Tbsp. unsalted butter, cubed
      Vanilla ice cream or whipped cream

1. Preheat oven to 375°. Combine pears, brown sugar and Chinese five-spice powder; toss to coat. Place half the pear mixture in a greased 2½-qt. baking dish. Layer with half the bread crumbs and half the butter. Repeat layers.

2. Bake, covered, 40 minutes. Uncover and bake until bubbly and golden brown, 25-30 minutes longer. Serve warm with vanilla ice cream or whipped cream.

1 SERVING: 358 cal., 15g fat (9g sat. fat), 38mg chol., 66mg sod., 58g carb. (44g sugars, 6g fiber), 2g pro.

HOLIDAY HELPER

For a crisp, crumble or brown betty, you'll want a pear that will retain its shape but not stay too crunchy. This recipe calls for Bartlett pears, but you could also use Anjou or Bosc.

ORNAMENT TREES

Nothing brings a shine to the holidays like ornaments. Here, ornaments show they don't belong just on the tree—they can dress up a dinner table as a marvelous centerpiece too!

WHAT YOU'LL NEED
- Spray paint
- Plastic foam cones (in a variety of sizes)
- Ornaments (small, medium and large)
- Greening pins
- Hot glue gun
- Optional: Garland, pearls and ribbons of your choice

INSTRUCTIONS
1. Spray-paint foam cones, then let them dry.
2. Experiment with your ornament arrangement by using greening pins to attach them to the cones. (Place large ornaments first, then medium, then small.)
3. When you're satisfied with the arrangement, glue ornaments to the cone and surrounding ornaments.
4. Embellish with garland, pearls and ribbons if desired.

HONEY-ROASTED HEIRLOOM POTATOES

Colorful! Salty! Sweet! A wonderful spin on the spot that the typical mashed potato dish takes at the holiday table. So versatile, they're delicious with a main course of ham, turkey or beef roast.
—*Linda Povlock, Hampstead, MD*

Prep: 15 min. • **Bake:** 35 min.
Makes: 6 servings

- 2 lbs. fingerling potatoes, halved lengthwise
- ¼ cup finely chopped onion
- 3 Tbsp. olive oil
- 2 Tbsp. honey
- 2 garlic cloves, minced
- 2 tsp. ground mustard
- 1 tsp. dried parsley flakes
- 2 tsp. sea salt
- ½ tsp. coarsely ground pepper
  Additional honey, optional

Preheat oven to 375°. Place potatoes in a greased 15x10x1-in. baking pan. In a small bowl, combine the remaining ingredients. Pour over potatoes; toss to coat. Bake, uncovered, until golden and tender, 35-40 minutes, stirring once halfway through cooking. If desired, drizzle with additional honey.

1 CUP: 225 cal., 7g fat (1g sat. fat), 0 chol., 659mg sod., 37g carb. (8g sugars, 3g fiber), 4g pro.

HOLIDAY HELPER

Fingerling potatoes are perfect for roasting because of their small size and delicate skin. There are different heirloom varieties in an array of colors. Choose potatoes that are roughly the same size; you can cut larger ones in half lengthwise to ensure even cooking.

ROAST PORK LOIN WITH THYME-HONEY MUSTARD SAUCE

Pork loin marinated with thyme, honey and spicy mustard makes a spectacular roast. The flavor is out of this world. A pro chef even complimented me on it!
—*Kelly Williams, Forked River, NJ*

Prep: 25 min. + marinating.
Bake: 1 hour + standing
Makes: 6 servings

- 1   boneless pork loin roast (2 to 3 lbs.)
- 1   cup chicken stock
- ½   cup honey
- ¼   cup unsweetened pineapple juice
- ¼   cup canola oil
- 1   tsp. dried thyme
- ½   tsp. spicy brown mustard
- ½   tsp. salt
- ½   tsp. coarsely ground pepper
  Coarse sea salt

1. Place pork roast in a large bowl or shallow dish. In a small bowl, whisk the stock, honey, pineapple juice, oil, thyme and mustard until blended; add to bowl. Turn pork to coat; cover and refrigerate 1-2 hours.
2. Preheat oven to 375°. Transfer roast and marinade to a greased 13x9-in. baking dish. Sprinkle roast with salt and pepper.
3. Bake until a thermometer reads 145°, 60-70 minutes. Remove roast from baking dish; tent with foil. Let stand for 10 minutes before slicing.
4. Meanwhile, transfer juices from baking dish to a small saucepan. Bring to a boil; cook until the liquid is reduced by half, 8-10 minutes, stirring occasionally. Spoon over roast; sprinkle with sea salt.

4 OZ. COOKED PORK: 366 cal., 16g fat (3g sat. fat), 75mg chol., 331mg sod., 25g carb. (24g sugars, 0 fiber), 30g pro.

MAPLE-GLAZED GREEN BEANS

After I picked my first green beans one year, I wanted to make a savory dish that was original, quick and packed with flavor. I loved this so much I couldn't stop eating it, so the next day I picked more beans and made this delicious side dish again.
—*Merry Graham, Newhall, CA*

Takes: 25 min. • **Makes:** 4 servings

- 3   cups cut fresh green beans
- 1   large onion, chopped
- 4   bacon strips, cut into 1-in. pieces
- ½   cup dried cranberries
- ¼   cup maple syrup
- ¼   tsp. salt
- ¼   tsp. pepper
- 1   Tbsp. bourbon, optional

1. In a large saucepan, place beans in a steamer basket over 1 in. water. Bring water to a boil. Reduce heat to maintain a low boil; steam, covered, until crisp-tender, 4-5 minutes.
2. Meanwhile, in a large skillet, cook onion and bacon over medium heat until the bacon is crisp; drain. Stir cranberries, maple syrup, salt, pepper and, if desired, bourbon into the onion mixture. Add beans; heat through, tossing to combine.

¾ CUP: 173 cal., 3g fat (1g sat. fat), 7mg chol., 302mg sod., 35g carb. (24g sugars, 4g fiber), 4g pro.

CARROT FRUITCAKE

Even those who don't care for fruitcake love this special holiday dessert. It's a fun way to dress up that old favorite, carrot cake. Try it—your friends and family will agree.
—*Ann Parden, Chunchula, AL*

Prep: 20 min.
Bake: 1¼ hours + cooling
Makes: 16 servings

- 1½ cups chopped nuts
- 1 cup chopped mixed candied fruit
- 1 cup chopped dates
- 1 cup raisins
- 3 cups all-purpose flour, divided
- 2 cups sugar
- 1½ cups canola oil
- 4 large eggs
- 2 tsp. baking powder
- 2 tsp. baking soda
- 2 tsp. ground cinnamon
- 1 tsp. salt
- 3 cups finely shredded carrots

ICING

- 1 cup confectioners' sugar
- 1 to 2 Tbsp. 2% milk

1. Preheat oven to 350°. In a small bowl, combine the nuts, candied fruit, dates and raisins. Add ½ cup flour; toss to coat.
2. In a large bowl, combine sugar and oil. Add eggs, 1 at a time, beating well after each addition. In another bowl, mix the remaining 2½ cups flour, the baking powder, baking soda, cinnamon and salt. Gradually add to sugar mixture, beating until smooth. (Batter will be stiff.) Fold in carrots and the nut mixture. Transfer to a greased and floured 10-in. tube pan.
3. Bake for 75-80 minutes or until a toothpick inserted in the center comes out clean. Cool in pan for 15 minutes before removing to a wire rack to cool completely.
4. In a small bowl, mix confectioners' sugar and enough milk to reach desired consistency; drizzle over cake.
1 PIECE: 565 cal., 29g fat (3g sat. fat), 53mg chol., 395mg sod., 75g carb. (49g sugars, 4g fiber), 8g pro.

ROASTED ASPARAGUS

Since asparagus is so abundant here in the spring, I like to put it to great use with this recipe. We all look forward to this side dish each year.
—*Vikki Rebholz, West Chester, OH*

Takes: 25 min. • **Makes:** 12 servings

- 4 lbs. fresh asparagus, trimmed
- ¼ cup olive oil
- ½ tsp. salt
- ¼ tsp. pepper
- ¼ cup sesame seeds, toasted

Preheat oven to 400°. Arrange asparagus in a single layer in 2 foil-lined 15x10x1-in. baking pans. Drizzle with oil. Sprinkle with salt and pepper. Bake, uncovered, until crisp-tender, 12-15 minutes, turning once. Sprinkle with sesame seeds.
1 SERVING: 73 cal., 6g fat (1g sat. fat), 0 chol., 122mg sod., 4g carb. (1g sugars, 2g fiber), 2g pro. **DIABETIC EXCHANGES:** 1 vegetable, 1 fat.

HOLIDAY HELPER

Before you roast the asparagus, rinse it and pat it dry. To trim asparagus, gently bend each stalk and, feeling where it wants to break, snap off the stalk end.

CHEDDAR MASHED CAULIFLOWER

Want an alternative to mashed potatoes? Try cauliflower jazzed up with cheddar cheese and rosemary.
—*Chrystal Baker, Studio City, CA*

Takes: 15 min. • **Makes:** 6 servings

- 2 medium heads cauliflower, broken into florets
- ⅓ cup 2% milk
- 1 Tbsp. minced fresh rosemary
- ½ tsp. salt
- 1 cup shredded sharp cheddar cheese
  Coarsely ground black pepper, optional

1. In a Dutch oven, bring 1 in. water to a boil. Add cauliflower; cover and cook until tender, 5-10 minutes. Drain.
2. Mash cauliflower with the milk, rosemary and salt. Stir in cheese until melted. If desired, top with additional fresh rosemary and coarsely ground black pepper.
¾ CUP: 122 cal., 6g fat (4g sat. fat), 21mg chol., 374mg sod., 12g carb. (5g sugars, 5g fiber), 8g pro.

HOLIDAY HELPER

If you like, you can substitute a different kind of cheese in this recipe. Go for a milder cheddar if you prefer. It would also do nicely with Swiss, Gruyere or Asiago.

FENNEL SALAD WITH ORANGE-BALSAMIC VINAIGRETTE

A sweet balsamic vinaigrette always pulls everything together in a delicious harmony of flavors. Raspberries are one of my very favorite fruits, so I'm always eager to find a new use for them.
—*Susan Gauthier, Falmouth, ME*

Takes: 25 min. • **Makes:** 8 servings

- ¼ cup balsamic vinegar
- ¼ cup maple syrup
- 2 Tbsp. orange marmalade
- 2 Tbsp. seedless raspberry preserves
- ½ tsp. ground mustard
- ¼ tsp. salt
- ⅛ tsp. pepper
- ½ cup olive oil

SALAD
- 1 pkg. (5 oz.) spring mix salad greens
- 2 fennel bulbs, thinly sliced
- 1 can (15 oz.) mandarin oranges, drained
- ¼ cup coarsely chopped pistachios, toasted

1. In a small bowl, whisk the first 7 ingredients. Gradually whisk in oil until blended.
2. In a large bowl, combine salad greens, fennel and oranges. Divide salad green mixture among 8 plates. Sprinkle with pistachios; drizzle with dressing.
1½ CUPS: 240 cal., 16g fat (2g sat. fat), 0 chol., 133mg sod., 25g carb. (18g sugars, 3g fiber), 2g pro.

BEEF TRIANGLES & CHUTNEY DIP

When I brought these crisp, golden brown triangles to a friend's housewarming party, they were gone in minutes. The spices in the beef make them unusual and delicious.
—*Carla DeVelder, Mishawaka, IN*

Prep: 45 min. • **Bake:** 10 min./batch
Makes: 56 appetizers (1 cup sauce)

- 1 lb. ground beef
- 1 small onion, finely chopped
- ⅓ cup dried currants
- ½ tsp. salt
- ½ tsp. ground cumin
- ¼ tsp. ground cinnamon
- ¼ tsp. ground nutmeg
- ⅛ tsp. cayenne pepper
- ⅛ tsp. pepper
- 1 Tbsp. cornstarch
- ½ cup water
- 28 sheets phyllo dough (14x9 in.)
  Butter-flavored cooking spray
- ½ cup plain yogurt
- ½ cup chutney

1. In a large skillet, cook beef and onion over medium heat until beef is no longer pink and onion is tender, 5-7 minutes, breaking up beef into crumbles; drain.

Stir in currants and seasonings. Combine the cornstarch and water until smooth; gradually stir into the beef mixture. Bring to a boil; cook and stir until thickened, 2 minutes. Remove from the heat.
2. Place 1 sheet of phyllo dough on a work surface with a short end facing you; spray sheet with butter-flavored spray. Place another sheet of phyllo on top and spritz with spray. (Keep the remaining phyllo covered with a damp towel to prevent it from drying out.) Cut the 2 layered sheets into four 14x2¼-in. strips. Preheat oven to 400°.
3. Place 1 rounded tsp. filling on the lower corner of each strip. Fold dough over filling, forming a triangle. Fold triangle up, then fold triangle over, forming another triangle. Continue folding, like a flag, until you come to the end of the strip. Spritz end of dough with spray and press onto triangle to seal. Turn triangle and spritz top with spray. Repeat with remaining phyllo and filling.
4. Place triangles on baking sheets coated with cooking spray. Bake until golden brown, 8-10 minutes. Combine yogurt and chutney. Serve with warm appetizers.
1 TRIANGLE WITH ¾ TSP. SAUCE: 41 cal., 1g fat (0 sat. fat), 4mg chol., 51mg sod., 5g carb. (2g sugars, 0 fiber), 2g pro.

GLAZED CORNISH HENS

If you're looking to add a touch of elegance to your Christmas dinner table, our Test Kitchen experts suggest these Cornish game hens topped with a sweet apricot glaze.
—Taste of Home *Test Kitchen*

Prep: 5 min. • **Bake:** 1 hour
Makes: 4 servings

- 2 Cornish game hens (20 to 24 oz. each), split lengthwise
- ¼ tsp. salt
- ⅛ tsp. white pepper
- ⅓ cup apricot spreadable fruit
- 1 Tbsp. orange juice

1. Preheat oven to 350°. Place hens, breast side up, on a rack in a shallow roasting pan. Sprinkle with salt and pepper. Bake, uncovered, 30 minutes.
2. In a small bowl, combine spreadable fruit and orange juice. Spoon some of the apricot mixture over the hens. Bake until golden brown and juices run clear, 30-35 minutes, basting several times with remaining apricot mixture. Let stand 5 minutes before serving.
½ HEN: 402 cal., 24g fat (7g sat. fat), 175mg chol., 233mg sod., 14g carb. (11g sugars, 0 fiber), 30g pro.

SEASONAL SIDE DISH CASSEROLES

Hearty and comforting, casseroles are a convenient and always welcome side dish. They come together quickly and most often can be made in advance, so they fit into a busy holiday cooking schedule with little fuss.

PANCETTA BRIOCHE DRESSING

I crave this creamy, crunchy stuffing every year. And I suspect my guests do too. It's usually gone before the turkey!
—*Jamie Brown-Miller, Napa, CA*

Prep: 15 min. • **Bake:** 25 min. • **Makes:** 12 servings

- 16 cups cubed brioche bread (about 1¾ lbs.)
- 2 cups diced red onions
- ¼ tsp. kosher salt
- ⅛ tsp. pepper
- 2 Tbsp. olive oil
- 2 cups chopped radicchio
- 1½ cups chicken broth
- 5 oz. pancetta, diced
- 2 large eggs, lightly beaten
- 2 Tbsp. minced fresh rosemary
- ¼ cup crumbled Roquefort or blue cheese

1. Preheat oven to 400°. Spread bread cubes on a baking sheet; bake until dried (do not brown), 6-8 minutes. Set aside.
2. Meanwhile, in a large skillet, cook the onions, salt and pepper in oil over medium-high heat until onions begin to brown. Stir in radicchio; remove from the heat.
3. In a large bowl, combine the bread cubes, radicchio mixture, chicken broth, pancetta, eggs and rosemary; gently toss to combine. Transfer to a greased 13x9-in. baking dish. Sprinkle with crumbled cheese. Bake, uncovered, until golden brown, 25-30 minutes.
¾ CUP: 169 cal., 7g fat (2g sat. fat), 32mg chol., 485mg sod., 20g carb. (3g sugars, 1g fiber), 6g pro.

CURRIED CARROTS WITH CRUNCHY PEANUT TOPPING

I use this recipe to make the most of my homegrown carrots. Warm curry spice and a crunchy peanut topping make this a no-leftovers dish. If you want to add a burst of green, use half carrots and half broccoli florets.
—*Trisha Kruse, Eagle, ID*

Prep: 20 min. • **Bake:** 20 min. • **Makes:** 6 servings

- 2 lbs. fresh carrots, cut into ½-in. slices
- 2 medium onions, halved and sliced ¼ in. thick
- ¾ cup mayonnaise
- ⅓ cup half-and-half cream
- 1 to 2 Tbsp. curry powder
- 1 tsp. salt
- ¼ tsp. pepper
- 20 Ritz crackers, crushed (about 1 cup)
- ½ cup chopped salted peanuts
- 2 Tbsp. butter, melted

1. Preheat oven to 350°. In a large saucepan, bring 2 in. water to a boil. Add carrots; return to a boil. Reduce heat; simmer 4 minutes. Add onions; return to a boil. Reduce heat; simmer until the carrots are tender, 4-5 minutes. Drain vegetables; return to pan.
2. Whisk together mayonnaise, cream, curry powder, salt and pepper. Pour over vegetables; toss to coat. Transfer to a greased 11x7-in. or 8-in. square baking dish. Combine crushed crackers and peanuts; sprinkle over carrots. Drizzle melted butter over top. Bake, uncovered, until bubbly, 20-25 minutes.
⅔ CUP: 438 cal., 35g fat (8g sat. fat), 19mg chol., 820mg sod., 28g carb. (10g sugars, 6g fiber), 6g pro.

EGGPLANT NAPOLEON CASSEROLE

When dining at the Kenyon Inn in Ohio, I tried their eggplant Napoleon—such a fantastic blend of texture and flavor! I created my own at home, and it's now my all-time favorite dish, home or away.
—*Brenda Scheiderer, Fredericktown, OH*

Prep: 1½ hours • **Bake:** 45 min. + standing
Makes: 15 servings

CRANBERRY SAUCE
- ½ cup sugar
- ¼ cup packed brown sugar
- ½ cup water
- ½ cup orange juice
- 1 pkg. (12 oz.) fresh or frozen cranberries
- 1 medium apple, peeled and chopped
- 1 tsp. vanilla extract
- ½ tsp. ground cinnamon

MASHED SWEET POTATOES
- 3 lbs. sweet potatoes, peeled and chopped
- ¼ cup packed brown sugar
- 2 Tbsp. butter

RISOTTO
- 4 cups vegetable broth
- 1 Tbsp. olive oil
- 1 large onion, chopped
- 1 cup uncooked arborio rice
- ½ cup whole milk
- ¼ cup grated Parmesan cheese
- ½ tsp. garlic salt

ASSEMBLY
- 1 large egg
- ¼ cup whole milk
- ¾ cup crushed cornflakes
- ¾ cup seasoned bread crumbs
- 1 medium eggplant, sliced into ¼-in. slices
  Cooking spray

1. In a small saucepan, bring sugars, water and orange juice to a boil over high heat. Add cranberries and apple; reduce heat and simmer, stirring occasionally, until the berries pop and sauce begins to thicken, about 30 minutes. Remove from heat; add vanilla and cinnamon.

2. Meanwhile, place sweet potatoes in a Dutch oven; add water to cover. Bring to a boil. Reduce heat; cook, uncovered, until tender, 15-20 minutes. Drain; place potatoes in a large bowl. Mash potatoes, gradually adding brown sugar and butter.

3. For risotto, in a small saucepan, bring broth to a simmer; keep hot. In the same Dutch oven used for potatoes, heat olive oil over medium heat. Add onion; cook and stir until softened, 6-8 minutes. Stir in rice, cook until rice is coated, 1-2 minutes. Add milk. Reduce heat to maintain a simmer; cook and stir until milk is absorbed. Add hot broth, ½ cup at a time, cooking and stirring until broth has been absorbed after each addition, until rice is tender but firm to the bite and risotto is creamy. Remove from heat; stir in Parmesan cheese and garlic salt. Spread risotto into a greased 13x9-in. baking dish; keep warm.

4. Preheat oven to 350°. In a shallow bowl, whisk together egg and milk until combined. In a second shallow bowl, combine cornflakes and bread crumbs. Dip eggplant in egg mixture, then into bread crumb mixture. Place on greased baking sheets; spritz with cooking spray. Bake until tender and golden brown, 15-20 minutes, turning once.

5. Layer half the eggplant slices on top of risotto; top with mashed sweet potatoes. Spread half the cranberry sauce over sweet potatoes. Top with remaining eggplant; spread remaining cranberry sauce over eggplant slices. Bake, uncovered, until bubbly, 45-50 minutes. Let stand 15 minutes before serving.

1 PIECE: 302 cal., 4g fat (2g sat. fat), 14mg chol., 399mg sod., 62g carb. (29g sugars, 5g fiber), 5g pro.

HOLIDAY HELPER

To save on time, much of this dish can be prepared in advance. The cranberry sauce, sweet potatoes and risotto can each be made ahead of time, or the whole thing can be made and assembled, and then placed in the refrigerator until ready to bake. Take the casserole out of the refrigerator 30-60 minutes before baking to let it come to room temperature.

MINTED PARSNIP SOUFFLE

These elegant souffles make wonderful use of a root vegetable that is often overlooked. The subtle mint pairs well with a variety of meats.
—*Catherine Wilkinson, Prescott, AZ*

Prep: 50 min. • **Bake:** 20 min.
Makes: 6 servings

- 3 large eggs
- 3 Tbsp. butter, divided
- 3 Tbsp. all-purpose flour, divided
- 1½ lbs. medium parsnips, peeled and sliced
- 2 Tbsp. finely chopped onion
- ½ cup water
- 2 tsp. lemon juice
- 3 Tbsp. sugar
- 1 tsp. salt
- 1 cup half-and-half cream
- 2 Tbsp. minced fresh mint

1. Separate eggs; let stand at room temperature for 30 minutes. Preheat oven to 350°. Grease six 8-oz. ramekins with 1 Tbsp. butter and dust with 1 Tbsp. flour.
2. Place the parsnips, onion and water in a large microwave-safe bowl. Cover and microwave on high until parsnips are tender, 5-7 minutes. Let stand for 5 minutes; drain. Place parsnip mixture and lemon juice in a food processor; cover and process until blended. Set aside.
3. In a small saucepan over medium heat, melt remaining butter. Stir in the sugar, remaining flour and the salt until blended. Gradually whisk in cream. Bring to a boil, stirring constantly; cook, stirring until thickened, 1-2 minutes longer. Transfer to a large bowl; stir in mint.
4. Stir a small amount of the hot mixture into the egg yolks; return all to the bowl, stirring constantly. Cool slightly; stir in the parsnip mixture.
5. In another bowl with clean beaters, beat egg whites until stiff peaks form. Stir a fourth of the egg whites into the egg yolk mixture until no white streaks remain. Fold in remaining egg whites until combined. Transfer to prepared ramekins.
6. Bake until the tops are puffed and center appears set, 20-25 minutes. Serve immediately.

1 SOUFFLE: 256 cal., 13g fat (7g sat. fat), 141mg chol., 500mg sod., 30g carb. (13g sugars, 4g fiber), 6g pro.

BACON RANCH CAULIFLOWER CASSEROLE

I was looking for something instead of potatoes or rice that could be prepped for a large group, and this cauliflower casserole with crowd-pleasing ranch and bacon flavors was just the thing. You can use low-fat mayo or substitute plain yogurt for the mayo to make it healthier.
—*Sandie Heindel, Liberty, MO*

Prep: 35 min. • **Bake:** 15 min.
Makes: 16 servings

- 2 medium heads cauliflower, broken into florets (about 12 cups)
- ⅛ tsp. salt
- ⅛ tsp. pepper
- 1 cup shredded mozzarella cheese
- 1 cup shredded Colby-Monterey Jack cheese, divided
- 10 bacon strips, cooked and crumbled
- ⅔ cup sour cream
- ⅔ cup mayonnaise
- ⅓ cup prepared ranch salad dressing
- ¼ cup grated Parmesan cheese
- ¼ cup thinly sliced green onions, divided
- 3 garlic cloves, minced
- 1 Tbsp. minced fresh parsley, divided

1. Preheat oven to 425°. Place the cauliflower in a 15x10x1-in. baking pan. Sprinkle with salt and pepper. Roast until the florets are tender and lightly browned, 30-35 minutes, stirring once.
2. In a small bowl, combine mozzarella, ½ cup Colby-Monterey Jack, bacon, sour cream, mayonnaise, ranch dressing, Parmesan, 2 Tbsp. green onions, garlic and 1½ tsp. parsley.
3. Transfer roasted cauliflower to a greased 13x9-in. baking dish. Dollop sour cream mixture over top; sprinkle with the remaining ½ cup Colby-Monterey Jack, 2 Tbsp. green onions and 1½ tsp. parsley.
4. Bake, uncovered, until heated through and cheese is melted, 12-15 minutes.

¾ CUP: 195 cal., 17g fat (6g sat. fat), 30mg chol., 339mg sod., 5g carb. (2g sugars, 2g fiber), 7g pro.

PATTERN PLAY

A little paint can transform plain white baskets into cozy catchalls. Celebrate the arrival of sweater weather by painting a basket in a pattern inspired by Nordic woolens.

WHAT YOU'LL NEED
- Baskets from a local craft or department store
- Pencil
- Fabric paint
- Flat brushes
- Rag for wiping away paint

INSTRUCTIONS
1. With a pencil, rough in the outline of your chosen design.
2. Squeeze some fabric paint, in colors of your choice, onto a paper plate.
3. Use a flat brush to apply the paint, wiping away smudges with a damp rag.
4. Once the paint is dry, fill the basket with seasonal decor, such as birch branches or a potted pine tree.

EASY APPLE SWEET POTATO BAKE

I've been cooking since I was 7 years old, and I still get excited when I find a recipe that is not only good but quick and easy to make. This sweet and nutty side dish is the perfect example.
—*Valerie Walker, Canton, IL*

Prep: 45 min. • **Bake:** 45 min.
Makes: 8 servings

- 2½ lbs. sweet potatoes
- ½ cup packed brown sugar
- ⅓ cup chopped walnuts
- 1 tsp. ground cinnamon
- ⅛ tsp. salt
- 3 cups thinly sliced peeled tart apples
- 4 Tbsp. butter, divided

1. Place the sweet potatoes in a large saucepan and cover with water. Bring to a boil. Reduce heat; cover and simmer 30 minutes or until tender. Drain. When cool enough to handle, peel potatoes and cut into ½-in. slices.

2. Preheat oven to 375°. In a small bowl, combine the brown sugar, walnuts, cinnamon and salt; set aside. In a large skillet, saute apples in 2 Tbsp. butter until tender, 3-4 minutes.

3. In a greased 1½-qt. baking dish, layer half the sweet potatoes, apples and brown sugar mixture. Repeat layers.

4. Dot with remaining 2 Tbsp. butter. Cover and bake 30 minutes. Uncover; bake until bubbly, 15 minutes longer.

1 SERVING: 284 cal., 9g fat (4g sat. fat), 15mg chol., 163mg sod., 50g carb. (38g sugars, 5g fiber), 3g pro.

HOLIDAY HELPER

To save on time, this side dish could be prepared and assembled ahead of time, then kept in the refrigerator overnight and baked before serving.

After baking, there will be some brown-sugar syrup in the bottom of the dish; if you like, use a spoon to scoop it up and drizzle it over the top of each serving.

GRANDPA'S PARTY POTATOES

My grandpa, who gave me this recipe, liked the way the cream cheese and onion dip created a wonderful velvety texture. I often assemble these potatoes the night before, then pop them in the oven the next day.
—*Mary Kay Elert, St. Paul Park, MN*

Prep: 20 min. + chilling • **Bake:** 50 min. • **Makes:** 14 servings

    12 medium potatoes, peeled and quartered
     2 Tbsp. butter
     2 Tbsp. 2% milk
    ¾ tsp. salt
    ¼ tsp. pepper
     1 pkg. (8 oz.) cream cheese, softened
     1 carton (8 oz.) French onion dip
        Paprika

1. Place potatoes in a large saucepan and cover with water. Bring to a boil. Reduce heat; cover and cook until tender, 15-20 minutes. Drain. Mash the potatoes with butter, milk, salt and pepper until smooth. Add cream cheese and onion dip; mix well.
2. Spread in a greased 2½-qt. baking dish. Sprinkle with paprika. Cover and refrigerate 8 hours or overnight.
3. Remove from the refrigerator 30 minutes before baking. Preheat oven to 350°. Bake, uncovered, until heated through, 50-60 minutes.
1 CUP: 181 cal., 10g fat (6g sat. fat), 22mg chol., 316mg sod., 21g carb. (2g sugars, 2g fiber), 4g pro.

HONEY BAKED LENTILS

This recipe originally had bacon in it, but I eliminated it in order to make a vegetarian dish. I added liquid smoke and additional vegetables. Serve with brown rice and additional soy sauce.
—*Suzanne Rumsey, Fort Wayne, IN*

Prep: 30 min. • **Bake:** 1 hour • **Makes:** 10 servings

     1 pkg. (16 oz.) dried lentils, rinsed
     6 cups water, divided
     2 tsp. salt
     1 bay leaf
     2 cups chopped onions
     4 medium carrots, finely chopped
     1 Tbsp. reduced-sodium soy sauce
     1 tsp. ground mustard
     1 tsp. liquid smoke
    ¼ tsp. ground ginger
    ⅓ cup honey

1. Preheat oven to 350°. In a large saucepan, combine the lentils, 5 cups water, the salt and bay leaf. Bring to a boil. Reduce heat; cover and simmer until the lentils are tender, 20-25 minutes. Discard bay leaf.
2. In a large bowl, combine onions, carrots, soy sauce, mustard, liquid smoke, ginger and the remaining 1 cup water. Gently stir in lentils. Transfer to a greased 13x9-in. baking dish. Drizzle with honey.
3. Bake, covered, 30 minutes. Uncover; bake until the carrots are tender, 30-35 minutes longer.
¾ CUP: 219 cal., 1g fat (0 sat. fat), 0 chol., 551mg sod., 43g carb. (13g sugars, 6g fiber), 12g pro.

BRUSSELS SPROUTS GRATIN

If you don't typically enjoy Brussels sprouts, this recipe will change your mind. It's creamy, savory and delicious.
—*Kevin Lieberman, Oklahoma City, OK*

Prep: 45 min. • **Bake:** 10 min.
Makes: 10 servings

- 2 lbs. Brussels sprouts, quartered
- 2 Tbsp. butter, melted
- ¾ tsp. salt
- ⅛ tsp. pepper

CREAM SAUCE
- 1 large onion, chopped
- 3 Tbsp. butter
- 3 Tbsp. all-purpose flour
- 1 cup whole milk
- 1 cup heavy whipping cream
- ⅛ tsp. white pepper
  Dash ground nutmeg

TOPPING
- ½ cup shredded Gruyere cheese
- ¼ cup grated Parmesan cheese

1. Preheat oven to 425°. In a large bowl, combine the Brussels sprouts, butter, salt and pepper; toss to coat. Transfer to a greased 13x9-in. baking dish. Bake, uncovered, for 25-30 minutes or until Brussels sprouts are tender, stirring occasionally.
2. Meanwhile, for the sauce, in a large skillet, saute onion in butter until tender. Stir in flour until blended; gradually add milk and cream. Bring to a boil; cook and stir for 2 minutes or until thickened. Stir in pepper and nutmeg.
3. Pour sauce over the Brussels sprouts. Sprinkle with cheeses. Reduce heat to 350°. Bake, uncovered, for 10-15 minutes or until heated through and the cheeses are melted.
¾ CUP: 233 cal., 18g fat (11g sat. fat), 58mg chol., 309mg sod., 13g carb. (4g sugars, 4g fiber), 7g pro.

HOLIDAY HELPER

Gruyere is rightfully prized for its complex, earthy flavor and smooth melt, but it can be pricey. If Gruyere isn't in your budget, you can substitute Swiss, Emmenthaler or Jarlsburg. Gouda or Comte would also work well in this recipe but would have a different flavor.

DELUXE CORNBREAD STUFFING

When my husband and I were newlyweds and far from family, we invited friends over for a holiday feast. I searched for dressing recipes and combined several to create this pleasing one.
—*Pamela Rickman, Valdosta, GA*

Prep: 20 min. • **Bake:** 55 min.
Makes: 12 servings

- 6 cups crumbled cornbread
- 2 cups white bread cubes, toasted
- 1 cup chopped pecans
- ¼ cup minced fresh parsley
- 1 tsp. dried thyme
- ½ tsp. rubbed sage
- ½ tsp. salt
- ½ tsp. pepper
- 1 lb. bulk pork sausage
- 2 Tbsp. butter
- 2 large tart apples, diced
- 1 cup diced celery
- 1 medium onion, finely chopped
- 1¾ to 2¼ cups chicken broth

1. Preheat oven to 350°. In a large bowl, combine the cornbread, bread cubes, pecans and seasonings; set aside.
2. Crumble sausage into a large cast-iron or other ovenproof skillet; cook over medium heat until no longer pink, breaking into crumbles. Remove with slotted spoon; drain on paper towels.
3. Add butter to drippings; saute the apples, celery and onion until tender. Add to bread mixture; stir in sausage and enough broth to moisten.
4. Spoon the mixture into cast-iron skillet; cover and bake for 45 minutes. Uncover and bake just until set, about 10 minutes longer.
1 CUP: 326 cal., 18g fat (4g sat. fat), 19mg chol., 780mg sod., 35g carb. (8g sugars, 4g fiber), 8g pro.

CHEESY CORN SPOON BREAD

Homey and comforting, this custardlike side dish is a much-requested recipe at potlucks and holiday dinners. The jalapeno adds just the right bite. Second helpings of this tasty casserole are common—leftovers aren't.
—*Katherine Franklin, Carbondale, IL*

Prep: 15 min. • **Bake:** 35 min. • **Makes:** 15 servings

- ¼ cup butter, cubed
- 1 medium onion, chopped
- 2 large eggs
- 2 cups sour cream
- 1 can (15¼ oz.) whole kernel corn, drained
- 1 can (14¾ oz.) cream-style corn
- ¼ tsp. salt
- ¼ tsp. pepper
- 1 pkg. (8½ oz.) cornbread/muffin mix
- 2 medium jalapeno peppers, divided
- 2 cups shredded cheddar cheese, divided

1. Preheat oven to 375°. In a large skillet, heat butter over medium-high heat. Add onion; saute until tender. Set aside.
2. Beat eggs; add sour cream, both cans of corn, salt and pepper. Stir in cornbread mix just until blended. Mince 1 jalapeno pepper; fold into corn mixture with sauteed onion and 1½ cups cheese.
3. Transfer to a greased shallow 3-qt. baking dish. Sprinkle with remaining ½ cup cheese. Bake, uncovered, until a toothpick inserted in center comes out clean, 35-40 minutes; cool slightly. Slice remaining jalapeno; sprinkle over dish.
NOTE: Wear disposable gloves when cutting hot peppers; the oils can burn exposed skin. Avoid touching your face.
1 SERVING: 266 cal., 17g fat (9g sat. fat), 56mg chol., 470mg sod., 21g carb. (7g sugars, 2g fiber), 8g pro.

FESTIVE WILD RICE CASSEROLE

My favorite holiday dish as a child was my Grandma Adeline's wild rice casserole. I always went back for seconds ... or thirds! As an adult I received the recipe, but it didn't taste as good as I remembered, so I began to play around with it. This is now my version—bigger, better and a staple at holiday dinners. To make this more of a main dish, consider adding some leftover ham or turkey.
—*Virginia Louden, Anoka, MN*

Prep: 30 min. • **Bake:** 25 min. • **Makes:** 6 servings

- 3 Tbsp. butter
- ½ lb. whole fresh mushrooms, chopped
- 1 small onion, chopped
- 1 Tbsp. minced garlic
- 1 pkg. (8 oz.) cream cheese, softened
- ½ cup sour cream
- ½ tsp. salt
- ½ tsp. pepper
- 1 cup cooked wild rice
- ½ cup slivered almonds, toasted, divided
- ½ cup dried cranberries, divided

1. Preheat oven to 350°. Melt butter in a large skillet over medium-high heat. Add mushrooms and onion; cook for 2-3 minutes. Add garlic; cook and stir until mushrooms are soft and lightly browned, 8-10 minutes.
2. Meanwhile, in a large bowl, mix together cream cheese, sour cream, salt and pepper until smooth and creamy. Stir in the mushroom mixture, cooked rice, 6 Tbsp. toasted almonds and 6 Tbsp. cranberries until blended.
3. Transfer mixture to a greased 9-in. pie plate. Top with remaining 2 Tbsp. almonds and 2 Tbsp. cranberries. Bake until heated through, about 25 minutes.
½ CUP: 360 cal., 28g fat (14g sat. fat), 67mg chol., 372mg sod., 24g carb. (14g sugars, 3g fiber), 7g pro.

SCALLOPED PINEAPPLE SIDE DISH CASSEROLE

If you like pairing pineapple with your Christmas ham, you'll love this side dish. It's also a wonderful choice for potlucks and church suppers.
—*Diana Loewen, Benton Harbor, MI*

Prep: 10 min. • **Bake:** 40 min. • **Makes:** 8 servings

- 3 large eggs
- ½ cup sugar
- ½ cup butter, melted
- ½ cup sweetened condensed milk
- 1 can (20 oz.) unsweetened crushed pineapple, undrained
- 4 cups cubed bread

1. Preheat oven to 350°. In a large bowl, whisk the eggs, sugar, butter and milk. Stir in pineapple with juice; fold in bread cubes. Transfer to a greased 8-in. square baking dish.
2. Bake, uncovered, until a thermometer inserted in the center reads 160°, 40-45 minutes. Let stand for 10 minutes before serving.
⅔ CUP: 328 cal., 16g fat (9g sat. fat), 107mg chol., 229mg sod., 43g carb. (34g sugars, 1g fiber), 6g pro.

SPINACH-PARM CASSEROLE

For those who ignore Popeye and won't eat their spinach, I find that spinach with garlicky butter and Parmesan helps change their minds.
—*Judy Batson, Tampa, FL*

Takes: 25 min. • **Makes:** 6 servings

- 2 lbs. fresh baby spinach
- 5 Tbsp. butter
- 3 Tbsp. olive oil
- 3 garlic cloves, minced
- 1 Tbsp. Italian seasoning
- ¾ tsp. salt
- 1 cup grated Parmesan cheese

1. Preheat oven to 400°. In a stockpot, bring 5 cups water to a boil. Add spinach; cook, covered, 1 minute or just until wilted. Drain well.
2. In a small skillet, heat butter and oil over medium-low heat. Add garlic, Italian seasoning and salt; cook and stir until garlic is tender, 1-2 minutes.
3. Spread spinach in a greased 1½-qt. or 8-in. square baking dish. Drizzle with butter mixture; sprinkle with cheese. Bake, uncovered, until cheese is lightly browned, 10-15 minutes.
⅔ CUP: 239 cal., 21g fat (9g sat. fat), 37mg chol., 703mg sod., 7g carb. (1g sugars, 3g fiber), 10g pro.

GREEN BEAN CASSEROLE

This casserole has always been one of my favorite dishes—it's so easy to put together! You can make it before any guests arrive and keep it refrigerated until baking time.
—*Anna Baker, Blaine, WA*

Prep: 15 min. • **Bake:** 30 min.
Makes: 10 servings

- 2 cans (10¾ oz. each) condensed cream of mushroom soup, undiluted
- 1 cup 2% milk
- 2 tsp. soy sauce
- ⅛ tsp. pepper
- 2 pkg. (16 oz. each) frozen green beans, cooked and drained
- 1 can (6 oz.) french-fried onions, divided

1. Preheat oven to 350°. In a bowl, combine soup, milk, soy sauce and pepper. Gently stir in beans. Spoon half the mixture into a 13x9-in. baking dish. Sprinkle with half the onions. Spoon the remaining bean mixture over the top. Sprinkle with the remaining onions.
2. Bake until heated through and onions are brown and crispy, 30-35 minutes.
1 CUP: 163 cal., 11g fat (3g sat. fat), 5mg chol., 485mg sod., 14g carb. (2g sugars, 1g fiber), 2g pro.

BOXING DAY LUNCHEON

Boxing Day is celebrated the day after Christmas—so it's an ideal time to use up the leftovers from the holiday feast! Use these recipes to make second-day delicacies that are all first rate.

MANDARIN STEAK SALAD

Your family will think you spent hours on this luscious salad, but it couldn't be easier to pull together. What an impressive way to use up leftover flank steak—or any other cut of beef!
—Taste of Home *Test Kitchen*

Takes: 25 min. • **Makes:** 4 servings (1 cup vinaigrette)

⅓ cup olive oil
¼ cup cider vinegar
¼ cup orange juice
2 Tbsp. minced fresh parsley
2 Tbsp. honey
1 garlic clove, minced
1 tsp. chili sauce
½ tsp. salt
4 cups torn romaine
1 lb. cooked beef sirloin steak, sliced
1 cup sliced fresh strawberries
1 small red onion, sliced
1 can (11 oz.) mandarin oranges, drained
2 cups pecan halves, toasted
1 pkg. (5.3 oz.) fresh goat cheese, crumbled

In a small bowl, whisk the first 8 ingredients; set aside. Divide romaine among 4 plates; top with steak, strawberries, onion, oranges, pecans and cheese. Serve with vinaigrette.
1 SERVING: 926 cal., 69g fat (12g sat. fat), 118mg chol., 549mg sod., 39g carb. (28g sugars, 8g fiber), 45g pro.

CHICKEN CURRY POT PIE

This savory pie combines two of my favorite things: comfort food and Indian food! Using precooked chicken makes it an easy and delicious way to use up leftovers.
—Angela Spengler, Niceville, FL

Prep: 10 min. • **Bake:** 30 min. • **Makes:** 6 servings

⅓ cup plus 1 tsp. butter, divided
1 small onion, chopped
⅓ cup all-purpose flour
2 tsp. plus ¼ tsp. curry powder, divided
¼ tsp. salt
¼ tsp. pepper
1½ cups chicken broth
⅔ cup 2% milk
2 cups cubed cooked chicken
1 can (15 oz.) sweet potatoes
¾ cup frozen peas
¾ cup frozen sliced carrots
Dough for double-crust pie

1. Preheat oven to 425°. In a large skillet heat ⅓ cup butter over medium-high heat. Add onion; cook and stir until tender, 3-5 minutes. Stir in flour, 2 tsp. curry powder, salt and pepper until blended; gradually whisk in broth and milk. Bring to a boil, stirring constantly; cook and stir until thickened, about 2 minutes. Stir in chicken, sweet potatoes, peas and carrots.
2. On a lightly floured surface, roll half of the dough to a ⅛-in.-thick circle; transfer to a 9-in. pie plate. Trim even with rim. Add filling. Roll remaining dough to a ⅛-in.-thick circle. Place over filling. Trim, seal and flute edge. Cut slits in top.
3. Bake until crust is golden brown and filling is bubbly, 30-35 minutes. Rub top with remaining butter and sprinkle with remaining ¼ tsp. curry powder.
DOUGH FOR DOUBLE-CRUST PIE: Combine 2½ cups all-purpose flour and ½ tsp. salt; cut in 1 cup cold butter until crumbly. Gradually add ⅓-⅔ cup ice water, tossing with a fork until dough holds together when pressed. Divide dough in half and shape into disks; wrap and refrigerate 1 hour.
1 PIECE: 777 cal., 47g fat (28g sat. fat), 154mg chol., 944mg sod., 67g carb. (15g sugars, 5g fiber), 23g pro.

HOMEMADE TURKEY SOUP

You can make the most of even the smallest pieces of leftover meat on your holiday turkey with this homemade turkey soup. I simmer the bones to get the rich flavor then easily remove any meat that remains. I add rice, vegetables and cream soup for a hearty soup that's tasty and economical.
—*June Sangrey, Manheim, PA*

Prep: 30 min. • **Cook:** 2 hours 35 min.
Makes: 10 servings (about 2½ qt.)

- 1 leftover turkey carcass (from a 10- to 12-lb. turkey)
- 2 qt. water
- 1 medium onion, cut into wedges
- ½ tsp. salt
- 2 bay leaves
- 1 cup chopped carrots
- 1 cup uncooked long grain rice
- ⅓ cup chopped celery
- ¼ cup chopped onion
- 1 can (10½ oz.) condensed cream of chicken or cream of mushroom soup, undiluted

1. Place the turkey carcass in a stockpot; add the water, onion, salt and bay leaves. Slowly bring to a boil over low heat; cover and simmer for 2 hours.
2. Remove carcass; cool. Strain broth and skim fat. Discard onion and bay leaves. Return broth to the pan. Add the carrots, rice, celery and chopped onion; cover and simmer until rice and vegetables are tender.
3. Remove turkey meat from bones; discard bones and cut turkey into bite-sized pieces. Add turkey and cream soup to broth; heat through.
1 CUP: 128 cal., 2g fat (1g sat. fat), 3mg chol., 391mg sod., 21g carb. (1g sugars, 1g fiber), 3g pro.

HOLIDAY HELPER

This soup is a great base for your own additions of vegetables and herbs. If you prefer noodles in your soup, use egg noodles instead of the rice, but add the noodles later in the cooking time so they just simmer until done. For extra depth of flavor, stir some leftover gravy into the soup as well.

SWEET POTATO & CARAMELIZED ONION SHELLS

Gorgonzola cheese and sweet potatoes add a fun and flavorful twist. Delicious with a sprinkle of Parmesan, the shells can be topped with leftover gravy too.
—*Robin Haas, Cranston, RI*

Prep: 40 min. • **Bake:** 10 min.
Makes: 7 servings

- 2 large onions, chopped
- 3 Tbsp. butter
- 1 tsp. garlic powder
- ¼ tsp. salt
- 21 uncooked jumbo pasta shells
- ¼ cup reduced-sodium chicken broth
- 1 Tbsp. sherry or apple cider
- 1 tsp. dried thyme
- ½ tsp. pepper
- 1½ cups mashed sweet potatoes
- 1½ cups crumbled Gorgonzola cheese
- ½ cup grated Parmesan cheese
- 2 Tbsp. minced fresh parsley
- 1 cup turkey gravy, warmed

1. In a large skillet, saute onions in butter until softened. Add garlic powder and salt. Reduce heat to medium-low; cook, stirring occasionally, until deep golden brown, 25-30 minutes.
2. Meanwhile, cook the pasta shells according to package directions. Drain pasta; set aside.
3. Stir broth, sherry, thyme and pepper into onions. Bring to a boil; cook until liquid is almost evaporated. Remove from the heat. Stir in sweet potatoes and Gorgonzola cheese.
4. Spoon sweet potato mixture into shells; place filled shells in a greased 11x7-in. baking dish. Sprinkle with Parmesan cheese.
5. Bake, covered, at 375° until heated through, 10-15 minutes. Sprinkle with parsley. Serve with gravy.
3 STUFFED SHELLS: 341 cal., 14g fat (9g sat. fat), 42mg chol., 758mg sod., 41g carb. (7g sugars, 4g fiber), 13g pro. **DIABETIC EXCHANGES:** 2 starch, 1 high-fat meat.

SOUTHWESTERN PORK SALAD

As pork producers, we're proud to cook and serve the delicious product we raise. This tempting, versatile salad is a succulent showcase for pork. I know your family will enjoy it as much as we do.
—*Sue Cunningham, Prospect, OH*

Prep: 15 min. + chilling • **Makes:** 4 servings

- 2   cups cooked pork loin strips
- 1   can (16 oz.) kidney beans, rinsed and drained
- 1   medium onion, chopped
- 1   large green pepper, chopped
- 1   large tomato, chopped
- ½   cup sliced ripe olives
- ¼   cup cider vinegar
- ¼   cup canola oil
- 2   Tbsp. sugar
- 2   Tbsp. minced fresh parsley
- 1   tsp. ground mustard
- 1   tsp. ground cumin
- 1   tsp. dried oregano
- ½   tsp. salt

In a large bowl, combine the pork, beans, onion, green pepper, tomato and olives. In a small bowl, whisk remaining ingredients. Pour over salad; toss gently to coat. Cover and refrigerate for 4-6 hours, stirring occasionally.

1½ CUPS: 450 cal., 22g fat (4g sat. fat), 63mg chol., 675mg sod., 35g carb. (14g sugars, 8g fiber), 29g pro.

HOLIDAY HELPER

Adjust this salad to your own tastes by swapping out different vegetables. Try black or pinto beans instead of the kidney beans, or green olives instead of ripe olives. Yellow and red peppers will give it different bursts of color and sweetness too.

PARMESAN CHICKEN COUSCOUS

My two children love Parmesan couscous, and this recipe is a no-fuss way for me to get them to eat spinach. It's also a go-to dish for using up leftover chicken.
—*Lisa Abbott, New Berlin, WI*

Takes: 20 min. • **Makes:** 4 servings

- ½   cup chopped walnuts
- 2   tsp. olive oil, divided
- 3   garlic cloves, minced
- 2   cups chopped fresh spinach
- 1½   cups cubed cooked chicken
- 1¼   cups water
- 2   tsp. dried basil
- ¼   tsp. pepper
- 1   pkg. (5.9 oz.) Parmesan couscous
- ¼   cup grated Parmesan cheese

1. In a large saucepan, cook walnuts over medium heat in 1 tsp. oil until toasted, 2-3 minutes. Remove and set aside.
2. In the same pan, cook garlic in remaining 1 tsp. oil for 1 minute. Add the spinach, chicken, water, basil and pepper. Bring to a boil. Stir in couscous. Remove from the heat; cover and let stand until water is absorbed, 5-10 minutes. Fluff with a fork. Stir in walnuts and sprinkle with cheese.

1 CUP: 391 cal., 18g fat (3g sat. fat), 51mg chol., 490mg sod., 34g carb. (1g sugars, 3g fiber), 25g pro. **DIABETIC EXCHANGES:** 3 lean meat, 2 starch, 2 fat.

ROASTED BANANA BREAD PUDDING

Old-fashioned banana bread pudding gets a decadent upgrade: The addition of eggnog and the golden brown topping are a match made in heaven. You could even add a little rum to take it up another notch. Leftover crusty bread or dinner rolls make a perfect base for this dish.
—*Devon Delaney, Westport, CT*

Prep: 25 min. • **Bake:** 40 min. • **Makes:** 15 servings

- 2   medium bananas, unpeeled
- 4   large eggs
- 1   cup eggnog or heavy whipping cream
- 1   cup whole milk
- ⅔   cup sugar
- ¼   tsp. ground cinnamon
- ¼   tsp. salt
- 10 cups cubed day-old bread
- 1   cup peanut butter chips
- ⅓   cup chopped pecans, toasted
     Vanilla ice cream
     Toasted peanuts, optional

1. Preheat oven to 400°. Place unpeeled bananas on a foil-lined baking sheet; roast until fragrant and skins have blackened, 12-15 minutes. Cool slightly. Reduce oven setting to 350°.
2. In a large bowl, whisk together eggs, eggnog, milk, sugar, cinnamon and salt. Peel and mash bananas; stir into egg mixture.
3. Spread bread cubes evenly in a greased 13x9-in. baking dish. Sprinkle with peanut butter chips and pecans. Pour egg mixture over the top.
4. Bake, uncovered, until puffed, golden brown and a knife inserted near the center comes out clean, 40-45 minutes. Serve warm with ice cream and, if desired, peanuts.
1 PIECE WITH 1 TBSP. SAUCE: 231 cal., 8g fat (3g sat. fat), 61mg chol., 217mg sod., 32g carb. (19g sugars, 2g fiber), 7g pro.

TURKEY PINTO BEAN SALAD WITH SOUTHERN MOLASSES DRESSING

This salad is a welcome alternative to the usual post-feast fare. It's a tasty main dish loaded with good-for-you protein.
—*Lily Julow, Lawrenceville, GA*

Prep: 35 min. + chilling • **Makes:** 6 servings

- ½   cup oil-packed sun-dried tomatoes
- 1   garlic clove, peeled and halved
- ½   cup molasses
- 3   Tbsp. cider vinegar
- 1   tsp. prepared mustard
- ½   tsp. salt
- ¼   tsp. coarsely ground pepper
- 3   cups cubed cooked turkey breast
- 2   cans (15 oz. each) pinto beans, rinsed and drained
- 1   medium green pepper, diced
- 2   celery ribs, diced
- 1   cup chopped sweet onion
- ¼   cup minced fresh parsley
     Lettuce leaves, optional

1. Drain tomatoes, reserving 2 Tbsp. oil. Place garlic and tomatoes in a food processor; cover and process until chopped. Add the molasses, vinegar, mustard, salt, pepper and reserved oil. Cover and process until smooth.
2. In a large bowl, combine the turkey, pinto beans, green pepper, celery, onion and parsley. Add dressing and toss to coat. Cover and refrigerate for at least 2 hours. If desired, serve with lettuce leaves.
1⅓ CUPS: 379 cal., 7g fat (1g sat. fat), 60mg chol., 483mg sod., 49g carb. (19g sugars, 7g fiber), 29g pro. **DIABETIC EXCHANGES:** 4 lean meat, 2½ starch, 1 vegetable, 1 fat.

BUBBLE & SQUEAK LEFTOVER POTATO CAKES

Nothing gets wasted in my kitchen, including leftover mashed potatoes! This classic British breakfast recipe is traditionally fried as one dish, but I love individual portions.
—*Jas Brechtl, South Bend, IN*

Prep: 15 min. + chilling. • **Cook:** 20 min.
Makes: 4 servings

- 1 Tbsp. canola oil
- 2 cups thinly sliced Brussels sprouts
- ½ cup diced carrots, optional
- 3 to 4 cups leftover mashed potatoes (with added milk and butter)
- 4 green onions, thinly sliced
- 1 tsp. ground cumin, optional
- ½ tsp. salt
- ½ tsp. pepper
- 3 Tbsp. all-purpose flour
  Oil for frying
  Optional: Poached or fried eggs, bacon, sausage and additional sliced green onions

1. In a large skillet, heat oil over medium heat. Add Brussels sprouts and, if desired, carrots; cook and stir until tender, 5 minutes. Remove from skillet.
2. In a large bowl, combine mashed potatoes and the cooled Brussels sprouts mixture. Add onion, cumin if desired, salt and pepper until blended.
3. Divide mixture and form into eight 1-in. cakes, packing well. Place on a large plate; cover. Chill until firm, 30 minutes.
4. Dip each cake into flour to lightly coat. In a deep cast-iron or electric skillet, heat ¼ in. oil to 375°. Working in batches, place a few cakes at a time in hot oil. Fry until golden brown, 3-4 minutes on each side. Drain on paper towels.
5. If desired, serve with eggs, bacon or breakfast sausage and sprinkle with green onions.
2 POTATO CAKES: 339 cal., 22g fat (5g sat. fat), 17mg chol., 808mg sod., 33g carb. (4g sugars, 5g fiber), 5g pro.

HOLIDAY HELPER

This is a classic way to use up leftovers—any cooked vegetables from your holiday dinner can be added to the potatoes. Try crumbling in bacon bits or ham too.

CHRISTMAS PORK PIE

When my mother was growing up, her mom made mince pies with meat. I created this main-dish pie with my grandmother in mind, and served it for the first time at my mother's 1999 Christmas party—to rave reviews.
—*Candice Salazar, Los Alamos, NM*

Prep: 35 min. • **Bake:** 30 min. + cooling
Makes: 6 servings

- 2 cups beef broth
- ¾ cup chopped onion
- ½ cup chopped dried apricots
- ½ cup raisins
- ½ cup whole-berry cranberry sauce
- ½ cup undrained crushed pineapple
- ½ tsp. curry powder
- ¼ tsp. ground cinnamon
- 1 Tbsp. cornstarch
- 1 Tbsp. water
- 3 cups cubed cooked pork
- ½ cup chopped pecans
- ½ tsp. salt
  Dough for double-crust pie
  Milk and sugar

1. Preheat oven to 400°. In a large saucepan, combine first 8 ingredients. Cook over medium heat for 20 minutes.
2. Combine cornstarch and water until smooth; stir into the fruit mixture. Bring to a boil; cook and stir until thickened, about 2 minutes. Remove from heat; stir in pork, pecans and salt.
3. On a lightly floured surface, roll half of the dough to a ⅛-in.-thick circle; transfer to a 9-in. pie plate. Trim even with rim. Fill with meat mixture. Roll remaining dough to a ⅛-in.-thick circle; make decorative cutouts in crust. Set cutouts aside. Place top crust over filling; trim, seal and flute edge.
4. Brush crust and cutouts with milk; place cutouts on top of pie. Sprinkle with sugar. Bake until golden brown, 30-35 minutes. Cool 10 minutes before serving. Refrigerate leftovers.
DOUGH FOR DOUBLE-CRUST PIE: Combine 2½ cups all-purpose flour and ½ tsp. salt; cut in 1 cup cold butter until crumbly. Gradually add ⅓-⅔ cup ice water, tossing with a fork until dough holds together when pressed. Divide dough in half. Shape each into a disk; wrap and refrigerate 1 hour.
1 PIECE: 665 cal., 33g fat (11g sat. fat), 77mg chol., 795mg sod., 69g carb. (27g sugars, 3g fiber), 25g pro.

HAM & BROCCOLI CORNBREAD

Leftovers haunt me. Often nobody wants to eat them, and I hate to see them go to waste. A cornbread casserole is an excellent way to leverage many combinations of leftover meat and veggies into exciting new meals that everyone will love.
—*Fay Moreland, Wichita Falls, TX*

Prep: 15 min. • **Bake:** 35 min. + standing
Makes: 12 servings

- 5 Tbsp. butter, divided
- 2 large eggs
- 1 cup 2% milk
- ½ cup sour cream
  Pinch cayenne pepper
- 2 pkg. (8½ oz. each) cornbread/muffin mix
- 2 cups chopped fresh broccoli
- 1½ cups shredded sharp cheddar cheese
- 1½ cups cubed fully cooked ham
- 3 green onions, thinly sliced

1. Preheat oven to 375°. Place 3 Tbsp. butter in a 12-in. cast-iron skillet; place pan in oven until butter is melted, 3-5 minutes. Carefully tilt pan to coat bottom and sides with butter.
2. Melt the remaining 2 Tbsp. butter. In a large bowl, whisk together eggs, milk, sour cream, cayenne pepper and melted butter until blended. Add muffin mixes; stir just until moistened. Fold in the remaining ingredients. Pour into hot pan.
3. Bake until top is golden brown and a toothpick inserted in center comes out clean, 35-40 minutes. Let stand for 15 minutes before serving.
1 PIECE: 338 cal., 18g fat (9g sat. fat), 73mg chol., 700mg sod., 31g carb. (10g sugars, 3g fiber), 12g pro.

HOLIDAY HELPER

You can add practically anything to the cornbread batter. A protein such as cubed cooked chicken, turkey or fish can replace the ham, and your choice of vegetables can stand in for the broccoli. This is an unusual use for leftover roasted or boiled potatoes—cubed and mixed in, they become soft and creamy in the finished cornbread.

CREAMY TURKEY ENCHILADAS

This is a fantastic way to use leftover turkey. It's always in the rotation during the week after a holiday feast. The recipe works with chicken just as nicely.
—*Brenda Baskerville, Fair Oaks, CA*

Prep: 20 min. • **Bake:** 20 min.
Makes: 4 servings

- ¼ cup chopped onion
- 3 Tbsp. butter, divided
- 1 garlic clove, minced
- 2 cups cubed cooked turkey
- 1 can (4 oz.) chopped green chiles
- ½ tsp. dried oregano
- 3 Tbsp. all-purpose flour
- 2 cups chicken broth
- ½ cup sour cream
- 8 corn tortillas (6 in.)
- 1½ cups (6 oz.) Colby-Monterey Jack cheese
- 1 can (3.8 oz.) sliced ripe olives, drained

1. Preheat oven to 375°. In a large skillet, saute onion in 1 Tbsp. butter until tender. Add garlic; cook 1 minute longer. Add the turkey, chiles and oregano; heat through.
2. In a small saucepan, melt remaining 2 Tbsp. butter. Stir in flour until blended; gradually add broth. Bring to a boil; cook, stirring, until thickened, 2 minutes. Remove from heat; stir in sour cream. Stir ½ cup sauce into the turkey mixture and set aside.
3. Spread ¼ cup sauce mixture into a greased 13x9-in. baking dish. Dip both sides of each tortilla in sauce mixture. Place ⅓ cup turkey mixture down the center of each tortilla and sprinkle with 2 Tbsp. cheese. Roll up and place seam side down in prepared dish.
4. Pour the remaining sauce mixture over top; sprinkle with olives and the remaining cheese. Bake, uncovered, until heated through and the cheese is melted, 20-25 minutes.
2 ENCHILADAS: 636 cal., 37g fat (21g sat. fat), 145mg chol., 1,340mg sod., 36g carb., 4g fiber, 38g pro.

WHAT IS BOXING DAY?

Boxing Day is the day after Christmas and is observed as a holiday in the United Kingdom and in British Commonwealth countries. While the origin isn't exactly certain, the day is traditionally associated with charitable giving.

In one explanation, the boxes in question were alms boxes in churches where parishioners donated money throughout Advent; the sums collected were distributed to the poor on the day after Christmas.

In the other most common tradition, Dec. 26 was when aristocratic households boxed up small gifts, money and leftovers from the Christmas feast and gave them to household servants (who of course had to work on Christmas!).

Whichever is more accurate, the emphasis is on giving and sharing. A worthy theme for a Boxing Day luncheon would involve collecting funds or needed items for a neighborhood cause. And of course, it would be a fitting idea to have boxes on hand to send your guests home with tasty leftovers!

TRACEY BUXTON // A COTTAGE INDUSTRY

TURKEY PUFFS WITH CRANBERRY CABERNET SAUCE

Caramelized onions and mushrooms revitalize leftover turkey, while the sweet cranberry sauce balances the rich pastry and cream cheese.
—*Suzanne Clark, Phoenix, AZ*

Prep: 40 min. • **Bake:** 20 min.
Makes: 4 servings

- 1 cup chicken broth
- 1 cup dried wild mushrooms
- 1 medium onion, thinly sliced
- 2 Tbsp. butter
- 1 tsp. minced fresh tarragon or ¼ tsp. dried tarragon
- ¼ tsp. salt
- ¼ tsp. pepper
- 1 pkg. (17.3 oz.) frozen puff pastry, thawed
- 8 oz. thinly sliced cooked turkey
- ½ cup spreadable chive and onion cream cheese
- 1 large egg, beaten

SAUCE
- 1 cup chicken broth
- 1 cup dry red wine or additional chicken broth
- ½ cup balsamic vinegar
- ¾ cup jellied cranberry sauce

1. Preheat oven to 400°. In a small saucepan, combine broth and mushrooms; bring to a boil.

Remove from the heat; let stand until mushrooms are softened, 15-20 minutes. Using a slotted spoon, remove mushrooms; coarsely chop. Strain remaining broth through a fine mesh strainer. Set aside mushrooms and broth.

2. In a large skillet, cook and stir onion in butter until softened. Reduce heat to medium-low; cook, stirring occasionally, until golden brown, about 10 minutes. Add tarragon, salt, pepper, mushrooms and broth. Bring to a boil; cook over medium heat until liquid is evaporated.

3. On a lightly floured surface, unfold the puff pastry. Roll each sheet into a 12x10-in. rectangle; cut each into 2 pieces. Transfer pastries to a greased baking sheet. Spoon the mushroom mixture onto each pastry; top with turkey and cream cheese.

4. Lightly brush pastry edges with water. Bring long sides over filling, pinching seams and ends to seal. Turn pastries seam side down. Cut small slits into pastry. Brush tops with egg. Bake until golden brown, 20-25 minutes.

5. Meanwhile, in a small saucepan, combine the broth, wine and vinegar. Bring to a boil; cook until liquid is reduced by half. Stir in cranberry sauce until melted. Serve with pastries.

1 FILLED PASTRY WITH 3 TBSP. SAUCE: 1037 cal., 53g fat (19g sat. fat), 144mg chol., 1295mg sod., 103g carb. (22g sugars, 12g fiber), 31g pro.

LAMB RATATOUILLE

This quick and easy recipe is a colorful way to use up leftover lamb—and it's so yummy, your family will never guess it's a second-day dish. It's also good made with beef.
—*Maxine Cenker, Weirton, WV*

Prep: 30 min. • **Cook:** 20 min. • **Makes:** 6 servings

1   pkg. (6.8 oz.) beef-flavored rice and vermicelli mix
2   Tbsp. butter
2½ cups water
3   medium tomatoes, peeled, seeded and chopped
1   medium zucchini, sliced
1½ cups sliced fresh mushrooms
1   small onion, chopped
6   green onions, sliced
3   garlic cloves, minced
2   Tbsp. olive oil
1   lb. cooked lamb or beef, cut into thin strips

1. Set rice seasoning packet aside. In a large skillet, cook and stir the rice mix in butter until browned. Add water and contents of seasoning packet; bring to a boil. Reduce heat; cover and simmer for 15 minutes.
2. Meanwhile, in another skillet, saute vegetables in oil until crisp-tender. Add lamb and vegetables to the rice. Simmer, covered, until the rice is tender, 5-10 minutes.
1 SERVING: 369 cal., 16g fat (6g sat. fat), 76mg chol., 580mg sod., 31g carb. (6g sugars, 3g fiber), 25g pro.

SWEET POTATO CRANBERRY CAKE

Plan on extra sweet potatoes for your holiday feast so you can make this next-day cake! The recipe uses delicious items you probably already have in your pantry (especially at Christmastime), like dried cranberries, coconut and chocolate chips. The secret ingredient, however, is a bit of chili powder.
—*Amie Valpone, New York, NY*

Prep: 15 min. • **Bake:** 30 min. + cooling • **Makes:** 20 servings

1   pkg. white cake mix (regular size)
2   cups mashed sweet potatoes
½   cup buttermilk
2   large eggs, room temperature
2   Tbsp. canola oil
1   tsp. vanilla extract
1   pkg. (8 oz.) reduced-fat cream cheese
¾   cup confectioners' sugar
1   tsp. ground cinnamon
¾   tsp. chili powder
½   cup dried cranberries
⅓   cup sweetened shredded coconut, toasted
¼   cup dark chocolate chips

1. Preheat oven to 350°. In a large bowl, combine the cake mix, sweet potatoes, buttermilk, eggs, oil and vanilla. Beat on low speed for 30 seconds; beat on medium for 2 minutes longer.
2. Pour batter into a 13x9-in. baking pan coated with cooking spray. Bake until a toothpick inserted in the center comes out clean, 28-33 minutes. Cool on a wire rack.
3. In a small bowl, combine the cream cheese, confectioners' sugar, cinnamon and chili powder. Spread over cake. Sprinkle with cranberries, coconut and chocolate chips. Refrigerate any leftovers.
1 PIECE: 235 cal., 8g fat (4g sat. fat), 29mg chol., 250mg sod., 37g carb. (22g sugars, 1g fiber), 4g pro.

CHRISTMAS CAKES

Holiday time means it's time for cake! Gorgeous, decadent dessert cakes as the finale to Christmas dinner, snack cakes to delight a houseful of guests, or showstopping contributions to a potluck or office party—there's a cake for every occasion here.

GINGER-GLAZED LEMON BUNDT

Spicy ginger, tart lemon and puckery cranberries make this melt-in-your-mouth cake as crisp—and gorgeous—as autumn.
—Taste of Home *Test Kitchen*

Prep: 20 min. • **Bake:** 1 hour + cooling
Makes: 12 servings

SUGARED CRANBERRIES
- 3 Tbsp. light corn syrup
- 1 cup fresh or frozen cranberries, thawed
- ⅓ cup sugar

CAKE
- 1 cup butter, softened
- 2 cups sugar
- 4 large eggs, room temperature
- 2 Tbsp. grated lemon zest
- 1 tsp. lemon extract
- 2½ cups all-purpose flour
- 2 tsp. baking powder
- ½ tsp. salt
- 1 cup fat-free vanilla Greek yogurt

GLAZE
- ⅔ cup confectioners' sugar
- 2 Tbsp. butter, melted
- 1 to 3 tsp. lemon juice
- ½ tsp. ground ginger

1. For sugared cranberries, heat corn syrup in a microwave until warm; gently toss cranberries in syrup, allowing excess to drip off. Toss in sugar to coat. Place on waxed paper; let stand until set, about 1 hour.
2. Meanwhile, preheat oven to 325°. Grease and flour a 10-in. fluted tube pan. In a large bowl, cream butter and sugar until light and fluffy, 5-7 minutes. Add eggs, 1 at a time, beating well after each addition. Beat in lemon zest and extract.
3. In another bowl, whisk flour, baking powder and salt; add to creamed mixture alternately with yogurt, beating well after each addition.
4. Transfer to prepared pan. Bake until a toothpick inserted in center comes out clean, 60-70 minutes. Cool in pan 10 minutes before removing to a wire rack to cool completely.
5. Mix confectioners' sugar, butter, lemon juice and ginger until smooth. Drizzle over cake. Top with sugared cranberries.
1 PIECE: 468 cal., 19g fat (12g sat. fat), 108mg chol., 350mg sod., 69g carb. (48g sugars, 1g fiber), 7g pro.

WHITE CHOCOLATE RASPBERRY CHEESECAKE

As a dairy farmer's wife, I have a lot of experience making cheesecake. In fact, most anything containing milk products is tasty in my book. If I'm out of cream cheese, it's time to go to the grocery store!
—Wendy Barkman, Breezewood, PA

Prep: 25 min.
Bake: 1 hour 20 min. + chilling
Makes: 12 servings

- 1½ cups graham cracker crumbs
- ¼ cup sugar
- ⅓ cup butter, melted

FILLING
- 3 pkg. (8 oz. each) cream cheese, softened
- ¾ cup sugar
- ⅓ cup sour cream
- 3 Tbsp. all-purpose flour
- 1 tsp. vanilla extract
- 3 large eggs, room temperature, lightly beaten
- 1 pkg. (10 to 12 oz.) white baking chips
- ¼ cup seedless raspberry jam

1. Preheat oven to 325°. In a small bowl, combine the graham cracker crumbs, sugar and butter. Press crumb mixture onto the bottom of a greased 9-in. springform pan; set aside.
2. In a large bowl, beat cream cheese and sugar until smooth. Beat in the sour cream, flour and vanilla. Add eggs; beat on low speed just until combined. Fold in the baking chips. Pour over crust.
3. In a microwave, melt raspberry jam; stir until smooth. Drop by teaspoonfuls over batter; cut through batter with a knife to swirl.
4. Place pan on a double thickness of heavy-duty foil (about 18 in. square). Securely wrap foil around pan. Place in a large baking pan; add 1 in. hot water to larger pan.
5. Bake until the center is just set, 80-85 minutes. Cool on a wire rack for 10 minutes. Carefully run a knife around edge of pan to loosen; cool 1 hour longer. Cover and refrigerate overnight. Remove side of pan.
1 PIECE: 403 cal., 23g fat (13g sat. fat), 97mg chol., 211mg sod., 45g carb. (23g sugars, 0 fiber), 6g pro.

RUSTIC HONEY CAKE

When my boys were young, they couldn't drink milk but they could have yogurt. This was a cake they could eat. And it's one dessert that doesn't taste overly sweet, which is always a nice change of pace.
—*Linda Leuer, Hamel, MN*

Prep: 15 min. • **Bake:** 30 min. + cooling
Makes: 12 servings

- ½   cup butter, softened
- 1   cup honey
- 2   large eggs, room temperature
- ½   cup plain yogurt
- 1   tsp. vanilla extract
- 2   cups all-purpose flour
- 2   tsp. baking powder
- ½   tsp. salt
     Assorted fresh fruit and
     additional honey
     Chopped pistachios, optional

1. Preheat oven to 350°. Grease a 9-in. cast-iron skillet; set aside.

2. In a large bowl, beat butter and honey until blended. Add eggs, 1 at a time, beating well after each addition. Beat in yogurt and vanilla. In another bowl, whisk flour, baking powder and salt; add to butter mixture. Transfer batter to the prepared skillet.

3. Bake until a toothpick inserted in center comes out clean, 30-35 minutes. Cool completely in pan on a wire rack. Serve with fruit, additional honey and, if desired, chopped pistachios.

FREEZE OPTION: Securely wrap cooled cake in foil; freeze. To use, thaw at room temperature and top as directed.

1 PIECE: 248 cal., 9g fat (5g sat. fat), 53mg chol., 257mg sod., 40g carb. (24g sugars, 1g fiber), 4g pro.

HOLIDAY HELPER

This cake is delicious all on its own, but we know some folks can't imagine a cake without frosting. If you're in that camp, spread cream cheese frosting on the cooled cake before adding the fresh fruit and nuts, and skip the additional honey.

CRANBERRY SAUCE CAKE

This delicious cake comes together fast and is so easy to make. Slice it at the table so everyone can see how beautiful it is.
—*Marge Clark, West Lebanon, IN*

Prep: 10 min. • **Bake:** 55 min. + cooling
Makes: 16 servings

- 1½   cups sugar
- 1   cup mayonnaise
- ⅓   cup orange juice
- 1   Tbsp. grated orange zest
- 1   tsp. orange extract
- 3   cups all-purpose flour
- 1   tsp. baking soda
- 1   tsp. salt
- 1   can (14 oz.) whole-berry cranberry sauce
- 1   cup chopped walnuts

ICING
- 1   cup confectioners' sugar
- 1   to 2 Tbsp. orange juice

1. Preheat oven to 350°. In a large bowl, combine sugar and mayonnaise until blended. Beat in orange juice, zest and extract. Combine the flour, baking soda and salt until blended; gradually add to the sugar mixture. Stir in cranberry sauce and walnuts.

2. Cut parchment to fit the bottom of a 10-in. tube pan. Spray the pan and paper with cooking spray. Pour batter into the prepared pan.

3. Bake until a toothpick inserted in the center comes out clean, 55-65 minutes. Cool in pan 10 minutes before removing to a wire rack to cool completely. In a small bowl, combine icing ingredients; drizzle over cake.

1 PIECE: 379 cal., 16g fat (2g sat. fat), 5mg chol., 308mg sod., 56g carb. (33g sugars, 1g fiber), 4g pro.

CRANBERRY LAYER CAKE

I adapted a Bundt cake recipe to create this layer cake. Cranberries, walnuts and homemade frosting make it so delicious that you'd never guess it starts with a convenient cake mix.
—*Sandy Burkett, Galena, OH*

Prep: 20 min. • **Bake:** 30 min. + cooling
Makes: 16 servings

- 1 pkg. white cake mix (regular size)
- 1⅓ cups water
- 3 large eggs, room temperature
- ⅓ cup canola oil
- 1 Tbsp. grated orange zest
- 1 cup fresh or frozen cranberries, thawed and coarsely chopped
- 1 cup finely chopped walnuts

CREAM CHEESE FROSTING
- 1 pkg. (8 oz.) cream cheese, softened
- ½ cup butter, softened
- 1 tsp. vanilla extract
- 3½ cups confectioners' sugar
- ½ tsp. grated orange zest
- ¼ cup finely chopped walnuts

1. Preheat oven to 350°. Line bottoms of 2 greased 9-in. round baking pans with parchment; grease paper. In a large bowl, combine the first 5 ingredients; beat on low speed 30 seconds. Increase speed to medium; beat 2 minutes longer. Stir in cranberries and walnuts. Transfer batter to prepared pans.
2. Bake until a toothpick inserted in center comes out clean, 30-35 minutes. Cool in pans 10 minutes before removing to wire racks; remove paper. Let cool completely.
3. For frosting, In a large bowl, beat cream cheese, butter and vanilla until blended. Gradually beat in confectioners' sugar and orange zest until smooth. Spread frosting between layers and over top and side of cake. Sprinkle with walnuts. Refrigerate leftovers.
1 PIECE: 441 cal., 24g fat (8g sat. fat), 64mg chol., 329mg sod., 55g carb. (40g sugars, 2g fiber), 5g pro.

HOLIDAY HELPER

Before assembling a layer cake, place a dab of frosting in the middle of the cake plate—it will prevent the cake from sliding around as you frost and decorate it.

COCONUT ITALIAN CREAM CAKE

I'd never tasted an Italian cream cake before moving to Colorado. Now I bake for people in the area, and this beauty is one of the most requested.
—*Ann Bush, Colorado City, CO*

Prep: 50 min. • **Bake:** 20 min. + cooling
Makes: 16 servings

- 5 large eggs, separated
- 1 cup butter, softened
- 1⅔ cups sugar
- 1½ tsp. vanilla extract
- 2 cups all-purpose flour
- ¾ tsp. baking soda
- ½ tsp. salt
- 1 cup buttermilk
- 1⅓ cups sweetened shredded coconut
- 1 cup chopped pecans, toasted

FROSTING
- 12 oz. cream cheese, softened
- 6 Tbsp. butter, softened
- 2¼ tsp. vanilla extract
- 5⅔ cups confectioners' sugar
- 3 to 4 Tbsp. heavy whipping cream
- ½ cup chopped pecans, toasted
- ¼ cup toasted sweetened shredded coconut, optional

1. Place egg whites in a small bowl; let stand at room temperature 30 minutes. Line bottoms of 3 greased 9-in. round baking pans with parchment. Grease paper; set pans aside.
2. Preheat oven to 350°. In a large bowl, cream butter and sugar until light and fluffy, 5-7 minutes. Add egg yolks, 1 at a time, beating well after each addition. Beat in vanilla. In another bowl, whisk flour, baking soda and salt; add to the creamed mixture alternately with buttermilk, beating well after each addition. Fold in coconut and pecans.
3. With clean beaters, beat egg whites on medium speed until stiff peaks form. Gradually fold into batter. Transfer to prepared pans. Bake until a toothpick inserted in center comes out clean, 20-25 minutes. Cool in pans 10 minutes before removing to wire racks; remove paper. Cool completely.
4. For frosting, in a large bowl, beat cream cheese and butter until smooth. Beat in vanilla. Gradually beat in confectioners' sugar and enough cream to reach spreading consistency. Spread frosting between layers and over top and sides of cake. Sprinkle with pecans and, if desired, coconut. Refrigerate leftovers.
NOTE: To toast pecans and coconut, spread 1 kind at a time in a 15x10x1-in. baking pan. Bake each pan at 350° for 5-10 minutes or until lightly browned, stirring occasionally.
1 PIECE: 667 cal., 36g fat (18g sat. fat), 128mg chol., 402mg sod., 82g carb. (68g sugars, 2g fiber), 7g pro.

HAZELNUT CAKE SQUARES

Whenever one of my daughters is asked to bring a dish to a church function, a birthday party or any special occasion, she asks me for this recipe. It is so easy to prepare because it starts with a cake mix. It doesn't need icing, so it's perfect for bake sales too.
—Brenda Melancon, McComb, MS

Prep: 10 min. • **Bake:** 25 min. + cooling • **Makes:** 15 servings

- 1   pkg. yellow cake mix (regular size)
- 3   large eggs
- ⅔   cup water
- ⅔   cup Nutella
- ¼   cup canola oil
- ½   cup semisweet chocolate chips
- ½   cup chopped hazelnuts, toasted
- ½   cup brickle toffee bits, optional
     Confectioners' sugar, optional

1. Preheat oven to 350°. Grease a 13x9-in. baking pan; set aside.
2. In a large bowl, combine cake mix, eggs, water, Nutella and oil; beat on low speed 30 seconds. Increase speed to medium; beat 2 minutes longer. Fold in chocolate chips, hazelnuts and, if desired, toffee bits.
3. Transfer batter to prepared pan. Bake until a toothpick inserted in center comes out clean, 25-30 minutes.
4. Cool completely in pan on a wire rack. Dust with confectioners' sugar if desired.
1 PIECE: 280 cal., 14g fat (3g sat. fat), 37mg chol., 245mg sod., 38g carb. (24g sugars, 2g fiber), 4g pro.

OLD-FASHIONED MOLASSES CAKE

This old-time spice cake is lower in fat but big on flavor. Serve it warm for breakfast on a frosty morning or have a square with hot cider on a snowy afternoon. It's an ideal cold-weather treat.
—Deanne Bagley, Bath, NY

Prep: 15 min. • **Bake:** 25 min. + cooling • **Makes:** 9 servings

- 2   Tbsp. butter, softened
- ¼   cup sugar
- 1   large egg, room temperature
- ½   cup molasses
- 1   cup all-purpose flour
- 1   tsp. baking soda
- ¼   tsp. ground ginger
- ¼   tsp. ground cinnamon
- ⅛   tsp. salt
- ½   cup hot water
- 9   Tbsp. fat-free whipped topping, optional

1. Preheat oven to 350°. In a small bowl, beat butter and sugar until crumbly, about 2 minutes. Beat in egg and molasses. Combine the flour, baking soda, ginger, cinnamon and salt; add to the butter mixture alternately with hot water, mixing well after each addition.
2. Transfer batter to a 9-in. square baking pan coated with cooking spray. Bake until a toothpick inserted in the center comes out clean, 25-30 minutes. Cool on a wire rack. Cut into squares; garnish with whipped topping.
1 PIECE: 155 cal., 3g fat (2g sat. fat), 27mg chol., 208mg sod., 30g carb. (19g sugars, 0 fiber), 2g pro. **DIABETIC EXCHANGES:** 2 starch, ½ fat

SPICED APPLE CAKE WITH CARAMEL ICING

Easy to prepare and popular with my friends and family, this apple cake is one of my all-time favorite recipes. A slice of this soft treat is delicious with a hot cup of coffee or tea.
—*Monica Burns, Fort Worth, TX*

Prep: 45 min. • **Bake:** 1¼ hours + cooling
Makes: 16 servings

- 3 cups chopped peeled Gala or Braeburn apples (about 3 medium)
- ½ cup bourbon
- 2 cups sugar
- 1½ cups canola oil
- 3 large eggs, room temperature
- 2 tsp. vanilla extract
- 3 cups all-purpose flour
- 2 tsp. apple pie spice
- 1 tsp. salt
- 1 tsp. baking soda
- 1 cup chopped walnuts, toasted

ICING
- ¼ cup butter, cubed
- ½ cup packed brown sugar
- 1 Tbsp. 2% milk
- 1 Tbsp. bourbon
  Dash salt
- ⅛ tsp. vanilla extract

1. Preheat oven to 350°. Grease and flour a 10-in. tube pan. In a large bowl, toss apples with bourbon.
2. In a second large bowl, beat sugar, oil, eggs and vanilla until well blended. In another bowl, whisk flour, pie spice, salt and baking soda; gradually beat into the sugar mixture. Stir in apple mixture and walnuts.
3. Transfer to prepared pan. Bake until a toothpick inserted in center comes out clean, 1¼-1½ hours. Cool in pan 10 minutes; remove to a wire rack to cool completely.
4. In a small heavy saucepan, combine butter, brown sugar, milk, bourbon and salt. Bring to a boil over medium heat, stirring occasionally; cook and stir 3 minutes. Remove from heat; stir in vanilla. Drizzle over warm cake. Cool completely.
NOTE: To remove cakes easily, use solid shortening to grease tube pans.
1 PIECE: 499 cal., 30g fat (4g sat. fat), 43mg chol., 275mg sod., 54g carb. (34g sugars, 2g fiber), 5g pro.

FESTIVE CRANBERRY-TOPPED CHEESECAKE

When my daughter was 4 months old, my husband and I hosted both of our families for Christmas dinner. I served this memorable cheesecake for dessert.
—*Stacy Dutka, Bienfait, SK*

Prep: 40 min. • **Bake:** 45 min. + chilling
Makes: 12 servings

- 2 cups crushed shortbread cookies
- 2 Tbsp. sugar
- ¼ cup butter, melted

FILLING
- 3 pkg. (8 oz. each) cream cheese, softened
- ¾ cup sugar
- 2 Tbsp. orange juice
- 1 Tbsp. grated orange zest
- 2 tsp. vanilla extract
- ½ tsp. ground cinnamon
- 3 large eggs, room temperature, lightly beaten

TOPPING
- 3 cups fresh or frozen cranberries, coarsely chopped
- 1¼ cups sugar
- 1 cup water
- 2 Tbsp. cornstarch
- ¼ cup orange juice
- ½ cup coarsely chopped pecans, toasted

1. Preheat oven to 325°. In a small bowl, combine cookie crumbs and sugar; stir in butter. Press onto the bottom of a greased 9-in. springform pan. Place pan on a baking sheet. Bake until set, 6-8 minutes. Cool on a wire rack.
2. For filling, in a large bowl, beat the cream cheese and sugar until smooth. Beat in juice, zest, vanilla and cinnamon. Add eggs; beat on low speed just until combined. Pour filling over crust.
3. Return pan to baking sheet. Bake until center is almost set, 45-50 minutes. Cool on a wire rack for 10 minutes. Carefully run a knife around edge of pan to loosen; cool 1 hour longer. Refrigerate overnight.
4. For topping, in a large saucepan, combine the cranberries, sugar and water. Bring to a boil. Reduce heat; simmer, uncovered, for 3 minutes. Combine cornstarch and orange juice until smooth; stir into cranberry mixture. Bring to a boil; cook and stir until thickened, about 2 minutes.
5. Remove from the heat; cool to room temperature. Stir in pecans. Spoon over cheesecake. Refrigerate until chilled.
1 PIECE: 537 cal., 33g fat (17g sat. fat), 129mg chol., 299mg sod., 55g carb. (37g sugars, 2g fiber), 8g pro.

ORANGE RICOTTA CAKE ROLL

I come from a big Italian family. When I was growing up, my mom cooked and baked many delicious meals and desserts from scratch. Now I do the same for my family. This cake is my finale to our special-occasion dinners.
—*Cathy Banks, Encinitas, CA*

Prep: 45 min. • **Bake:** 10 min. + chilling • **Makes:** 12 servings

- 4   large eggs, separated, room temperature
- ¼   cup baking cocoa
- 2   Tbsp. all-purpose flour
- ⅛   tsp. salt
- ⅔   cup confectioners' sugar, sifted, divided
- 1   tsp. vanilla extract
- ½   tsp. cream of tartar

FILLING
- 1   container (15 oz.) ricotta cheese
- 3   Tbsp. mascarpone cheese
- ⅓   cup sugar
- 1   Tbsp. Kahlua (coffee liqueur)
- 1   Tbsp. grated orange zest
- ½   tsp. vanilla extract
     Additional confectioners' sugar

1. Place egg whites in a bowl. Preheat oven to 325°. Line bottom of a greased 15x10x1-in. baking pan with parchment; grease paper. Sift cocoa, flour and salt together twice.
2. In a large bowl, beat egg yolks until slightly thickened. Gradually add ⅓ cup confectioners' sugar, beating on high speed until thick and lemon-colored. Beat in vanilla. Fold in cocoa mixture (batter will be very thick).
3. Add cream of tartar to egg whites; with clean beaters, beat on medium until soft peaks form. Gradually add remaining ⅓ cup confectioners' sugar, 1 Tbsp. at a time, beating on high after each addition until sugar is dissolved. Continue beating until soft glossy peaks form. Fold a fourth of the whites into the batter, then fold in the remaining whites. Transfer to prepared pan, spreading evenly.
4. Bake until the top springs back when lightly touched, 9-11 minutes. Cover cake with waxed paper; cool completely on a wire rack.
5. Remove waxed paper; invert cake onto an 18-in.-long sheet of waxed paper dusted with confectioners' sugar. Gently peel off parchment.
6. In a small bowl, beat cheeses and sugar until blended. Stir in Kahlua, orange zest and vanilla. Spread over cake to within ½ in. of edges. Roll up jelly-roll style, starting with a short side. Trim ends; place on a platter, seam side down.
7. Refrigerate, covered, at least 1 hour before serving. To serve, dust with confectioners' sugar.

1 PIECE: 169 cal., 9g fat (5g sat. fat), 94mg chol., 95mg sod., 17g carb. (14g sugars, 0 fiber), 7g pro. **DIABETIC EXCHANGES:** 2 fat, 1 starch.

HOLIDAY FRUITCAKE

After some experimenting in the kitchen, I finally came up with my ideal fruitcake. I think it has just the right mix of nuts and fruit.
—*Allene Spence, Delbarton, WV*

Prep: 20 min. • **Bake:** 2 hours + cooling • **Makes:** 16 servings

- 1½ cups whole red candied cherries
- 1½ cups whole green candied cherries
- 3   cups diced candied pineapple
- 10 oz. golden raisins
- 1   lb. walnut halves
- 1   cup shortening
- 1   cup sugar
- 5   large eggs, room temperature
- 4   Tbsp. vanilla extract
- 3   cups all-purpose flour
- 3   tsp. baking powder
- 1   tsp. salt

1. Preheat oven to 300°. Grease and flour a 10-in. tube pan; set aside. Combine fruits and nuts. In another bowl, cream shortening and sugar until light and fluffy, 5-7 minutes. Beat in eggs and vanilla. Combine flour, baking powder and salt; add to creamed mixture and mix well. Pour over fruit mixture; stir to coat.
2. Transfer to prepared pan. Bake until a toothpick inserted in center comes out clean, about 2 hours. Cool 10 minutes; remove from pan to a wire rack to cool completely. Wrap tightly and store in a cool place. Bring to room temperature before serving; slice with a serrated knife.

1 PIECE: 686 cal., 32g fat (5g sat. fat), 58mg chol., 342mg sod., 92g carb. (61g sugars, 4g fiber), 10g pro.

CINNAMON TWIRL ROLY-POLY

My whole house smells incredible when this cake is in the oven. Change it up with other extracts too—maple is heavenly.
—*Holly Balzer-Harz, Malone, NY*

Prep: 40 min. + chilling
Bake: 10 min. + cooling • **Makes:** 12 servings

- 3 large eggs, room temperature
- ¾ cup sugar
- ⅓ cup water
- 1 tsp. vanilla extract
- 1 cup all-purpose flour
- 1½ tsp. baking powder
  Dash salt
- 6 Tbsp. butter, softened
- ½ cup packed brown sugar
- 2 tsp. ground cinnamon

FILLING
- 4 oz. cream cheese, softened
- ¼ cup butter, softened
- 1 cup confectioners' sugar
- ½ tsp. ground cinnamon
- 1 to 2 tsp. half-and-half cream or 2% milk
- ¼ cup finely chopped walnuts, optional

GLAZE
- ¼ cup butter
- 1½ cups confectioners' sugar
- 1 tsp. vanilla extract
- 2 to 3 Tbsp. half-and-half cream or 2% milk
- ¼ cup chopped walnuts, optional

1. Preheat oven to 375°. Line bottom and sides of a greased 15x10x1-in. baking pan with parchment; grease parchment.
2. Beat eggs on high speed until thick and pale, about 5 minutes. Gradually beat in sugar until well mixed. Reduce speed to low; beat in water and vanilla. In another bowl, whisk together the flour, baking powder and salt; add to the egg mixture, mixing just until combined.
3. Transfer batter to prepared pan. Bake until cake springs back when lightly touched, 10-12 minutes. Cool 5 minutes. Invert onto a kitchen towel dusted with confectioners' sugar. Gently peel off parchment. Roll up cake in the towel jelly-roll style, starting with a short side. Cool completely on a wire rack.
4. Meanwhile, beat butter, brown sugar and cinnamon until creamy. Unroll cake; spread brown sugar mixture over cake to within ½ in. of edges.

5. For filling, beat cream cheese and butter until creamy. Beat in the confectioners' sugar and cinnamon; gradually add cream until mixture reaches a spreadable consistency. Spread filling over brown sugar mixture. If desired, sprinkle with walnuts. Roll up again, without towel; trim ends if needed. Place on a platter, seam side down.
6. For glaze, heat butter in a small saucepan over medium-low heat until foamy and golden, 6-8 minutes. Remove from heat. Stir in confectioners' sugar and vanilla, then add cream 1 Tbsp. at a time, stirring well, until mixture reaches a pourable consistency. Slowly pour glaze over top of cake, allowing some to flow over sides. If desired, top with walnuts. Refrigerate, covered, for at least 2 hours before serving.

1 PIECE: 396 cal., 18g fat (11g sat. fat), 93mg chol., 341mg sod., 56g carb. (47g sugars, 1g fiber), 4g pro.

HOLIDAY HELPER

This easy-to-make cake is perfect for the holidays since it can be made at least a day ahead. It's important to let the cake cool completely while it's rolled up in the towel. Letting it cool in a roll will make it easier to roll after it's been filled and will prevent cracking.

STICKY TOFFEE PUDDING WITH BUTTERSCOTCH SAUCE

Sticky toffee pudding is a classic dessert in Britain. I love that I can enjoy the traditional treat with its rich butterscotch sauce at home.
—*Agnes Ward, Stratford, ON*

Prep: 30 min. + cooling • **Bake:** 50 min.
Makes: 15 servings (2½ cups sauce)

- 2 cups coarsely chopped pitted dates (about 12 oz.)
- 2½ cups water
- 2 tsp. baking soda
- 1⅔ cups sugar
- ½ cup butter, softened
- 4 large eggs, room temperature
- 2 tsp. vanilla extract
- 3¼ cups all-purpose flour
- 2 tsp. baking powder

BUTTERSCOTCH SAUCE

- 7 Tbsp. butter, cubed
- 2¼ cups packed brown sugar
- 1 cup half-and-half cream
- 1 Tbsp. brandy
- ¼ tsp. vanilla extract
  Whipped cream, optional

1. Preheat oven to 350°. In a small saucepan, combine dates and water; bring to a boil. Remove from the heat; stir in baking soda. Cool to lukewarm.
2. In a large bowl, cream sugar and butter until light and fluffy, 5-7 minutes. Add eggs, 1 at a time, beating well after each addition. Beat in vanilla. In another bowl, mix flour and baking powder; gradually add to the creamed mixture. Stir in date mixture.
3. Transfer to a greased 13x9-in. baking pan. Bake until a toothpick inserted in center comes out clean, 50-60 minutes. Cool slightly in pan on a wire rack.
4. Meanwhile, for the sauce, in a small saucepan, melt butter; add brown sugar and cream. Bring to a boil over medium heat, stirring constantly. Remove from the heat. Stir in brandy and vanilla. Serve warm with warm cake. If desired, top with whipped cream.

1 PIECE WITH ABOUT 2 TBSP. SAUCE: 521 cal., 15g fat (9g sat. fat), 88mg chol., 361mg sod., 93g carb. (70g sugars, 3g fiber), 6g pro.

SANTA CUPCAKES

My children decorate these cute cupcakes every year for Christmas. We use chocolate chips for Santa's eyes and a Red Hot for his nose, but you can use any kind of candy you like.
—*Sharon Skildum, Maple Grove, MN*

Prep: 30 min. • **Bake:** 20 min. + cooling
Makes: about 1½ dozen

- 1 pkg. white cake mix (regular size)
- 1 can (16 oz.) vanilla frosting (about 1⅔ cups)
  Red gel or paste food coloring
  Miniature marshmallows
  Brown M&M's minis
  Red Hots
  Red jimmies
  Sweetened shredded coconut

1. Prepare and bake cake mix according to package directions for cupcakes, filling 18 or more paper-lined muffin cups two-thirds full. Cool in pans 10 minutes before removing to wire racks; cool completely.
2. Tint ⅔ cup frosting red with food coloring. Place 3 Tbsp. white frosting in a food-safe plastic bag; cut a ¼-in. hole in a corner and reserve for piping.
3. Use remaining white frosting to cover two-thirds of each cupcake. For hats, cover remaining third of each cupcake with red frosting. Pipe fur trim with white frosting; add marshmallows for pompoms. Decorate with M&M's, Red Hots and jimmies for faces; add coconut for beards.

1 CUPCAKE: 276 cal., 12g fat (2g sat. fat), 31mg chol., 249mg sod., 40g carb. (28g sugars, 0 fiber), 2g pro.

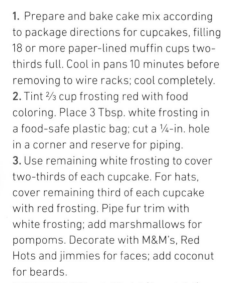

MOTHER'S WALNUT CAKE

Even though Mother baked this tall, beautiful cake often when I was growing up, it was a real treat every time. I like the walnuts in the cake and the frosting. Mother frequently used black walnuts from our trees.
—*Helen Vail, Glenside, PA*

Prep: 20 min. • **Bake:** 20 min. + cooling
Makes: 16 servings

- ½ cup butter, softened
- ½ cup shortening
- 2 cups sugar
- 4 large eggs, room temperature
- 3½ cups all-purpose flour
- 2 tsp. baking soda
- ½ tsp. salt
- 1½ cups buttermilk
- 2 tsp. vanilla extract
- 1½ cups ground walnuts

FROSTING
- 11 oz. cream cheese, softened
- ¾ cup butter, softened
- 5 to 5½ cups confectioners' sugar
- 1½ tsp. vanilla extract
- ⅓ cup finely chopped walnuts

1. Preheat oven to 350°. Grease and flour three 9-in. round pans; set aside. Cream butter, shortening and granulated sugar until light and fluffy, 5-7 minutes. Add eggs, 1 at a time, beating well after each addition. Combine flour, baking soda and salt; gradually add to the creamed mixture alternately with buttermilk and vanilla. Beat on low speed just until combined. Stir in ground walnuts.
2. Pour into prepared pans. Bake until a toothpick inserted in the center comes out clean, 20-25 minutes. Cool 5 minutes; remove from pans to wire racks to cool completely.
3. For frosting, beat cream cheese and butter until smooth. Add confectioners' sugar; mix well. Beat in vanilla until smooth. Spread frosting between layers and over the top and sides of cake. Sprinkle with walnuts. Refrigerate.
1 PIECE: 685 cal., 35g fat (16g sat. fat), 114mg chol., 475mg sod., 86g carb. (61g sugars, 1g fiber), 9g pro.

MASCARPONE CHEESECAKE

This rich dessert is sure to delight with its creamy filling, whipped topping and sweet caramel drizzle. It makes a fitting ending to a special meal.
—*Deanna Polito-Laughinghouse, Raleigh, NC*

Prep: 30 min. • **Bake:** 1 hour + chilling
Makes: 16 servings

- ¾ cup graham cracker crumbs
- 3 Tbsp. sugar
- 3 Tbsp. butter, melted

FILLING
- 2 pkg. (8 oz. each) cream cheese, softened
- 2 cartons (8 oz. each) Mascarpone cheese
- 1 cup sugar
- 1 Tbsp. lemon juice
- 1 Tbsp. vanilla extract
- 4 large eggs, room temperature, lightly beaten

TOPPING
- 1 carton frozen whipped topping, thawed
- 1 Tbsp. caramel ice cream topping

1. Preheat oven to 325°. Place a greased 9-in. springform pan on a double thickness of heavy-duty foil (about 18 in. square). Securely wrap foil around pan.
2. In a small bowl, combine cracker crumbs and sugar; stir in butter. Press mixture onto the bottom of prepared pan. Place pan on a baking sheet. Bake 10 minutes. Cool on a wire rack.
3. For filling, in a large bowl, beat the cheeses, sugar, lemon juice and vanilla until smooth. Add eggs; beat on low speed just until combined. Pour over crust. Place springform pan in a large baking pan; add 1 in. hot water to the larger pan.
4. Bake until center is just set and top appears dull, 1-1¼ hours. Remove springform pan from water bath. Cool on a wire rack for 10 minutes. Carefully run a knife around the edge of pan to loosen; cool 1 hour longer.
5. Refrigerate overnight. Remove sides of pan. Garnish cheesecake with whipped topping; drizzle with caramel. Refrigerate any leftovers.
1 PIECE: 339 cal., 26g fat (15g sat. fat), 121mg chol., 160mg sod., 21g carb. (18g sugars, 0 fiber), 6g pro.

SUPER HOLIDAY CUPCAKES

These peppermint cupcakes are so festive for the holidays! Everyone loves the kiss hidden inside each one. They are impressive decorated as a pull-apart wreath, but I also like to top them individually with untinted white frosting and a sprinkle of crushed candy canes.
—*Jenn Arata, tasteofhome.com*

Prep: 20 min. • **Bake:** 20 min.
Makes: 2 dozen

- 4 large eggs
- 2 cups sugar
- 1 cup 2% milk
- ¾ cup canola oil
- 1 tsp. vanilla extract
- 2½ cups all-purpose flour
- 2¼ tsp. baking powder
- 24 candy cane-flavored kisses
- 1 to 2 candy canes, crushed

FROSTING
- ⅔ cup butter, softened
- 4 cups confectioners' sugar
- 2 tsp. vanilla extract
- 3 to 4 Tbsp. 2% milk

Red and green food coloring paste, optional
- 4 oz. ready-to-use rolled fondant
Optional: Miniature candy canes, jumbo mint balls, red Sixlets and white sugar pearls

1. Preheat oven to 375°. In a large bowl, beat the eggs and sugar until thick and lemon-colored. Beat in the milk, oil and vanilla. Combine the flour and baking powder; gradually beat into the egg mixture until blended.
2. Fill 24 paper-lined muffin cups three-fourths full. Bake until a toothpick inserted near the center comes out with moist crumbs, about 15 minutes. Press a candy cane kiss, point side down, into the center of each cupcake. Bake 1-2 minutes longer. Sprinkle tops with crushed candy cane. Cool for 10 minutes before removing from pans to wire racks to cool completely.
3. For frosting, in a large bowl, combine the butter, confectioners' sugar and vanilla; beat until smooth. Add enough milk to achieve a spreading consistency.

If desired, add food coloring paste to tint frosting. Frost cupcakes. Arrange 15 cupcakes on a platter in a 14-in. circle; place remaining 9 cupcakes in the center of the ring to form a 8-in. circle.
4. Make fondant bow and snowflakes (see below). Carefully transfer bow to cupcake wreath; arrange snowflakes on wreath. If desired, decorate wreath with mini candy canes, jumbo mint balls, red Sixlets and white sugar pearls.

1 CUPCAKE WITH 2 TBSP. FROSTING:
357 cal., 15g fat (5g sat. fat), 47mg chol., 108mg sod., 54g carb. (43g sugars, 0 fiber), 3g pro.

MAKING A FONDANT BOW

1. Tint half the fondant red; wrap the remaining white fondant well and set aside.
2. Roll red fondant into a 10x4-in. rectangle on a surface lightly dusted with confectioners' sugar. Cut two 10x1½-in. strips.
3. Fold an end of 1 strip toward the center of the strip, forming 1 loop and 1 tail of the bow; repeat with the second strip.
4. Connect the 2 pieces, placing 1 loop on the left and the second loop on the right; pinch center together.
5. From remaining red fondant, cut a 2½x¾-in. strip. Wrap around the center of the bow; pinch to seal. Trim ends.

NOTE: For snowflakes, roll out reserved white fondant to ⅛-in. thickness. Cut shapes using a snowflake cutter dusted with confectioners' sugar.

SEASONAL GET-TOGETHERS

Make your holiday gathering one your guests will be talking about all year! Plan a party for the kids, pull out the stops for a Mexican-themed celebration or create a jaw-dropping charcuterie board.

FELIZ NAVIDAD

Celebrate the season with Mexican and Tex-Mex flavors! From classic recipes to brand-new combinations, these dishes will make everyone happy.

CHICKEN TAMALES

I love making tamales. They take a little time to make but are so worth the effort. I usually make them for Christmas, but my family wants them more often, so I'll freeze a big batch.
—Cindy Pruitt, Grove, OK

Prep: 2½ hours + soaking • **Cook:** 45 min.
Makes: 20 tamales

- 24 dried corn husks
- 1 broiler/fryer chicken (3 to 4 lbs.), cut up
- 1 medium onion, quartered
- 2 tsp. salt
- 1 garlic clove, crushed
- 3 qt. water

DOUGH

- 1 cup shortening
- 3 cups masa harina

FILLING

- 6 Tbsp. canola oil
- 6 Tbsp. all-purpose flour
- ¾ cup chili powder
- ½ tsp. salt
- ¼ tsp. garlic powder
- ¼ tsp. pepper
- 2 cans (2¼ oz. each) sliced ripe olives, drained
  Hot water

1. Cover corn husks with cold water; soak until softened, at least 2 hours.
2. Place chicken, onion, salt and garlic in a 6-qt. stockpot. Pour in 3 qt. water; bring to a boil. Reduce heat; simmer, covered, until chicken is tender, 45-60 minutes. Remove chicken from broth. When cool enough to handle, remove bones and skin; discard. Shred chicken. Strain cooking juices; skim off fat. Reserve 6 cups stock.
3. For dough, beat shortening until light and fluffy, about 1 minute. Beat in small amounts of masa harina alternately with small amounts of reserved stock, using no more than 2 cups stock. Drop a small amount of dough into a cup of cold water; dough should float. If not, continue beating, retesting every 1-2 minutes.
4. For filling, heat the oil in a Dutch oven; stir in flour until blended. Cook and stir over medium heat until lightly browned, 7-9 minutes. Stir in seasonings, chicken and the remaining stock; bring to a boil. Reduce heat; simmer, uncovered, stirring occasionally, until thickened, about 45 minutes.

5. Drain corn husks and pat dry; tear 4 husks to make 20 strips for tying tamales. (To prevent husks from drying out, cover with a damp towel until ready to use.) On wide end of each remaining husk, spread 3 Tbsp. dough to within ½ in. of side edges; top each with 2 Tbsp. chicken filling and 2 tsp. olives. Fold long sides of husk over filling, overlapping slightly. Fold over narrow end of husk; tie with a strip of husk to secure.
6. Place a large steamer basket in the stockpot over water; place tamales upright in steamer. Bring to a boil; steam, covered, adding hot water as needed, until dough peels away from husks, about 45 minutes.

2 TAMALES: 564 cal., 35g fat (7g sat. fat), 44mg chol., 835mg sod., 43g carb. (2g sugars, 7g fiber), 20g pro.

ABOUT MASA

Fresh masa (dough made from stone-ground corn flour, called masa harina) is the foundation of a perfect tamale. You can find masa harina and corn husks in the international foods aisle.

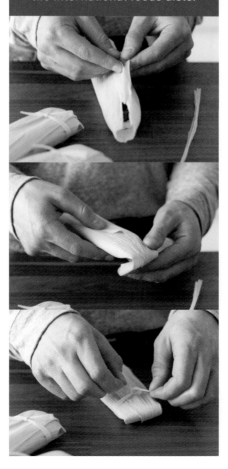

MOLE NEW MEXICAN WEDDING COOKIES

Heat and sweetness is an amazing combination. I added chili powder and chocolate chips to give a new twist to traditional Mexican cookies. They melt in your mouth, and then the spice hits you. I just love them.
—Marla Clark, Albuquerque, NM

Prep: 30 min.
Bake: 15 min./batch + cooling
Makes: 2½ dozen

- ½ cup butter, softened
- ¾ cup confectioners' sugar, divided
- 1 tsp. vanilla extract
- 1 cup all-purpose flour
- ½ cup ground pecans
- 1 tsp. chili powder
- ¼ tsp. ground cinnamon
- ¼ tsp. ground cloves
- ¼ tsp. ground allspice
- ½ cup miniature semisweet chocolate chips

1. Preheat oven to 350°. Cream butter and ⅓ cup confectioners' sugar until light and fluffy; beat in vanilla. In another bowl, whisk together next 6 ingredients. Gradually beat into creamed mixture. Fold in chocolate chips.
2. Shape dough into 1-in. balls. Place 1 in. apart on ungreased baking sheets. Bake until the bottoms are lightly browned, 12-15 minutes. Remove from pans to wire racks to cool 5 minutes. Roll in remaining confectioners' sugar. Cool completely.

1 COOKIE: 81 cal., 5g fat (3g sat. fat), 8mg chol., 27mg sod., 8g carb. (5g sugars, 1g fiber), 1g pro.

HOMEMADE CHURROS

These fried cinnamon-sugar goodies are best served fresh and hot. Try them with a cup of coffee or hot chocolate. Don't be surprised if people start dunking, and then go back for more!
—Taste of Home *Test Kitchen*

Prep: 15 min. + cooling • **Cook:** 20 min.
Makes: about 1 dozen

- ½ cup water
- ½ cup 2% milk
- 1 Tbsp. canola oil
- ¼ tsp. salt
- 1 cup all-purpose flour
- 1 large egg, room temperature
- ¼ tsp. grated lemon zest
  Additional oil for frying
- ½ cup sugar
- ¼ tsp. ground cinnamon

1. In a large saucepan, bring the water, milk, oil and salt to a boil. Add flour all at once and stir until a smooth ball forms. Transfer to a large bowl; let stand for 5 minutes.

2. Beat on medium-high speed for 1 minute or until the dough softens. Add egg and lemon zest; beat for 1-2 minutes. Set aside to cool.
3. In a deep cast-iron or heavy skillet, heat 1 in. oil to 375°. Insert a large star tip in a pastry bag; fill with dough. On a baking sheet, pipe dough into 4-in. strips.
4. Transfer strips to skillet; fry until golden brown on both sides. Drain on paper towels. Combine the sugar and cinnamon; sprinkle mixture over churros. Serve warm.
1 CHURRO: 122 cal., 5g fat (1g sat. fat), 17mg chol., 60mg sod., 17g carb. (9g sugars, 0 fiber), 2g pro.

HOLIDAY HELPER

Fry your churros in batches to prevent overcrowding the skillet. The cooked churros should be crispy on the outside and tender inside. If they split, it's a sign your cooking oil is too hot. If the oil isn't hot enough, the churros will absorb it and will be greasy and undercooked rather than crispy.

PRESSURE-COOKER EASY PORK POSOLE

Looking for a meal in a bowl? Sit down to a Mexican classic full of cubed pork, sliced sausage, hominy and more. It all goes into the pressure cooker, making it a great option for a weeknight dinner or a party where you have your hands full preparing different foods.
—Greg Fontenot, The Woodlands, TX

Prep: 30 min. • **Cook:** 15 min.
Makes: 8 servings (2 qt.)

- 1 Tbsp. canola oil
- ½ lb. boneless pork shoulder butt roast, cubed
- ½ lb. fully cooked andouille sausage links, sliced
- 2 medium tomatoes, seeded and chopped
- 1 can (15 oz.) hominy, rinsed and drained
- 1 cup minced fresh cilantro
- 1 medium onion, chopped
- 4 green onions, chopped
- 1 jalapeno pepper, seeded and chopped
- 2 garlic cloves, minced
- 1 Tbsp. chili powder
- 1 tsp. ground cumin
- ½ tsp. cayenne pepper
- ½ tsp. coarsely ground pepper
- 6 cups reduced-sodium chicken broth
  Optional: Corn tortillas, chopped onion, minced fresh cilantro and lime wedges

1. Select saute setting on a 6-qt. electric pressure cooker and adjust for medium heat; add oil. When oil is hot, cook and stir the cubed pork and sausage until browned; drain. Return all to pressure cooker. Press cancel.
2. Add the next 12 ingredients. Lock lid; close pressure-release valve. Adjust to pressure-cook on high for 10 minutes. Allow pressure to release naturally for 5 minutes, then quick-release any remaining pressure. If desired, serve with tortillas, onion, cilantro and lime wedges.
NOTE: Wear disposable gloves when cutting hot peppers; the oils can burn skin. Avoid touching your face.
1 CUP: 189 cal., 11g fat (3g sat. fat), 54mg chol., 954mg sod., 11g carb. (2g sugars, 3g fiber), 14g pro.

SOUTH-OF-THE-BORDER CITRUS SALAD

Orange, grapefruit and jicama add color and texture to this out-of-the-ordinary fruit salad. Sometimes I'll toss in slices of mango and cucumber for extra fun.
—Mary Fuller, SeaTac, WA

Takes: 20 min. • **Makes:** 6 servings

3   medium pink grapefruit
3   medium oranges
1   cup julienned peeled jicama
2   Tbsp. minced fresh cilantro
2   Tbsp. lime juice
¼   tsp. ground cinnamon

1. Cut a thin slice from the top and bottom of each grapefruit and orange; stand fruit upright on a cutting board. With a knife, cut the peel and outer membrane from fruit. Cut fruit crosswise into slices; place in a large bowl.
2. Add remaining ingredients; toss to combine. Transfer to a platter; refrigerate, covered, until serving.
¾ CUP: 70 cal., 0 fat (0 sat. fat), 0 chol., 2mg sod., 17g carb. (13g sugars, 3g fiber), 1g pro. **DIABETIC EXCHANGES:** 1 fruit.

FIERY STUFFED POBLANOS

I love Southwest-inspired cuisine, but the dishes are often unhealthy. As a dietitian, I try to come up with nutritious twists on recipes, which is how my stuffed peppers dish was born.
—Amber Massey, Argyle, TX

Prep: 50 min. + standing • **Bake:** 20 min.
Makes: 8 servings

8   poblano peppers
1   can (15 oz.) black beans, rinsed and drained
1   medium zucchini, chopped
1   small red onion, chopped
4   garlic cloves, minced
1   can (15¼ oz.) whole kernel corn, drained
1   can (14½ oz.) fire-roasted diced tomatoes, undrained
1   cup cooked brown rice
1   Tbsp. ground cumin
1   to 1½ tsp. ground ancho chile pepper
¼   tsp. salt
¼   tsp. pepper
1   cup shredded reduced-fat Mexican cheese blend, divided
3   green onions, chopped
½   cup reduced-fat sour cream

1. Broil peppers 3 in. from heat until skins blister, about 5 minutes. With tongs, rotate peppers a quarter turn. Broil and rotate until all sides are blistered and blackened. Immediately place peppers in a large bowl; cover and let stand for 20 minutes.
2. Meanwhile, in a small bowl, coarsely mash beans; set aside. In a large nonstick skillet, cook and stir zucchini and onion until tender. Add garlic; cook 1 minute longer. Add the corn, tomatoes, rice, seasonings and beans. Remove from heat; stir in ½ cup cheese. Set aside.
3. Preheat oven to 375°. Peel charred skins from poblanos and discard. Cut a lengthwise slit through each pepper, leaving stem intact; discard membranes and seeds. Spoon ⅔ cup of the filling into each pepper.
4. Place peppers in a 13x9-in. baking dish coated with cooking spray. Bake until heated through, 18-22 minutes, sprinkling with green onions and remaining cheese during last 5 minutes of baking. Serve with sour cream.
NOTE: Wear disposable gloves when cutting hot peppers; the oils can burn skin. Avoid touching your face.
1 STUFFED PEPPER: 223 cal., 5g fat (2g sat. fat), 15mg chol., 579mg sod., 32g carb. (9g sugars, 7g fiber), 11g pro. **DIABETIC EXCHANGES:** 2 vegetable, 1 starch, 1 lean meat, 1 fat.

CLASSIC TRES LECHES CAKE

A classic in Mexican kitchens for generations, this cake gets its name from the three types of milk—evaporated, sweetened condensed and heavy whipping cream—used to create a super moist and tender texture.
—Taste of Home *Test Kitchen*

Prep: 45 min. • **Bake:** 20 min. + chilling
Makes: 10 servings

- 4 large eggs, separated, room temperature
- ⅔ cup sugar, divided
- ⅔ cup cake flour
  Dash salt
- ¾ cup heavy whipping cream
- ¾ cup evaporated milk
- ¾ cup sweetened condensed milk
- 2 tsp. vanilla extract
- ¼ tsp. rum extract

TOPPING

- 1¼ cups heavy whipping cream, chilled
- 3 Tbsp. sugar
  Optional: Dulce de leche or sliced fresh strawberries

1. Place egg whites in a large bowl. Line bottom of a 9-in. springform pan with parchment; grease the paper.
2. Preheat oven to 350°. In another large bowl, beat the egg yolks until slightly thickened. Gradually add ⅓ cup sugar, beating on high speed until thick and lemon-colored, about 5 minutes. Fold in flour, a third at a time.
3. Add salt to egg whites; with clean beaters, beat on medium until soft peaks form. Gradually add remaining ⅓ cup sugar, 1 Tbsp. at a time, beating on high after each addition until the sugar is dissolved. Continue beating until soft glossy peaks form. Fold a third of the whites into batter, then fold in remaining whites. Gently spread into prepared pan.
4. Bake until top springs back when lightly touched, 20-25 minutes. Cool for 10 minutes before removing from pan to a wire rack to cool completely.
5. Place cake on a rimmed serving plate. Poke holes in top with a skewer. In a small bowl, mix cream, evaporated milk, sweetened condensed milk and extracts; brush or pour mixture slowly over cake. Refrigerate, covered, 2 hours.

6. For topping, beat the cream until it begins to thicken. Add sugar; beat until peaks form. Spread over top of cake. If desired, top cake with dulce de leche or strawberries just before serving.
1 PIECE: 392 cal., 23g fat (14g sat. fat), 142mg chol., 104mg sod., 40g carb. (33g sugars, 0 fiber), 8g pro.

HOLIDAY HELPER

You can make tres leches cake a day or two in advance (with the exception of the whipped cream topping). In fact, letting the cake sit overnight is ideal. Because of the fresh dairy, always store tres leches cake in the fridge. It will last 3 to 4 days. Be sure to keep it covered so no other fridge odors infiltrate your dessert. Due to the milk soak, this cake is not a good candidate for freezing.

SLOW SOAK

Be generous when poking holes into the cake so that the liquid will disperse evenly throughout the cake. Pour slowly, using a small spatula or pastry brush to guide the liquid over the cake. Be sure to let the cake rest for at least 2 hours to give the liquid a chance to absorb.

CHRISTMAS CHARCUTERIE BOARD

For a casual gathering for snacks and drinks, or as an appetizing precursor to a formal sit-down dinner, a beautifully assembled board is a delight.

ON THE BOARD

1. Wild Plum Jelly, p. 130
2. Candied Pecans, p. 128
3. Bacon, Cheddar & Swiss Cheese Ball, p. 130
4. Gentleman's Whiskey Bacon Jam, p. 127

GENTLEMAN'S WHISKEY BACON JAM

You can slather this smoky jam on pretty much anything. It lasts only a week in the fridge, so I freeze small amounts for a quick snack with crackers.
—Colleen Delawder, Herndon, VA

Prep: 15 min. • **Cook:** 30 min. • **Makes:** 3 cups

- 1½ lbs. thick-sliced bacon strips, finely chopped
- 8 shallots, finely chopped
- 1 large sweet onion, finely chopped
- 2 garlic cloves, minced
- 1 tsp. chili powder
- ½ tsp. paprika
- ¼ tsp. kosher salt
- ¼ tsp. pepper
- ½ cup whiskey
- ½ cup maple syrup
- ¼ cup balsamic vinegar
- ½ cup packed brown sugar
  Assorted crackers

1. In a large skillet, cook bacon over medium heat until crisp. Drain on paper towels. Discard all but 2 Tbsp. drippings. Add chopped shallots and onion to the drippings; cook over medium heat until caramelized, stirring occasionally.
2. Stir in garlic; cook 30 seconds. Add seasonings. Remove from heat; stir in whiskey and maple syrup. Increase heat to high; bring to a boil and cook 3 minutes, stirring constantly. Add the vinegar and brown sugar; cook, stirring constantly, 3 minutes longer.
3. Crumble bacon; add to skillet. Reduce heat to low and cook 12 minutes, stirring every few minutes. Allow jam to cool slightly. Transfer half the jam to a food processor and pulse until smooth; stir puree into remaining jam. Serve with assorted crackers.
2 TBSP.: 112 cal., 8g fat (3g sat. fat), 10mg chol., 118mg sod., 7g carb. (5g sugars, 0 fiber), 2g pro.

HOLIDAY HELPER

Make prep easier by freezing the bacon (it helps to cut it into chunks first) and then pulsing it in the food processor until finely chopped.

CRANBERRY-MANGO SALSA WITH TREE CHIPS

This delightfully different salsa features a nice balance of sweet, tart and spicy. The accompanying tree-shaped chips are fun and easy to make using tortillas and a cookie cutter.
—Janice Christofferson, Eagle River, WI

Prep: 40 min. + cooling
Bake: 5 min./batch
Makes: 3½ cups salsa (100 chips)

- 1 pkg. (12 oz.) fresh or frozen cranberries
- 1 cup sugar
- 1 cup water
- 1 Tbsp. cornstarch
- 1 Tbsp. lime juice
- 1 medium mango, peeled and chopped
- 1 jalapeno pepper, seeded and chopped
- 1 green onion, chopped
- 1 Tbsp. chopped red onion
- 1 Tbsp. minced fresh cilantro
- ¼ tsp. ground cumin
- 10 spinach, tomato and/or plain tortillas (8 in.)

1. In a large saucepan, combine the cranberries, sugar and water. Cook over medium heat until the berries pop, about 15 minutes. Combine cornstarch and lime juice until smooth; add to the cranberry mixture. Bring to a boil; cook and stir until thickened, 1-2 minutes. Transfer to a large bowl; stir in mango, jalapeno, onions, cilantro and cumin. Cool. Refrigerate, covered, until serving.
2. Preheat oven to 350°. Using a 3-in. tree-shaped cookie cutter, cut 10 tree shapes from each tortilla; place cutouts on ungreased baking sheets. Bake until crisp, 5-6 minutes. Remove to wire racks to cool completely. Serve with salsa.
NOTE: Wear disposable gloves when cutting hot peppers; the oils can burn skin. Avoid touching your face.
2 TBSP. SALSA WITH 4 CHIPS : 92 cal., 1g fat (0 sat. fat), 0 chol., 89mg sod., 19g carb. (9g sugars, 1g fiber), 2g pro.
DIABETIC EXCHANGES: 1 starch.

TOM & JERRY

It just wouldn't be Christmas without sipping a warm Tom & Jerry drink. I was surprised to find out that not everyone knows about this beverage treat. One sip and I'm sure you'll be hooked. It's a like a warm version of eggnog, only better.
—*James Schend, Pleasant Prairie, WI*

Takes: 25 min. • **Makes:** 10 servings

- 6   large pasteurized eggs, separated
- 2   cups sugar
- 2   Tbsp. brandy or rum
- 1   Tbsp. vanilla extract
- 2   tsp. pumpkin pie spice
- ½   tsp. bitters (preferably Angostura)
- ½   tsp. cream of tartar, optional

EACH SERVING
- ¾   cup boiling water or hot 2% milk
- 1   oz. brandy
- 1   oz. rum
      Freshly grated nutmeg, optional

1. In a large bowl, beat egg yolks until thin and loose, about 1 minute. Gradually beat in sugar, brandy, vanilla, pie spice and bitters; beat until thick and frothy, 3-5 minutes.
2. In another large bowl, with clean beaters beat egg whites (and, if desired, cream of tartar) on high speed just until stiff but not dry. Fold a fourth of the whites into the yolk mixture until no white streaks remain. Fold in the remaining whites until combined. Refrigerate mixture, covered, until serving.
3. For each serving, place ¾ cup mixture into a large mug. Add boiling water, brandy and rum; stir until blended. If desired, top with freshly grated nutmeg.
1 SERVING: 340 cal., 3g fat (1g sat. fat), 112mg chol., 44mg sod., 41g carb. (41g sugars, 0 fiber), 4g pro.

HOLIDAY HELPER

Try making this drink with Cognac, which is the traditional brandy to use for this Christmas cocktail. You could also add other spices and garnishes, like cinnamon or star anise.

CANDIED PECANS

I like to pack these crispy pecans in jars, tied with pretty ribbon, for family and friends. My granddaughter gave some to a doctor at the hospital where she works, and he said they were too good to be true!
—*Opal Turner, Hughes Springs, TX*

Prep: 25 min. • **Bake:** 30 min.
Makes: about 1 lb.

- 2¾ cups pecan halves
- 2   Tbsp. butter, softened, divided
- 1   cup sugar
- ½   cup water
- ½   tsp. salt
- ½   tsp. ground cinnamon
- 1   tsp. vanilla extract

1. Place pecans in a shallow baking pan in a 250° oven for 10 minutes or until warmed. Grease a 15x10x1-in. baking pan with 1 Tbsp. butter; set aside.
2. Grease the sides of a large heavy saucepan with remaining 1 Tbsp. butter; add the sugar, water, salt and cinnamon. Bring to a boil, stirring constantly to dissolve the sugar. Cover; cook 2 minutes longer to dissolve any sugar crystals that may form on the sides of pan.
3. Cook, without stirring, until a candy thermometer reads 236° (soft-ball stage). Remove from heat; add vanilla. Stir in warm pecans until evenly coated.
4. Spread onto prepared baking pan. Bake at 250° for 30 minutes, stirring every 10 minutes. Spread on a waxed paper-lined baking sheet to cool.
NOTE: We recommend you test your candy thermometer before each use by bringing water to a boil; the thermometer should read 212°. Adjust your recipe temperature up or down based on your test.
2 OZ. NUTS: 380 cal., 30g fat (4g sat. fat), 8mg chol., 177mg sod., 30g carb. (26g sugars, 4g fiber), 3g pro.

BACON, CHEDDAR & SWISS CHEESE BALL

When it's time for a party, everyone requests this ultimate cheese ball. It works as a spreadable dip and makes a fabulous hostess gift.
—Sue Franklin, Lake Saint Louis, MO

Prep Time: 20 min. + chilling • **Makes:** 2 cheese balls (4 cups each)

- 1 pkg. (8 oz.) cream cheese, softened
- ½ cup sour cream
- 2 cups shredded Swiss cheese
- 2 cups shredded sharp cheddar cheese
- 1 cup crumbled cooked bacon (about 12 strips), divided
- ½ cup chopped pecans, toasted, divided
- ½ cup finely chopped onion
- 1 jar (2 oz.) diced pimientos, drained
- 2 Tbsp. sweet pickle relish
- ¼ tsp. salt
- ¼ tsp. pepper
- ¼ cup minced fresh parsley
- 1 Tbsp. poppy seeds
  Assorted crackers

1. In a large bowl, beat cream cheese and sour cream until smooth. Stir in shredded cheeses, ½ cup bacon, ¼ cup pecans, the onion, pimientos, pickle relish, salt and pepper. Refrigerate, covered, at least 1 hour.
2. In a small bowl, mix parsley, poppy seeds and the remaining ½ cup bacon and ¼ cup pecans. Spread half the parsley mixture on a large plate. Shape half the cheese mixture into a ball; roll in parsley mixture to coat evenly. Cover. Repeat to make another cheese ball. Refrigerate at least 1 hour. Serve with crackers.
NOTE: To toast nuts, bake in a shallow pan in a 350°; oven for 5-10 minutes or cook in a skillet over low heat until lightly browned, stirring occasionally.
2 TBSP.: 116 cal., 10g fat (5g sat. fat), 22mg chol., 194mg sod., 2g carb. (1g sugars, 0 fiber), 6g pro.

WILD PLUM JELLY

I've had this wild plum jelly recipe for ages. Each year when the plums are ripe, I'll fill my pail and make this jelly. It's so good served with toast, pancakes or with crackers and a sharp cheese.
—Ludell Heuser, Mount Horeb, WI

Prep: 55 min. • **Process:** 5 min. • **Makes:** about 8 half-pints

- 5 lbs. wild plums, halved and pitted
- 4 cups water
- 1 pkg. (1¾ oz.) powdered fruit pectin
- 7½ cups sugar

1. In a stockpot, simmer plums and water until tender, about 30 minutes. Line a strainer with 4 layers of cheesecloth and place over a bowl. Place plum mixture in strainer; cover with edges of cheesecloth. Let stand until liquid in bowl measures 5½ cups, about 30 minutes.
2. Return liquid to the pan. Add pectin; stir and bring to a boil. Add sugar; bring to a full rolling boil. Boil 1 minute; stirring constantly.
3. Remove from heat; skim off any foam. Carefully ladle hot mixture into hot sterilized half-pint jars, leaving ¼ in. headspace. Remove air bubbles; wipe rims and put on lids. Process for 5 minutes in a boiling-water canner.
NOTE: The processing time listed is for altitudes of 1,000 feet or less. Add 1 minute for each 1,000 feet of additional altitude.
2 TBSP.: 108 cal., 0 fat (0 sat. fat), 0 chol., 0 sod., 28g carb. (27g sugars, 1g fiber), 0 pro.

STACKED CHRISTMAS TREE COOKIES

Prepared cookie dough gives you a head start to your own little forest of Christmas trees. Get the kids involved in this holiday craft and keep them busy making memories.
—*Sue Draheim, Waterford, WI*

Prep: 30 min. • **Bake:** 10 min. + cooling
Makes: 9 servings

- 1 tube (16½ oz.) refrigerated sugar cookie dough
- ½ tsp. vanilla extract
- ½ cup all-purpose flour
  Green colored sugar
- 1 can (16 oz.) vanilla frosting
- 9 unwrapped Rolo candies
  Necco wafer candies
  Smarties candies
  Yellow food coloring
  Water
  Red nonpareils

1. Preheat oven to 350°. Place cookie dough in a large bowl; let stand at room temperature to soften, 5-10 minutes. Beat in vanilla. Add flour; beat until blended.

2. On a lightly floured surface, roll out dough to ¼-in. thickness. Using a floured 2-in. round cookie cutter, cut out 18 cookies. Repeat with 1½-in. and 1-in. round cookie cutters. For remaining dough, use a floured ½-in. star-shaped cookie cutter to cut out 9 stars.

3. Sprinkle round cookies with colored sugar. Place 1 in. apart on ungreased baking sheets. Bake until edges are light brown, 6-9 minutes. Remove to wire racks to cool completely.

4. For each Christmas tree, pipe frosting on top of a Rolo candy for a trunk; top with a 2-in. cookie. Pipe frosting on top and bottom of a Necco wafer; place in center of cookie. Top with another 2-in. cookie. Repeat layers with two 1½-in. cookies and two 1-in. cookies, using Smarties between the smaller layers.

5. For stars, color a small amount of frosting yellow and pipe onto star-shaped cookies; attach to the tops of trees using additional frosting. Thin remaining frosting with water; drizzle over edges. Decorate with nonpareils.

1 CHRISTMAS TREE: 466 cal., 18g fat (6g sat. fat), 6mg chol., 278mg sod., 72g carb. (48g sugars, 1g fiber), 3g pro.

HOW TO BUILD A BASIC BOARD

Follow these steps when putting together a board or platter of your own.

1. Pull the cheeses out of the refrigerator about an hour before assembling the board. Place the cheese first. Pre-cut a few slices or crumble a corner of a wedge to demonstrate know how each cheese should be consumed.

2. Add small bowls. Bowls of different sizes and colors will add visual interest. Next, place any decorative elements—such lemon leaves, fig leaves or grape leaves—to avoid having to tuck them under foods later.

3. Add the meats. Fold slices of meat in different ways to add visual interest, texture and height. Keep meats of similar colors apart from one another on the board.

4. Arrange crackers and condiments, placing the items that pair best near each other.

5. Fill in some of the gaps with grapes and dried fruits.

6. Fill in the last open spaces with nuts and pickles.

7. Add mini utensils to the board, including cheese knives and spoons for condiments. Set out extra cheese knives, appetizer plates and napkins.

POLAR FROST PARTY

For a winter party the kids will love, create an eye-catching spread that's as fun to look at as it is delicious to eat!

SNOWFLAKE TOMATO SOUP

Our sensational soup features lots of pleasing ingredients, and is extra fun to eat when decorated with pretty snowflakes.
—Taste of Home *Test Kitchen*

Takes: 25 min. • **Makes:** 10 servings

2 cans (28 oz. each) crushed tomatoes
1 can (14½ oz.) chicken broth
2 Tbsp. minced fresh oregano
   or 2 tsp. dried oregano
1 to 2 Tbsp. sugar
1 cup heavy whipping cream
   Optional: Crackers and sliced white cheese

1. In a blender, process tomatoes, 1 can at a time, until smooth. Transfer to a large saucepan. Stir in the broth; bring to a boil. Reduce heat; cover and simmer for 10 minutes. Stir in oregano and sugar. Add a small amount of the hot tomato mixture to whipping cream; return all to saucepan. Cook until slightly thickened (do not boil).
2. If desired, cut snowflake shapes from sliced cheese using small cutter; arrange on top of crackers. Place the soup into serving bowl; top with crackers and cheese if desired.
1 CUP: 140 cal., 9g fat (6g sat. fat), 27mg chol., 451mg sod., 14g carb. (9g sugars, 3g fiber), 3g pro.

HOLIDAY HELPER

For the garnish on this soup, we used miniature pastry cutters to cut out pieces of cheese slices, then laid them on top of octagonal crackers. Cutters come in a wide variety of holiday themed shapes, so you can cut out snowmen, gingerbread men or anything you like.

For a different kind of decoration, try piping some sour cream on top of each serving to make a spiral pattern, a star shape, or any design you please!

OVERNIGHT REINDEER ROLLS

Have some family fun making these reindeer-shaped rolls with the kids. Make sure to take pictures of the final product because the rolls will be gone before you know it!
—*Chris O'Connell, San Antonio, TX*

Prep: 50 min. + chilling
Bake: 10 min. • **Makes:** 3 dozen

2 pkg. (¼ oz. each) active dry yeast
1½ cups warm water (110° to 115°)
2 large eggs, room temperature
½ cup butter, softened
½ cup sugar
2 tsp. salt
5¾ to 6¼ cups all-purpose flour
DECORATIONS
1 large egg
2 tsp. water
36 raisins (about 2 Tbsp.), halved
18 red candied cherries, halved

1. In a small bowl, dissolve yeast in warm water. In a large bowl, combine eggs, butter, sugar, salt, yeast mixture and 3 cups flour; beat on medium speed until smooth. Stir in enough remaining flour to form a very soft dough (dough will be sticky). Do not knead. Cover and refrigerate overnight.

2. Turn dough onto a floured surface; divide and shape into 36 balls. Roll each into a 5-in. log. Cut each log lengthwise halfway down the center. Pull the cut sections apart for antlers. Using kitchen shears, snip ½-in. cuts along outer sides for antler points. Flatten the uncut half of log for face.
3. Place 2 in. apart on greased baking sheets. Cover with kitchen towels; let rise in a warm place until doubled, about 30 minutes. Preheat oven to 400°.
4. In a small bowl, whisk egg and water until blended; brush over the rolls. Press raisin halves into dough for eyes; press cherry halves into dough for noses.
5. Bake until golden brown, 8-10 minutes. Serve warm.
1 ROLL: 116 cal., 3g fat (2g sat. fat), 24mg chol., 155mg sod., 19g carb. (5g sugars, 1g fiber), 3g pro.
KNOT-SHAPED ROLLS: Shape dough into 36 balls. Roll each into a 6-in. rope; tie into a loose knot. Tuck ends under; place 2 in. apart on greased baking sheets. Let rise and bake as recipe directs, increasing baking time to 10-12 minutes.
S-SHAPED ROLLS: Divide dough into 36 portions. Roll each into a 10-in. rope. Shape rope into an S, then coil each end until it touches the center; place 2 in. apart on greased baking sheets. Let rise and bake as recipe directs, increasing baking time to 10-12 minutes.

APPLE-GOUDA PIGS IN A BLANKET

For New Year's, I used to make beef and cheddar pigs in a blanket, but now I like apple and Gouda for an even better flavor celebration.
—Megan Weiss, Menomonie, WI

Takes: 30 min. • **Makes:** 2 dozen

- 1 tube (8 oz.) refrigerated crescent rolls
- 1 small apple, peeled and cut into 24 thin slices
- 6 thin slices Gouda cheese, quartered
- 24 miniature smoked sausages
  Honey mustard salad dressing, optional

1. Preheat oven to 375°. Unroll crescent dough and separate into 8 triangles; cut each lengthwise into 3 thin triangles. On the wide end of each triangle, place 1 slice apple, 1 folded piece cheese and 1 sausage; roll up tightly.
2. Place rolls 1 in. apart on parchment-lined baking sheets, point side down. Bake until golden brown, 10-12 minutes. If desired, serve with dressing.
1 APPETIZER: 82 cal., 6g fat (2g sat. fat), 11mg chol., 203mg sod., 5g carb. (1g sugars, 0 fiber), 3g pro.

CREAMY PINEAPPLE FLUFF SALAD

Guests of all ages will gravitate to this traditional fluff salad, chock-full of pineapple, marshmallows and cherry bits.
—Janice Hensley, Owingsville, KY

Takes: 25 min. • **Makes:** 16 servings

- 1 pkg. (8 oz.) cream cheese, softened
- 1 can (14 oz.) sweetened condensed milk
- ¼ cup lemon juice
- 2 cans (20 oz.) pineapple tidbits, drained
- 1½ cups multicolored miniature marshmallows, divided
- 1 carton (8 oz.) frozen whipped topping, thawed
- ½ cup chopped nuts
- ⅓ cup maraschino cherries, chopped

In a large bowl, beat the cream cheese, condensed milk and lemon juice until smooth. Add pineapple and 1 cup of the marshmallows; fold in whipped topping. Sprinkle with chopped nuts, cherries and the remaining ½ cup marshmallows. Refrigerate leftovers.
½ CUP: 161 cal., 10g fat (6g sat. fat), 16mg chol., 50mg sod., 17g carb. (12g sugars, 1g fiber), 2g pro.

HOLIDAY HELPER

This sweet, fluffy salad is a longtime favorite with many families, and you can make adjustments to make it your own. Some common additions include coconut, lemon zest and homemade whipped cream. If you can't find pineapple tidbits in your store, you can use crushed pineapple instead—just make sure to drain it well!

PRETZEL POLAR BEARS

Stick these cool cuties in a mug of hot chocolate or show them off on a holiday cookie tray. Covered in white chocolate and coconut, they're almost too adorable to eat. Almost.
—Taste of Home *Test Kitchen*

Prep: 30 min. + standing • **Makes:** 1 dozen

1½ cups sweetened shredded coconut
8   oz. white baking chocolate, melted
12 pretzel rods
    Assorted decorations: Candy coating disks, halved
    miniature marshmallows, white baking chips, miniature
    semisweet chocolate chips, sprinkles and Sixlets
    Fruit by the Foot fruit rolls, optional

1. Place coconut in a shallow bowl. Pour melted chocolate into 1 end of an 11x7-in. dish. Roll two-thirds of a pretzel rod in the chocolate, allowing excess to drip off. Place on waxed paper; let stand until chocolate just begins to lose its sheen. Repeat with the remaining pretzels. Sprinkle coated pretzels with coconut, patting to help adhere.
2. Decorate as desired, using some of the melted chocolate to attach candy coating disks to make faces, halved mini marshmallows or white chips to make ears, and mini chocolate chips, sprinkles and Sixlets to make eyes and noses.
3. Carefully stand bears upright in a tall glass or press the bottoms of the pretzel rods into holes cut into a 2-in.-thick piece of Styrofoam. If desired, cut fruit rolls into thin strips to make scarves; tie around bears. Let stand until set.
1 PRETZEL: 166 cal., 9g fat (7g sat. fat), 0 chol., 244mg sod., 22g carb. (14g sugars, 1g fiber), 2g pro.

SNOW PUNCH

Pretty as a fresh snowdrift, this creamy, fruity punch has been a Christmas tradition in our family for years—but it's a light and refreshing thirst-quencher in any season.
—Eloise Neeley, Norton, OH

Takes: 10 min. • **Makes:** 2½ qt.

1   cup lemon juice
5   medium ripe bananas
1   cup sugar
2   cups half-and-half cream
1   liter lemon-lime soda, chilled
1   pint lemon or pineapple sherbet
¼   cup sweetened shredded coconut, optional

1. In a blender, cover and process the lemon juice, bananas and sugar until smooth. Add cream; blend until smooth. Cover and refrigerate.
2. Just before serving, pour banana mixture into a punch bowl. Stir in soda. Top with lemon sherbet and, if desired, coconut.
1 CUP: 296 cal., 7g fat (4g sat. fat), 26mg chol., 56mg sod., 58g carb. (51g sugars, 2g fiber), 3g pro.

HOLIDAY HELPER

The banana mixture for these drinks can be made in advance and kept in the refrigerator until you're ready to serve. Instead of mixing it all in a punch bowl, you can scoop sherbet into individual glasses, then top with the banana mixture and soda.

SNOWMAN CAKE

This frosty figure will melt ... in your mouth! The cute-as-can-be character is completely edible, from its chocolate candy buttons and coconut snowflakes to the licorice scarf and gumdrop nose. What's more, you'll be able to build it without using a specially shaped pan. The finished cake will be 10 inches high and 6½ inches wide at the base.
—Taste of Home *Test Kitchen*

Prep: 40 min. • **Bake:** 1 hour + cooling
Makes: 24 servings

- 2   pkg. (16 oz. each) pound cake mix
- 1   cup shortening
- 1   cup butter, softened
- 8   cups confectioners' sugar
- 2   tsp. vanilla extract
- 4   to 6 Tbsp. 2% milk
- 3½ cups sweetened shredded coconut (about 10 oz.)
     M&M's: 2 brown, 3 green, 2 red
     Large gumdrops: 1 orange, 1 green
- 4½ tsp. miniature chocolate chips, melted
- 1   chocolate wafer
- 4   sour candy strips

1. Preheat oven to 350°. Prepare cake mixes according to package directions. Pour batter into 2 greased 1-qt. ovenproof bowls, 2 greased 10-oz. custard cups and 1 greased muffin cup.
2. Bake muffin cup for 18-20 minutes, custard cups for 45-50 minutes and bowls for 60-65 minutes or until a toothpick inserted in the center comes out clean. Cool for 5 minutes before removing cakes from pans to wire racks to cool completely. Use a serrated knife to level all the cakes and cupcake.
3. For frosting, cream the shortening and butter in a bowl. Beat in confectioners' sugar, vanilla and enough milk to reach spreading consistency.
BODY & HEAD:
1. For the body, place 1 large round cake flat side up on an 8-in. serving plate. Frost the top of the cake. Place the remaining large cake on top with the flat side down and edges even. Frost the top and side.
2. For the head, place 1 custard-cup cake, flat side up, on top of body. Frost the top of the cake. Place the remaining custard-cup cake on top with the flat side down

and edges even. Frost the top and side. Set aside ¼ cup of frosting for hat.
3. Press coconut over the top and sides of snowman, reserving some to sprinkle on plate later. Press 2 brown M&M's onto the face for eyes and 3 green M&M's onto the body for buttons.
4. Use your fingers to shape the orange gumdrop into a carrot shape. Press the wide end into the face for the nose.
HAT:
1. Place reserved frosting in a bowl. Stir melted chips into frosting until blended. Frost top of wafer. With top of cupcake down, place cupcake on top of frosted wafer. Frost cupcake with remaining frosting. Place hat on snowman's head.
2. Wrap 1 sour candy strip around hat just above brim and trim as needed; secure with toothpick if desired.
3. Flatten green gumdrop between pieces of waxed paper. Using sharp knife, cut a holly leaf shape from gumdrop; place on hat brim. Place 2 red M&M's on brim next to holly leaf for the berries.
FINISHING:
Wrap 2 sour candy strips around neck for scarf, trimming as needed; if desired, secure with toothpicks. Loop remaining sour candy strip around loop at neck to form hanging portion of scarf. Sprinkle plate with reserved coconut.

1 PIECE: 526 cal., 23g fat (12g sat. fat), 36mg chol., 239mg sod., 79g carb. (64g sugars, 1g fiber), 2g pro.

NO PURCHASE NEEDED

This cake is made using common baking equipment—1-qt. bowls, 10-oz. custard cups and a muffin tin. The bowls already have a slightly flattened bottom, so you won't need to level the rounded side of the cakes to prevent them from rolling on the plate.

BUON NATALE

Individual customs may differ, but some things are universal!
In Italy, Christmas is a time for family, fellowship and
lots of *buon cibo*—good food! Treat your *familia* to an
Italian-flavored holiday they won't soon forget!

CHOCOLATE & CHERRY STROMBOLI

This melty, chocolaty spin on stromboli is delicious as a dessert or as an indulgent breakfast. Serve it with a cup of coffee, and even the coldest winter day instantly feels more snug.
—Lorraine Caland, Shuniah, ON

Prep: 40 min. + rising
Bake: 20 min. + cooling
Makes: 1 loaf (12 pieces)

- 4 cups all-purpose flour
- 1 pkg. (¼ oz.) quick-rise yeast
- 1 tsp. salt
- 1 cup warm water (120° to 130°)
- 3 Tbsp. canola oil
- 2 Tbsp. honey
- 1 egg, room temperature, lightly beaten
- 1 tsp. lemon juice
- 8 oz. finely chopped bittersweet chocolate, divided
- ½ cup dried cherries, chopped
- 2 Tbsp. coarse sugar

1. Whisk 3 cups flour, the yeast and salt. In another bowl, mix water, oil and honey. Add to dry ingredients; beat on medium speed for 2 minutes. Stir in enough of the remaining flour to form a soft dough (dough will be sticky).
2. Turn dough onto a floured surface; knead for 3-5 minutes or until smooth and elastic. Place in a greased bowl, turning once to grease top. Cover; let rise in a warm place until doubled, about 30 minutes.
3. Preheat oven to 400°. Press dough into a greased 15x10x1-in. baking pan. Whisk the egg with lemon juice; brush dough with half of egg wash. Sprinkle half of chocolate evenly over dough; top with cherries. Starting with a long side, fold dough over filling into thirds. Do not pinch ends to seal. Brush with the remaining egg wash. Sprinkle with coarse sugar. Bake on lowest oven rack until bread sounds hollow when tapped, about 20 minutes. Cool on wire rack.
4. Meanwhile, in a microwave, melt the remaining chocolate. Drizzle over cooled bread.
1 PIECE: 248 cal., 8g fat (2g sat. fat), 16mg chol., 205mg sod., 36g carb. (10g sugars, 2g fiber), 5g pro.

ITALIAN HOLIDAY COOKIES

Many of our holiday traditions center around the foods my mother made while I was growing up. These cookies bring back wonderful memories.
—Sue Seymour, Valatie, NY

Prep: 20 min.
Cook: 5 min./batch + cooling
Makes: about 15 dozen

Oil for deep-fat frying
- 1 Tbsp. sugar
- 1 tsp. grated lemon zest
- 1 tsp. vanilla extract
- ½ tsp. salt
- 4 large eggs, room temperature
- 2½ cups all-purpose flour
- 1 cup honey
  Candy sprinkles

1. In an electric skillet or deep-fat fryer, heat oil to 350°. In a bowl, combine sugar, lemon zest, vanilla and salt. Add eggs and 2 cups flour; mix well. Turn onto a floured surface and knead in remaining ½ cup flour (dough will be soft).
2. With a floured knife or scissors, cut dough into 20 pieces. Roll each piece into pencil shapes. Cut into ½-in. pieces. Fry pieces, a few at a time, until golden brown, about 2 minutes per side. Drain on paper towels. Place in a large bowl.
3. Heat the honey to boiling; pour over cookies and mix well. With a slotted spoon, place on a serving platter; mound into a tree shape if desired. Decorate with candy sprinkles. Cool completely.
1 COOKIE: 18 cal., 1g fat (0 sat. fat), 4mg chol., 8mg sod., 3g carb. (2g sugars, 0 fiber), 0 pro.

SPICED PEAR RISOTTO

We love risotto and are always in search of fun and different ways to prepare it. I like to serve this fruity version with pork tenderloin.
—*Kim Berto, Port Orchard, WA*

Prep: 15 min. • **Cook:** 35 min. • **Makes:** 10 servings

    6   cups chicken broth
    ½   cup finely chopped sweet onion
    ½   cup finely chopped sweet red pepper
    1   garlic clove, minced
    3   Tbsp. butter
    3   cups uncooked arborio rice
    ½   tsp. Chinese five-spice powder
        Dash cayenne pepper
    ¼   cup apple cider or juice
    1   large pear, peeled and chopped
    ½   cup grated Parmesan cheese, divided
    ½   tsp. coarsely ground pepper
        Chopped chives, optional

1. In a large saucepan, heat broth and keep warm. In a Dutch oven, saute the onion, red pepper and garlic in butter until tender, about 3 minutes.
2. Add the rice, five-spice powder and cayenne; cook and stir for 2-3 minutes. Reduce heat to medium; add cider. Cook and stir until all the liquid is absorbed.
3. Add warm broth, ½ cup at a time, stirring constantly. Allow the liquid to absorb between additions. Cook just until risotto is creamy and rice is almost tender. (Cooking time is about 25 minutes.)
4. Add the pear, ¼ cup cheese and the pepper; cook and stir until heated through. Sprinkle with remaining ½ cup cheese. If desired, top with chopped chives.
¾ CUP: 293 cal., 5g fat (3g sat. fat), 16mg chol., 675mg sod., 54g carb. (4g sugars, 2g fiber), 6g pro.

MIXED OLIVE CROSTINI

These little toasts are pretty and irresistible—they're always a big hit. Even though they look as if you fussed, the ingredients are probably already in your pantry.
—*Laurie LaClair, North Richland Hills, TX*

Takes: 25 min. • **Makes:** 2 dozen

    1   can (4¼ oz.) chopped ripe olives
    ½   cup pimiento-stuffed olives, finely chopped
    ½   cup grated Parmesan cheese
    ¼   cup butter, softened
    1   Tbsp. olive oil
    2   garlic cloves, minced
    ¾   cup shredded part-skim mozzarella cheese
    ¼   cup minced fresh parsley
    1   French bread baguette (10½ oz.)

1. In a small bowl, combine the first 6 ingredients; stir in mozzarella cheese and parsley. Cut baguette into 24 slices; place on an ungreased baking sheet. Spread with olive mixture.
2. Broil 3-4 in. from the heat until edges are lightly browned and cheese is melted, 2-3 minutes.
1 SERVING: 102 cal., 6g fat (2g sat. fat), 9mg chol., 221mg sod., 10g carb. (0 sugars, 1g fiber), 3g pro.

HOLIDAY HELPER

The difference between crostini and bruschetta is the bread. While bruschetta is made with slices from a larger, rustic Italian loaf, crostini uses a slender, finer-textured bread. You can use this recipe to make bruschetta instead, if you prefer.

PORK WITH GORGONZOLA SAUCE

A tangy Gorgonzola cheese sauce dresses up tender slices of pork. Served alongside steamed broccoli, this special entree is sure to create a memorable meal.
—Taste of Home *Test Kitchen*

Prep: 15 min. • **Bake:** 10 min.
Makes: 6 servings

- ¼ cup Dijon mustard
- 1 Tbsp. olive oil
- 1 Tbsp. dried thyme
- 2 pork tenderloins (¾ lb. each)
  Salt and pepper to taste

SAUCE
- 1 garlic clove, minced
- 1 Tbsp. butter
- 1 Tbsp. all-purpose flour
- 1 cup heavy whipping cream
- ¼ cup dry white wine
- ¼ cup chicken broth
- 1 cup (4 oz.) crumbled Gorgonzola cheese
  Additional Gorgonzola cheese crumbles, optional

1. Preheat oven to 425°. In a small bowl, whisk the mustard, olive oil and thyme until blended; set aside. Sprinkle pork with salt and pepper. In a large nonstick skillet over high heat, brown pork on all sides, about 10 minutes.
2. Transfer pork to a foil-lined roasting pan that has been coated with cooking spray. Spread mustard mixture over all sides of pork. Bake until a thermometer reads 145°, 10-20 minutes. Remove from oven; let stand 5 minutes.
3. Meanwhile, in a small saucepan, over medium heat, saute garlic in butter for 30 seconds. Stir in the flour until well blended. Gradually whisk in the cream, wine and chicken broth. Bring to a boil; cook and stir 1 minute or until thickened. Add cheese. Cook and stir until sauce is reduced to desired consistency, about 5 minutes.
4. Slice pork and transfer to serving plates. Spoon sauce over pork. If desired, sprinkle with additional cheese.
1 SERVING : 398 cal., 28g fat (16g sat. fat), 139mg chol., 608mg sod., 6g carb. (0 sugars, 1g fiber), 28g pro.

SPUMONI SLICES

My sweet rectangles get their name from the old-fashioned tri-colored ice cream. Our whole family prefers them.
—Mary Chupp, Chattanooga, TN

Prep: 40 min. + chilling
Bake: 5 min./batch + cooling
Makes: about 7 dozen

- 1 cup butter, softened
- 1½ cups confectioners' sugar
- 1 large egg, room temperature
- 1 tsp. vanilla extract
- 2½ cups all-purpose flour
- 2 oz. semisweet chocolate, melted
- ½ cup chopped pecans
- 3 to 5 drops green food coloring
- ¼ cup finely chopped candied red cherries
- ½ tsp. almond extract
- 3 to 5 drops red food coloring

1. In a large bowl, cream butter and sugar until light and fluffy. Beat in egg and vanilla. Gradually add flour and mix well. Divide dough in 3 portions. Stir chocolate into 1 portion. Add pecans and green food coloring to the second portion. Add cherries, almond extract and red food coloring to the third.
2. Roll each portion between 2 pieces of waxed paper into an 8x6-in. rectangle. Remove waxed paper. Place chocolate rectangle on a piece of plastic wrap. Top with the green and pink rectangles; press together lightly. Wrap with plastic and chill overnight.
3. Preheat oven to 375°. Cut chilled dough in half lengthwise. Return 1 rectangle to the refrigerator. Cut remaining rectangle into ⅛-in. slices. Place 1 in. apart on ungreased baking sheets.
4. Bake until set, 5-7 minutes. Cool on pan for 2 minutes before removing to wire racks to cool completely. Repeat with remaining dough.
2 COOKIES: 101 cal., 6g fat (3g sat. fat), 17mg chol., 47mg sod., 11g carb. (5g sugars, 0 fiber), 1g pro.

HOLIDAY HELPER

Classic spumoni includes pistachio as its third flavor. You can alter this recipe, if you'd like, by exchanging the pecans for chopped pistachios and adding ½ tsp. of pistachio extract to the green layer.

TUSCAN CORNBREAD WITH ASIAGO BUTTER

I had some fresh basil and needed to find a use for it. Peering into my pantry, I saw a bag of cornmeal and figured that cornbread with a Tuscan twist would be delicious. Canned tomatoes mean it can be made any time of year, but during peak tomato season, I'll use fresh instead—just remove the skins, seed and finely dice.
—*Michelle Anderson, Eagle, ID*

Prep: 25 min. • **Bake:** 20 min.
Makes: 8 servings (1¼ cups butter)

- 2   oz. sliced pancetta or bacon strips, finely chopped
- 1   to 2 Tbsp. olive oil, as needed
- 1½ cups white cornmeal
- ½   cup all-purpose flour
- 2   tsp. baking powder
- ½   tsp. salt
- 2   large eggs, room temperature
- 1   cup buttermilk
- ¼   cup minced fresh basil
- 1   garlic clove, minced
- 1   can (14½ oz.) diced tomatoes, drained
- 1   can (2¼ oz.) sliced ripe olives, drained

ASIAGO BUTTER
- 1   cup butter, softened
- 2   Tbsp. olive oil
- ⅓   cup shredded Asiago cheese
- 2   Tbsp. thinly sliced green onion
- 1½ tsp. minced fresh basil
- ½   tsp. minced fresh oregano
- 1   garlic clove, minced, optional

1. Preheat oven to 400°. In a 10-in. cast-iron or other ovenproof skillet, cook pancetta over medium heat until crisp, stirring occasionally. Remove with a slotted spoon; drain on paper towels. Reserve drippings in skillet. If necessary, add enough oil to measure 2 Tbsp. drippings.
2. In a large bowl, whisk cornmeal, flour, baking powder and salt. In another bowl, whisk eggs, buttermilk, basil and garlic until blended; stir in tomatoes. Add to flour mixture; stir just until moistened. Fold in olives and pancetta.

3. Place skillet with drippings in oven; heat 2 minutes. Tilt pan to coat bottom and side with drippings. Add batter to hot pan. Bake until a toothpick inserted in center comes out clean, 20-25 minutes. Cool in pan on a wire rack.
4. Meanwhile, in a small bowl, beat the butter until light and fluffy. Beat in oil until blended; stir in cheese, green onion, basil, oregano and, if desired, garlic. Serve ½ cup butter mixture with warm cornbread (save remaining butter for another use).
NOTE: If desired, shape remaining butter into a log. Wrap in plastic; refrigerate for a week or freeze for several months. To use, unwrap and slice; serve with bread, pasta, vegetables, seafood or poultry.
1 WEDGE WITH 1 TBSP. BUTTER: 329 cal., 18g fat (8g sat. fat), 79mg chol., 695mg sod., 34g carb. (4g sugars, 2g fiber), 8g pro.

HOLIDAY IN ITALY

Italian Christmas celebrations begin with the Feast of the Immaculate Conception (Dec. 8) and don't end until Epiphany (Jan. 6). In between, there are costumes, music, games and food aplenty. Bagpipers dress as shepherds and play to crowds in town squares. *La Befana* (the good witch—left behind by the three wise men to do housework) is said to bring presents on Epiphany, and costumed witches can be seen sailing on Venetian canals. On New Year's Eve, some regions still practice *Lancio dei Cocci*, when glassware is hurled from windows, symbolic of being rid of the past year's misfortunes.

PRESSURE-COOKER CLAM SAUCE

I serve this bright and fresh clam sauce often, usually with pasta. But it's also delectable as a hot dip for special get-togethers.
—Frances Pietsch, Flower Mound, TX

Takes: 15 min. • **Makes:** 4 cups

- 4 Tbsp. butter
- 2 Tbsp. olive oil
- ½ cup finely chopped onion
- 8 oz. fresh mushrooms, chopped
- 2 garlic cloves, minced
- 2 cans (10 oz. each) whole baby clams
- ½ cup water
- ¼ cup sherry
- 2 tsp. lemon juice
- 1 bay leaf
- ¾ tsp. dried oregano
- ½ tsp. garlic salt
- ¼ tsp. white pepper
- ¼ tsp. Italian seasoning
- ¼ tsp. pepper
- 2 Tbsp. chopped fresh parsley
   Hot cooked pasta
   Grated Parmesan cheese, optional

1. Select saute setting on a 6-qt. electric pressure cooker. Adjust for medium heat; add butter and oil. When hot, cook and stir onion 2 minutes. Add mushrooms and garlic; cook 1 minute longer. Press cancel.
2. Drain clams, reserving liquid; coarsely chop. Add clams, reserved clam juice and the next 9 ingredients to pressure cooker. Lock lid; close pressure-release valve. Adjust to pressure-cook on high for 2 minutes. Quick-release pressure.
3. Discard bay leaf; stir in parsley. Serve with pasta. If desired, serve with grated Parmesan cheese and additional lemon juice and parsley.
½ CUP: 138 cal., 10g fat (4g sat. fat), 40mg chol., 580mg sod., 5g carb. (1g sugars, 0 fiber), 7g pro.

HOLIDAY HELPER

To make this in a slow cooker, first saute onion, mushroom and garlic on the stovetop. Then combine ingredients as instructed in a 5-qt. slow cooker. Cook, covered, on low 3 hours. Remove and discard bay leaf; stir in parsley.

APRICOT ALMOND TORTE

This pretty cake takes time, so I like to make the layers in advance and assemble it the day of serving, which makes it an easier option for entertaining.
—Trisha Kruse, Eagle, ID

Prep: 45 min. • **Bake:** 25 min. + cooling
Makes: 12 servings

- 3 large eggs, room temperature
- 1½ cups sugar
- 1 tsp. vanilla extract
- 1¾ cups all-purpose flour
- 1 cup ground almonds, toasted
- 2 tsp. baking powder
- ½ tsp. salt
- 1½ cups heavy whipping cream, whipped

FROSTING/ASSEMBLY
- 1 pkg. (8 oz.) cream cheese, softened
- 1 cup sugar
- ⅛ tsp. salt
- 1 tsp. almond extract
- 1½ cups heavy whipping cream, whipped
- 1 jar (10 to 12 oz.) apricot preserves
- ½ cup slivered almonds, toasted

1. Preheat oven to 350°. In a large bowl, beat eggs, sugar and vanilla on high speed until thick and lemon-colored. Combine flour, almonds, baking powder and salt; gradually fold into egg mixture alternately with the whipped cream.
2. Transfer batter to 2 greased and floured 9-in. round baking pans. Bake until a toothpick inserted in the center comes out clean, 22-28 minutes. Cool 10 minutes before removing from pans to wire racks to cool completely.
3. In a large bowl, beat cream cheese, sugar and salt until smooth. Beat in extract. Fold in whipped cream.
4. Cut each cake horizontally into 2 layers. Place the bottom layer on a serving plate; spread with 1 cup frosting. Top with another cake layer; spread with half the preserves. Repeat layers. Frost side of cake; decorate the top edge with remaining frosting. Sprinkle with toasted slivered almonds.
1 PIECE: 546 cal., 25g fat (12g sat. fat), 115mg chol., 284mg sod., 75g carb. (51g sugars, 2g fiber), 8g pro.

CHOCOLATE CANNOLI

We made two Italian treats into one with beautiful pizzelle cookies wrapped around a rich, chocolaty cannoli filling. The chopped pistachios are a pretty touch.
—Taste of Home *Test Kitchen*

Prep: 45 min. + cooling
Cook: 5 min./batch
Makes: 12 filled pizzelle

- 1 large egg, room temperature
- ¼ cup sugar
- ¼ cup butter, melted
- ½ tsp. vanilla extract
- ¼ tsp. grated lemon zest
- ⅛ tsp. almond extract
- ½ cup all-purpose flour
- ¼ tsp. baking powder

FILLING

- ¾ cup sugar
- 3 Tbsp. cornstarch
- 1 cup whole milk
- 1⅛ tsp. vanilla extract
- 1 drop cinnamon oil, optional
- 1¾ cups ricotta cheese
- 1 milk chocolate candy bar with almonds (4¼ oz.), chopped
- ½ cup chopped pistachios

1. In a large bowl, beat the egg, sugar, butter, vanilla, lemon zest and almond extract until blended. Combine flour and baking powder; stir into the egg mixture and mix well.

2. Bake in a preheated pizzelle iron according to manufacturer's directions until golden brown. Remove cookies and immediately shape into tubes. Place on wire racks to cool.

3. For filling, in a small saucepan, combine sugar and cornstarch. Stir in milk until smooth. Bring to a boil; cook and stir until thickened, about 2 minutes. Stir in vanilla and cinnamon oil if desired. Cool completely.

4. In a large bowl, beat ricotta cheese until smooth. Gradually beat in custard mixture. Fold in chocolate. Spoon or pipe filling into shells. Dip each end in chopped pistachios. Serve immediately. Refrigerate leftovers.

1 SERVING: 289 cal., 15g fat (8g sat. fat), 47mg chol., 124mg sod., 33g carb. (25g sugars, 1g fiber), 8g pro.

HAZELNUT TOFFEE ZUCCOTTO

As a grandmother and great-grandmother, I've always enjoyed cooking and creating recipes. In our home, we love to make Italian food because it's our favorite type of cuisine. *Zuccotto*, which means "little pumpkin" in Italian, is a traditional Italian dessert.
—*Patricia Harmon, Baden, PA*

Prep: 30 min. + chilling
Makes: 10 servings

- 1 loaf (10¾ oz.) frozen pound cake, thawed
- ⅓ cup Kahlua (coffee liqueur)
- 1 pkg. (8 oz.) cream cheese, softened
- ⅔ cup confectioners' sugar
- 1½ tsp. instant espresso powder
- 1 tsp. vanilla extract
- ⅔ cup heavy whipping cream
- 3 English toffee candy bars (1.4 oz. each), chopped
- ½ cup chopped hazelnuts, toasted
  Baking cocoa and additional confectioners' sugar

1. Line a 1½-qt. bowl with plastic wrap; set aside. Cut pound cake into ¼-in. slices; set aside 6 slices for the top. Line bottom and sides of prepared bowl with remaining cake, trimming slices to fit snugly. Brush cake in bowl with some Kahlua.

2. In a small bowl, beat cream cheese, confectioners' sugar, espresso powder and vanilla until blended. In another bowl, beat cream until stiff peaks form; fold into cream cheese mixture. Fold in chopped candy bars and hazelnuts. Spoon over cake.

3. Brush 1 side of reserved cake slices with the remaining Kahlua; place brushed sides down over the filling, trimming the slices to fit. Refrigerate, covered, 5 hours or overnight.

4. To serve, unmold onto a serving plate. Remove bowl and plastic wrap; dust cake with cocoa and additional confectioners' sugar. Cut into wedges.

NOTE: To toast nuts, bake in a shallow pan in a 350°; oven for 5-10 minutes or cook in a skillet over low heat until lightly browned, stirring occasionally.

1 PIECE: 409 cal., 26g fat (14g sat. fat), 97mg chol., 222mg sod., 36g carb. (26g sugars, 1g fiber), 5g pro.

HOLIDAY BISCOTTI

A twice-baked Italian cookie, biscotti makes a wonderful dunker. A pretty way to present a batch is on a Christmasy plate arranged in a wagon-wheel fashion.
—*Libia Foglesong, San Bruno, CA*

Prep: 20 min. + chilling • **Bake:** 50 min. • **Makes:** 2 dozen

- ½   cup butter, softened
- 1   cup sugar
- 3   large eggs, room temperature
- 2   tsp. vanilla extract
- 1   tsp. orange extract
- 3   cups all-purpose flour
- 2   tsp. baking powder
- ½   tsp. salt
- ⅔   cup dried cranberries, coarsely chopped
- ⅔   cup pistachios, coarsely chopped
- 2   Tbsp. grated orange zest

1. In a bowl, cream butter and sugar. Add the eggs, 1 at a time, beating well after each addition. Stir in extracts. Combine flour, baking powder and salt; gradually add to creamed mixture and mix well (dough will be sticky). Stir in cranberries, pistachios and orange zest. Chill 30 minutes.

2. Divide dough in half. On a floured surface, shape each half into a loaf 1½-2 in. in diameter. Place on an ungreased baking sheet. Bake at 350° for 30-35 minutes.

3. Cool for 5 minutes. Cut diagonally into ¾-in. thick slices. Place slices, cut side down, on an ungreased baking sheet. Bake 9-10 minutes. Turn slices over; bake until golden brown, 10 minutes longer. Cool on wire rack.

1 COOKIE: 164 cal., 6g fat (3g sat. fat), 37mg chol., 144mg sod., 24g carb. (11g sugars, 1g fiber), 3g pro.

SPINACH WITH PINE NUTS & RAISINS

A nice side dish for winter meat entrees, this bright and flavorful recipe is a delicious way to get your greens onto any table. The simple list of ingredients makes it easy to prepare.
—*Gretchen Whelan, San Francisco, CA*

Prep: 25 min. • **Cook:** 10 min. • **Makes:** 6 servings

- ⅓   cup golden raisins
- ⅓   cup pine nuts
- 3   garlic cloves, minced
- ¼   cup olive oil
- 2   pkg. (10 oz. each) fresh spinach, torn
- ¼   tsp. salt
- ⅛   tsp. pepper

1. Place raisins in a small bowl. Cover with boiling water; let stand for 5 minutes. Drain and set aside.

2. In a Dutch oven, cook pine nuts and garlic in oil over medium heat for 2 minutes. Stir in raisins; cook 1 minute longer. Stir in spinach, salt and pepper; cook just until tender, 4-5 minutes. Serve with a slotted spoon.

½ CUP: 171 cal., 13g fat (2g sat. fat), 0 chol., 175mg sod., 11g carb. (6g sugars, 3g fiber), 5g pro. **DIABETIC EXCHANGES:** 2 fat, 1 vegetable, ½ fruit.

HOLIDAY HELPER

Also known as pignolia or pinon, the pine nut is the small seed from 1 of several pine tree varieties. They are small elongated ivory-colored nuts measuring about ⅜ in. long and having a soft texture and a buttery flavor. Frequently used in Italian dishes and sauces such as pesto, pine nuts are often toasted to enhance their flavor.

BUTTERNUT RAVIOLI WITH BOURBON PECAN SAUCE

Each year our family receives 25 pounds of pecans from a friend. With that many nuts, it requires some imagination to create different recipes so not to tire of their goodness. These tender butternut ravioli draped in a rich bourbon pecan sauce is one way I beat recipe fatigue.
—*Michele Lucas, Media, PA*

Prep: 30 min. • **Cook:** 20 min.
Makes: 6 servings

- 2 cups cubed peeled butternut squash
- 1 can (14½ oz.) vegetable broth
- ⅛ tsp. ground cloves
- 1 cup ricotta cheese
- ¼ cup ground pecans, toasted
- ½ tsp. garlic powder
- ½ tsp. salt
- ¼ tsp. pepper
- 32 wonton wrappers

BOURBON PECAN SAUCE
- 2 Tbsp. butter
- 2 Tbsp. all-purpose flour
- ½ tsp. salt
- ¼ tsp. pepper
- ¾ cup half-and-half cream
- ⅔ cup 2% milk
- ½ cup finely chopped pecans, toasted
- 1 Tbsp. bourbon

GARNISH
   Minced fresh parsley and additional chopped pecans

1. In a large saucepan, combine squash and broth. Bring to a boil. Reduce heat; cover and simmer until squash is tender, 15-20 minutes. Drain. Mash squash with cloves. Transfer to a large bowl; cool to room temperature.
2. In a small bowl, combine the ricotta, pecans, garlic powder, salt and pepper; add to squash mixture.
3. Spoon 1 Tbsp. squash mixture off center on a wonton wrapper. (Keep wrappers covered with a damp paper towel until ready to use.) Moisten edges with water. Fold wonton over diagonally and seal edges of triangle with a fork. Repeat with remaining wrappers and filling. Refrigerate for 5-10 minutes.
4. In a Dutch oven, bring water to a boil. Reduce heat to a gentle simmer. Cook the ravioli in batches until they float, 1-2 minutes. Remove with a slotted spoon; keep warm.
5. Meanwhile, for the sauce, in a small skillet, melt butter. Stir in the flour, salt and pepper until smooth. Gradually stir in cream and milk. Bring to a boil; cook and stir until thickened, about 2 minutes. Stir in pecans and bourbon; heat through. Serve with ravioli. Sprinkle with parsley and additional pecans.

5 RAVIOLI WITH 3 TBSP. SAUCE: 415 cal., 22g fat (8g sat. fat), 48mg chol., 1071mg sod., 41g carb. (7g sugars, 3g fiber), 13g pro.

SWEET POTATO PANZANELLA

This is my favorite cool-weather salad. It is filled with flavor and texture but isn't too high in calories.
—*Mary Leverette, Columbia, SC*

Takes: 30 min. • **Makes:** 8 servings

- 2 cups cubed peeled sweet potatoes
- 4 cups cubed French bread
- 4 Tbsp. olive oil, divided
- ⅛ tsp. salt
- ⅛ tsp. pepper
- 4 cups fresh baby spinach
- ½ small red onion, thinly sliced
- ¼ cup minced fresh basil
- ¼ cup minced fresh cilantro
- ⅓ cup red wine vinegar

1. Preheat oven to 450°. Place sweet potatoes in a large saucepan; add water to cover. Bring to a boil. Reduce heat; cook, covered, until just tender, 8-12 minutes. Drain; cool slightly.
2. Toss bread cubes with 2 Tbsp. oil, salt and pepper. Spread evenly in an ungreased 15x10x1-in. pan. Bake until golden brown, about 5 minutes. Transfer to a large bowl; cool slightly.
3. Add spinach, red onion, herbs and sweet potatoes to toasted bread. In a small bowl, whisk together vinegar and remaining oil. Drizzle over salad; toss gently to combine.

¾ CUP: 142 cal., 7g fat (1g sat. fat), 0 chol., 150mg sod., 17g carb. (3g sugars, 2g fiber), 2g pro. **DIABETIC EXCHANGES:** 1½ fat, 1 starch.

WHITE BEAN SOUP WITH ESCAROLE

Pantry staples make this healthy soup oh, so simple to prepare. When I can't find escarole, I substitute fresh spinach. Just add to the soup pot moments before serving.
—*Gina Samokar, North Haven, CT*

Prep: 15 min. • **Cook:** 35 min. • **Makes:** 8 servings (2 qt.)

- 1 Tbsp. olive oil
- 1 small onion, chopped
- 5 garlic cloves, minced
- 3 cans (14½ oz. each) reduced-sodium chicken broth
- 1 can (14½ oz.) diced tomatoes, undrained
- ½ tsp. Italian seasoning
- ¼ tsp. crushed red pepper flakes
- 1 cup uncooked whole wheat orzo pasta
- 1 bunch escarole, coarsely chopped (about 8 cups)
- 1 can (15 oz.) cannellini beans, rinsed and drained
- ¼ cup shredded Parmesan cheese

1. In a Dutch oven, heat oil over medium heat. Add onion and garlic; cook and stir until tender. Add broth, tomatoes, Italian seasoning and pepper flakes; bring to a boil. Reduce heat; simmer, uncovered, 15 minutes.

2. Stir in orzo and escarole. Return to a boil; cook until orzo is tender, 12-14 minutes. Add beans; heat through, stirring occasionally. Sprinkle servings with cheese.

1 CUP SOUP WITH 1½ TSP. CHEESE: 174 cal., 3g fat (1g sat. fat), 2mg chol., 572mg sod., 28g carb. (3g sugars, 8g fiber), 9g pro.
DIABETIC EXCHANGES: 1 starch, 1 vegetable, 1 lean meat, ½ fat.

TUSCAN SAUSAGE & BEAN DIP

This is an adaptation of a Mexican dip I once had. The original was wicked good, but I was going through an I'm-so-over-Mexican-dip phase and decided to switch it up. Take this version to a party—I'll bet you no one else will bring anything like it!
—*Mandy Rivers, Lexington, SC*

Prep: 25 min. • **Bake:** 20 min. • **Makes:** 16 servings

- 1 lb. bulk hot Italian sausage
- 1 medium onion, finely chopped
- 4 garlic cloves, minced
- ½ cup dry white wine or chicken broth
- ½ tsp. dried oregano
- ¼ tsp. salt
- ¼ tsp. dried thyme
- 1 pkg. (8 oz.) cream cheese, softened
- 1 pkg. (6 oz.) fresh baby spinach, coarsely chopped
- 1 can (15 oz.) cannellini beans, rinsed and drained
- 1 cup chopped seeded tomatoes
- 1 cup shredded part-skim mozzarella cheese
- ½ cup shredded Parmesan cheese
  Assorted crackers or toasted French bread baguette slices

1. Preheat oven to 375°. In a large skillet, cook sausage, onion and garlic over medium heat until sausage is no longer pink, breaking up sausage into crumbles; drain. Stir in wine, oregano, salt and thyme. Bring to a boil; cook until liquid is almost evaporated.

2. Add cream cheese; stir until melted. Stir in spinach, beans and tomatoes; cook and stir until spinach is wilted. Transfer to a greased 8-in. square baking dish (if using an ovenproof skillet, leave in skillet). Sprinkle with cheeses.

3. Bake until bubbly, 20-25 minutes. Serve with crackers.

¼ CUP: 200 cal., 14g fat (7g sat. fat), 41mg chol., 434mg sod., 7g carb. (2g sugars, 2g fiber), 10g pro.

THE BEST EVER LASAGNA

My brother, Joe, created this lasagna based on our mom's recipe. It's a family favorite at Christmas, thanks to the special ingredients that make it *magnifico*.
—Stephanie Marchese, Whitefish Bay, WI

Prep: 2¾ hours • **Bake:** 1 hour + standing
Makes: 15 servings

- 1 medium onion, chopped
- 2 Tbsp. olive oil
- 4 garlic cloves, minced
- 1 can (6 oz.) tomato paste
- 2 cans (28 oz. each) crushed tomatoes in puree
- 6 cups water
- 1 cup chopped fresh basil
- 2¼ tsp. sugar, divided
- 1 tsp. salt
- 1 lb. bulk Italian sausage
- 4 Italian sausage links
- 1 carton (16 oz.) whole milk ricotta cheese
- 8 cups shredded mozzarella cheese, divided
- 1 large egg, beaten
- ¼ tsp. dried basil
- 12 sheets no-cook lasagna noodles
- 21 slices provolone cheese
- ⅓ cup grated Parmesan cheese

1. In a Dutch oven, cook onion in olive oil over medium heat until tender, 4-5 minutes. Add garlic; cook 1 minute. Stir in tomato paste and cook, stirring constantly, until fragrant, 3-4 minutes. Add crushed tomatoes, water, fresh basil, 2 tsp. sugar and the salt. Bring to a boil; reduce heat. Simmer 1 hour, stirring occasionally.

2. Meanwhile, cook the bulk sausage in a skillet over medium heat until no longer pink, 8-10 minutes, breaking into crumbles; drain. Add to sauce; simmer until the mixture is thickened, about 1 hour longer.

3. While sauce simmers, preheat oven to 350°. Place sausage links on a rimmed baking sheet; roast until cooked through, 35-40 minutes. Remove and let cool slightly; slice into ¼-in.-thick pieces.

4. In a small bowl, mix ricotta cheese, 1 cup mozzarella cheese, egg, dried basil and remaining ¼ tsp. sugar.

5. In a greased 13x9-in. baking dish, spread 2 cups sauce. Arrange 4 noodles over sauce; spread with a third of the ricotta mixture. Add 7 provolone slices, a third of the sliced sausage and 1½ cups mozzarella cheese. Repeat layers 2 more times, using only 1 cup sauce per layer. Spread with 2 cups sauce (reserve the remaining sauce for serving on the side), remaining 2½ cups mozzarella cheese and the Parmesan cheese (dish will be full).

6. Place dish on a rimmed baking sheet and bake, uncovered, until bubbly and deep golden brown, 60-65 minutes. Let stand 15 minutes before serving. Serve with remaining meat sauce.

1 PIECE: 509 cal., 33g fat (15g sat. fat), 106mg chol., 1185mg sod., 27g carb. (9g sugars, 3g fiber), 29g pro.

HOLIDAY HELPER

This lasagna recipes does take some work, mostly because it starts with making the sauce from scratch. That level of effort makes it appropriate for a holiday or special occasion. To save time, make the sauce ahead of time; it will keep in an airtight container in the refrigerator for 3-4 days.

If you prefer, you can use either sweet or hot Italian sausage, use a mixture of both, or use half ground beef.

CHOCOLATE COOKIES

Mixed into a rich dough, used as a tempting filling or drizzled
on top for a dazzling finish, a bit (or a lot!) of chocolate
has no match in making decadent, delicious treats
that will make your cookie tray a showstopper.

CHOCOLATE CARAMEL KISS COOKIES

I make this cookie every Christmas with my family. It's a fun twist on a classic peanut butter blossom because of the cinnamon in the batter and the caramel kiss on top. We love the cinnamon-caramel combination, but you could switch out the kiss for a different festive flavor.
—Kristen Heigl, Staten Island, NY

Prep: 15 min.
Bake: 10 min./batch + cooling
Makes: 2 dozen

- ½ cup butter, softened
- ½ cup packed brown sugar
- 1 cup sugar, divided
- 1 large egg plus 1 large egg yolk, room temperature
- 1½ tsp. vanilla extract
- 1¼ cups all-purpose flour
- ¾ cup baking cocoa
- 1 tsp. baking soda
- 1 tsp. ground cinnamon
- ¾ tsp. salt
- 24 caramel-filled milk chocolate kisses

1. Preheat oven to 350°. Cream butter, brown sugar and ½ cup sugar until light and fluffy, 5-7 minutes. Beat in egg, egg yolk and vanilla. In another bowl, whisk the next 5 ingredients; gradually beat into creamed mixture.
2. Shape rounded tablespoons of dough into balls. Roll in remaining ½ cup sugar. Place 2 in. apart on ungreased baking sheets. Bake until edges begin to brown, 8-10 minutes. Immediately press a kiss into the center of each cookie (cookie will crack around edges). Cool on pans 2 minutes. Remove to wire racks to cool.
1 COOKIE: 143 cal., 6g fat (3g sat. fat), 27mg chol., 170mg sod., 23g carb. (15g sugars, 1g fiber), 2g pro.

CHOCOLATE REINDEER COOKIES

Add a touch of whimsy to your holiday spread with these chocolaty treats. They're perfect for getting little ones involved.
—Taste of Home Test Kitchen

Prep: 55 min.
Bake: 15 min./batch + cooling
Makes: about 5 dozen

- 2¾ cups all-purpose flour
- 1¼ tsp. baking soda
- ½ tsp. salt
- ¾ cup butter, cubed
- 1½ cups packed brown sugar
- 2 Tbsp. water
- 2 cups semisweet chocolate chips
- 2 large eggs, room temperature
- ½ tsp. almond extract
- 1 can (16 oz.) chocolate frosting

DECORATIONS
- Candy eyes
- Reese's mini white peanut butter cups
- Miniature pretzels
- Peanut butter M&M's

1. Whisk together flour, baking soda and salt. Place butter, brown sugar and water in a large saucepan over low heat; cook, stirring, until butter is melted. Remove from heat; stir in chocolate chips until smooth. Stir in eggs and extract. Stir in flour mixture. Let stand until firm enough to shape, about 15 minutes.
2. Shape level tablespoons of dough into balls; flatten each to ¼-in. thickness. Place in a covered container, separating layers with waxed paper; freeze until firm. (May be frozen up to 3 months.)
3. To bake, preheat oven to 350°. Place frozen dough portions 2 in. apart on greased baking sheets. Bake until set, 12-14 minutes. Remove from pans to wire racks; cool completely.
4. Spread cookies with frosting, reserving a small amount for mouths. Decorate faces with candy eyes; add peanut butter cups for snouts, pretzels for antlers and M&M's for noses. Pipe mouths with reserved frosting.
1 COOKIE: 122 cal., 6g fat (3g sat. fat), 12mg chol., 83mg sod., 18g carb. (13g sugars, 1g fiber), 1g pro.

CHOCOLATE MINT SANDWICH COOKIES

I got this recipe from my daughter years ago. I've taken these chewy filled treats and the treasured recipe to many cookie exchanges.
—*Bertha Bratt, Lynden, WA*

Prep: 20 min. • **Bake:** 10 min./batch + cooling
Makes: 2½ dozen cookies

- 6 Tbsp. butter, cubed
- 1½ cups packed brown sugar
- 2 Tbsp. water
- 2 cups semisweet chocolate chips
- 2 large eggs, room temperature
- 1 tsp. vanilla extract
- 2½ cups all-purpose flour
- 1½ tsp. baking soda
- 1 tsp. salt

FILLING
- 2½ cups confectioners' sugar
- ¼ cup butter, softened
- 3 Tbsp. 2% milk
- ½ tsp. peppermint extract
     Dash salt
- 3 drops green food coloring, optional

1. Preheat oven to 350°. In a small saucepan, combine the butter, brown sugar, water and chocolate chips. Cook, stirring, over low heat until chips are melted. Cool. Beat in eggs and vanilla. Combine the flour, baking soda and salt; gradually add to the chocolate mixture.
2. Drop by rounded teaspoonfuls 2 in. apart onto ungreased baking sheets. Bake until firm, 10-12 minutes. Remove to wire racks to cool.
3. For the filling, in a large bowl, combine confectioners' sugar, butter, milk, extract, salt and, if desired, food coloring until smooth. Spread on the bottoms of half of the cookies; top with remaining cookies.
1 SANDWICH COOKIE: 213 cal., 8g fat (5g sat. fat), 23mg chol., 187mg sod., 36g carb. (27g sugars, 1g fiber), 2g pro.

CHEWY GERMAN CHOCOLATE COOKIES

When I want a cookie that's as chewy as a brownie, this is the recipe I reach for. Coffee granules add the right amount of mocha flavor.
—*Darlene Brenden, Salem, OR*

Prep: 25 min. • **Bake:** 10 min./batch • **Makes:** 4 dozen

- 12 oz. German sweet chocolate, chopped
- 2 Tbsp. shortening
- 1 tsp. instant coffee granules
- 3 large eggs, room temperature
- 1¼ cups sugar
- 1 tsp. vanilla extract
- 1 cup all-purpose flour
- ½ tsp. baking powder
- ½ tsp. salt
- ½ cup chopped pecans
- 48 pecan halves
     Confectioners' sugar, optional

1. Preheat oven to 350°. In a microwave, melt chocolate and shortening; stir until smooth. Stir in coffee granules; cool and set aside.
2. In a large bowl, beat eggs and sugar until light and lemon-colored. Beat in cooled chocolate and the vanilla. Combine the flour, baking powder and salt; add to the chocolate mixture and mix well. Stir in chopped pecans.
3. Working quickly, drop dough by tablespoonfuls 2 in. apart onto greased baking sheets. Place a pecan half in the center of each. Bake until cookies are set, 10-12 minutes. Cool for 1 minute before removing to wire racks. If desired, dust with confectioners' sugar.
1 COOKIE: 98 cal., 5g fat (2g sat. fat), 12mg chol., 34mg sod., 9g carb. (7g sugars, 1g fiber), 1g pro.

CHOCOLATE GINGERSNAPS

When my daughter Jennifer was 15 years old, she created this recipe as a way to combine two of her favorite flavors. The cookies are perfect with a glass of milk.
—*Paula Zsiray, Logan, UT*

Prep: 45 min. + chilling • **Bake:** 10 min./batch
Makes: about 3½ dozen

½ cup butter, softened
½ cup packed light brown sugar
¼ cup molasses
1 Tbsp. water
2 tsp. minced fresh gingerroot
1½ cups all-purpose flour
1 Tbsp. baking cocoa
1¼ tsp. ground ginger
1 tsp. baking soda
1 tsp. ground cinnamon
¼ tsp. ground nutmeg
¼ tsp. ground cloves
7 oz. semisweet chocolate, finely chopped
¼ cup coarse sugar

1. In a large bowl, cream butter and brown sugar until light and fluffy, 5-7 minutes. Beat in the molasses, water and gingerroot. Combine flour, cocoa, ground ginger, baking soda, cinnamon, nutmeg and cloves; gradually add to the creamed mixture and mix well. Stir in chocolate. Cover and refrigerate until easy to handle, about 2 hours.
2. Preheat oven to 350°. Shape dough into 1-in. balls; roll in sugar. Place 2 in. apart on greased baking sheets.
3. Bake until tops begin to crack, 10-12 minutes. Cool for 2 minutes before removing to wire racks.
1 COOKIE: 80 cal., 4g fat (2g sat. fat), 6mg chol., 47mg sod., 9g carb. (6g sugars, 0 fiber), 1g pro.

CHOCOLATE COCONUT OATIES

There are those nights when you just need a sweet treat. I hit the pantry and improvised this recipe on the fly. The secret is the mini chocolate chips—you get a little melty goodness in every single bite.
—*Emily Tyra, Lake Ann, MI*

Prep: 30 min. + chilling • **Bake:** 10 min./batch
Makes: about 4½ dozen

1¼ cups butter, softened
1 cup packed brown sugar
1 large egg, room temperature
2 cups all-purpose flour
2 cups quick-cooking oats
1 tsp. salt
1 cup miniature semisweet chocolate chips
1 cup sweetened shredded coconut

1. In a large bowl, cream butter and brown sugar until light and fluffy, 5-7 minutes. Beat in egg. In another bowl, whisk flour, oats and salt; gradually beat into the creamed mixture. Stir in chocolate chips and coconut.
2. Divide dough in half. Shape each into a disk. Cover and refrigerate 1 hour or until firm enough to roll.
3. Preheat oven to 350°. On a lightly floured surface, roll out each portion of dough to ¼-in. thickness. Cut with a floured 2¼-in. square cookie cutter. Place 1 in. apart on parchment-lined baking sheets.
4. Bake until edges are light brown, 9-11 minutes. Remove from pans to wire racks to cool.
FREEZE OPTION: Transfer wrapped disks to a freezer container; freeze. To use, thaw dough in refrigerator until soft enough to roll. Bake as directed.
1 COOKIE: 106 cal., 6g fat (4g sat. fat), 15mg chol., 85mg sod., 12g carb. (7g sugars, 1g fiber), 1g pro.

CHOCOLATE WALNUT CRESCENTS

Use a round cookie cutter to form the crescent shapes for these nutty favorites. They're so pretty sprinkled with sugar and drizzled with chocolate.
—TerryAnn Moore, Vineland, NJ

Prep: 40 min. + chilling
Bake: 10 min./batch + cooling
Makes: about 10½ dozen

1 cup butter, softened
½ cup sugar
1 tsp. vanilla extract
2 cups all-purpose flour
2 cups ground walnuts
3 Tbsp. baking cocoa
2 to 3 Tbsp. confectioners' sugar
2 cups semisweet chocolate chips
2 tsp. shortening

1. In a large bowl, cream butter and sugar until light and fluffy, 5-7 minutes. Beat in vanilla. Combine the flour, walnuts and cocoa; gradually add to creamed mixture and mix well. Cover and refrigerate dough for 1 hour or until easy to handle.

2. Preheat oven to 350°. On a lightly floured surface, roll out dough to ¼-in. thickness. Using a floured plain or finely scalloped 2-in. round cookie cutter, cut a semicircle off 1 corner of the dough, forming the inside of a crescent shape. Reposition cutter 1¼ in. from inside of crescent; cut cookie, forming a crescent 1¼ in. wide at its widest point. Repeat. Chill and reroll scraps if desired.

3. Place 1 in. apart on ungreased baking sheets. Bake until set, 9-11 minutes. Cool on pan for 1 minute before removing to wire racks to cool completely.

4. Sprinkle cookies with confectioners' sugar. In a microwave, melt chocolate chips and shortening; stir until smooth. Drizzle over cookies; let stand until set. Store in an airtight container.

1 COOKIE: 46 cal., 3g fat (2g sat. fat), 4mg chol., 12mg sod., 4g carb. (2g sugars, 0 fiber), 1g pro.

ADVENT WREATH

Stock this Advent calendar with sweet treats and tiny presents, and count down the days until Christmas!

WHAT YOU'LL NEED

- 12-in. flat wooden wreath
- Green spray paint
- 25 favor tins (2-in. diameter)
- Red ribbon
- Staple gun and staples
- Hot glue gun and glue
- Patterned paper
- Paper punches (2-in. diameter, 1-in. diameter)
- Number stickers (1-25)

INSTRUCTIONS

1. Spray-paint wooden wreath; let dry.
2. Arrange 24 tins around wreath form; glue them in place.
3. Use the 2-in. paper punch to make 25 paper circles; glue them to the tins.
4. Use the 1-in. paper punch to make 25 paper circles; glue them on top of larger circles.
5. Glue ribbon to back of the remaining tin; staple end of ribbon to the back of wreath so that the tin hangs in the center of wreath.
6. Cut two 36-in. pieces of red ribbon. Staple each to the back of wreath at a slight angle so they can be tied in a bow above wreath. Trim ends if necessary.
7. Place a number sticker on each of the tins, with No. 25 in the center. Fill tins with goodies.

PISTACHIO MERINGUE SANDWICH COOKIES

This fun, easy and casual spin on a labor-intensive traditional macaron features a rich chocolate filling and tasty pistachios. You can amp up the color by adding more food coloring.
—Taste of Home *Test Kitchen*

Prep: 35 min.
Bake: 10 min./batch + cooling
Makes: about 1½ dozen

- 1¼ cups confectioners' sugar
- ¾ cup pistachios
- 3 large egg whites, room temperature
  Dash salt
- ¼ cup sugar
  Green paste food coloring, optional

CHOCOLATE FILLING
- 4 oz. bittersweet chocolate, chopped
- ½ cup heavy whipping cream
- 2 tsp. corn syrup
- 1 Tbsp. butter
  Additional pistachios, finely chopped, optional

1. Preheat the oven to 350°. Pulse confectioners' sugar and pistachios in a food processor until powdery.
2. In a large bowl, beat egg whites and salt on medium speed until soft peaks form. Gradually add sugar, 1 Tbsp. at a time, beating on high until stiff peaks form. Fold in pistachio mixture and, if desired, green food coloring.
3. Cut a small hole in the tip of a pastry bag; insert a round tip. Transfer pistachio mixture to bag. Pipe 1-in.-diameter cookies 1 in. apart onto parchment-lined baking sheets. Bake until lightly browned and firm to the touch, 10-12 minutes. Cool completely on pans on wire racks.
4. For filling, place chocolate in a small bowl. In a small saucepan, bring cream and corn syrup just to a boil. Pour over chocolate; whisk until smooth. Whisk in butter. Cool, stirring occasionally, to room temperature or until filling reaches a spreading consistency, about 45 minutes.
5. Spread filling on the bottoms of half the cookies; cover with the remaining cookies. If desired, roll edges in finely chopped pistachios.
1 SANDWICH COOKIE: 160 cal., 9g fat (4g sat. fat), 10mg chol., 135mg sod., 16g carb. (14g sugars, 1g fiber), 3g pro.

CHOCOLATE-DRIZZLED RAVIOLI COOKIES

My daughter Madalyn came up with these Oreo-filled ravioli. Our family couldn't stop eating them. Even her teachers were asking her to make them and to share the recipe!
—Sarah Sandifer, Bamberg, SC

Prep: 45 min. + chilling
Bake: 15 min./batch + cooling
Makes: about 3½ dozen

- 1 cup shortening
- 1⅓ cups sugar
- 2 large eggs, room temperature
- 1 tsp. vanilla extract
- 2½ cups all-purpose flour
- 1 tsp. baking powder
- ½ tsp. salt

FILLING
- 12 Oreo cookies
- 1 pkg. (8 oz.) cream cheese, softened
- ¼ cup confectioners' sugar
- ½ tsp. coconut extract

DRIZZLE
- 1 cup semisweet chocolate chips
- 2 tsp. shortening
  Additional Oreo cookies, crushed, optional

1. In a large bowl, cream shortening and sugar until light and fluffy, 5-7 minutes. Beat in eggs and vanilla. In another bowl, whisk flour, baking powder and salt; gradually beat into creamed mixture.
2. Divide dough in half. Shape each into a disk; wrap. Refrigerate for 30 minutes or until firm enough to roll.
3. Meanwhile, preheat oven to 350°. For filling, place Oreos in a food processor; process until finely crushed. Add cream cheese, confectioners' sugar and extract; process until blended.
4. On a lightly floured surface, roll out 1 portion of dough to ⅛-in. thickness. Cut with a floured 2-in. round cookie cutter. Place about 1½ tsp. filling in center of half the cutouts. Cover with remaining cutouts. Press edges with a fork to seal. Place 1 in. apart on greased baking sheets. Repeat with remaining dough and filling.
5. Bake until the edges are light brown, 15-20 minutes. Cool on pans 2 minutes. Remove to wire racks to cool completely.
6. In a microwave, melt chocolate chips and shortening; stir until smooth. Drizzle over cookies. If desired, sprinkle with Oreo crumbs; let stand until set. Store in an airtight container in the refrigerator.
1 COOKIE: 155 cal., 9g fat (3g sat. fat), 15mg chol., 75mg sod., 18g carb. (11g sugars, 1g fiber), 2g pro.

COCONUT CHOCOLATE SLICES

These crispy cookies with a chewy coconut center travel really well. I've sent boxes to our son in the Army, and they've always arrived unbroken.
—Cheri Booth, Gering, NE

Prep: 30 min. + chilling • **Bake:** 10 min.
Makes: about 4 dozen

- 3 oz. cream cheese, softened
- ⅓ cup sugar
- 1 tsp. vanilla extract
- 1 cup sweetened shredded coconut
- ½ cup finely chopped nuts

COOKIE DOUGH

- 6 Tbsp. butter, softened
- 1 cup confectioners' sugar
- 1 large egg, room temperature
- 2 oz. semisweet chocolate, melted and cooled
- 1 tsp. vanilla extract
- 1½ cups all-purpose flour
- ½ tsp. baking soda
- ½ tsp. salt

1. Beat cream cheese, sugar and vanilla until smooth. Stir in coconut and nuts. Refrigerate 30 minutes or until easy to handle.
2. Meanwhile, cream the butter and confectioners' sugar until light and fluffy, 5-7 minutes. Beat in egg, chocolate and vanilla. Combine flour, baking soda and salt; gradually add to creamed mixture and mix well. Refrigerate until easy to handle, about 30 minutes.
3. Roll dough between waxed paper into a 14x4½-in. rectangle. Remove top piece of waxed paper. Shape coconut filling into a 14-in. roll; place on dough, 1 in. from a long side. Roll the dough around the filling and seal edges. Wrap and refrigerate 2-3 hours or overnight.
4. Preheat oven to 350°. Unwrap dough and cut into ¼-in. slices. Place slices 2 in. apart on greased baking sheets, reshaping if necessary. Bake until set, 8-10 minutes. Cool for 1 minute before removing to wire racks.
1 COOKIE: 75 cal., 4g fat (2g sat. fat), 9mg chol., 61mg sod., 8g carb. (5g sugars, 0 fiber), 1g pro.

TRIPLE CHOCOLATE CANDY CANE COOKIES

This dazzling cookie showcases one of my family's favorite flavors, peppermint. It's always one of the first to disappear from the cookie tray.
—Priscilla Yee, Concord, CA

Prep: 40 min.
Bake: 10 min./batch + cooling
Makes: about 3 dozen

- ¾ cup butter, softened
- 1 cup sugar
- 1 large egg, room temperature
- 1¾ cups all-purpose flour
- ½ cup baking cocoa
- ¼ tsp. salt
- ¼ tsp. baking soda
- 3 oz. semisweet chocolate, chopped
- 2 tsp. canola oil, divided
- 3 oz. white baking chocolate, chopped
- ¼ cup crushed candy canes (about 10 miniature)

1. Preheat oven to 350°. In a small bowl, cream butter and sugar until light and fluffy, 5-7 minutes. Beat in egg. In a second bowl, whisk flour, cocoa, salt and baking soda; gradually beat into the creamed mixture.
2. Shape dough into 1-in. balls; place 2 in. apart on ungreased baking sheets. Flatten to 2-in. rounds with the bottom of a glass. Bake until set (do not overbake), 6-8 minutes. Cool on pans 5 minutes. Remove to wire racks to cool completely.
3. In a microwave, melt the semisweet chocolate with 1 tsp. oil; stir until smooth. Dip half of each cookie into chocolate mixture. Melt white chocolate with the remaining 1 tsp. oil; drizzle over cookies. Sprinkle tops with crushed candy canes; let stand until set.
1 COOKIE: 115 cal., 6g fat (3g sat. fat), 15mg chol., 63mg sod., 15g carb. (9g sugars, 1g fiber), 1g pro.

DOES FLOUR EXPIRE?

All flour has a printed "best by" date somewhere on the package. You can generally use flour for 4-6 months past this date. Store flour in an airtight container in a cool, dry place. You can roughly double the flour's lifespan by keeping it in the freezer.

If flour is past its best-by date, check for signs of deterioration before using it. Flour should be white or cream-colored with a smooth, dry texture and a neutral aroma. If flour is gray or yellowing, contains lumps because of moisture, or smells musty, sour or unpleasant, discard it. If there are signs of insect or rodent infestation (i.e., brown or black spots in the flour or holes and tears in the bag), throw it away, regardless of the condition of the flour or its best-by date.

Most of the time, using expired flour won't make you sick, but it's not an item you want to leave in the pantry for too long. Expired flour won't have the same quality in flavor and texture, so your recipe won't turn out the same. In the case of self-rising flour, which contains baking powder, expired flour will result in baked goods that don't rise.

STACKED SNOWMAN COOKIES

Though they hold their cute snowman shape well, these cookies are still nice and soft. Kids love the design, and everyone loves the chocolate flavor packed into the cookie.
—*Evangeline Bradford, Covington, KY*

Prep: 1 hour + standing
Bake: 10 min./batch + cooling
Makes: 3 dozen

- 1 cup unsalted butter, softened
- 1¾ cups sugar
- 2 large eggs, room temperature
- 2 tsp. vanilla extract
- 2¾ cups all-purpose flour
- ¾ cup Dutch-processed cocoa
- 1 tsp. baking powder
- ½ tsp. salt

ICING
- 2 cups confectioners' sugar
- 4½ tsp. meringue powder
- ⅓ to ½ cup water
- ¼ tsp. almond extract, optional
  Black, orange and brown paste food coloring

1. In a large bowl, cream butter and sugar until light and fluffy, 5-7 minutes. Beat in eggs and vanilla. In another bowl, whisk flour, cocoa, baking powder and salt; gradually beat into the creamed mixture. Divide dough in half; shape each into a disk. Wrap and refrigerate until firm enough to roll, about 30 minutes.

2. Preheat oven to 350°. On a lightly floured surface, roll 1 portion of dough to ¼-in. thickness. With a 2-in. round cookie cutter, cut out 18 circles. Repeat with 1½-in. and 1-in. round cookie cutters. Place 1 in. apart on parchment-lined baking sheets. Bake until edges are set, 7-10 minutes. Repeat with remaining dough. Cool completely on wire racks.

3. For icing, combine confectioner's sugar, meringue powder, ⅓ cup water and, if desired, extract; beat on low speed just until combined. Beat on high until stiff peaks form, 4-5 minutes. Add enough remaining water until icing no longer holds a peak. Keep unused icing covered at all times with a damp cloth.

4. Using a pastry bag and #2 round tip, pipe icing over cookies. Let stand at least 5 minutes before gently stacking cookies to create snowmen. Let stand at room temperature several hours or until frosting is dry and firm. Using a new fine-tipped paintbrush, decorate snowmen with food coloring as desired.

1 SNOWMAN: 166 cal., 6g fat (4g sat. fat), 24mg chol., 54mg sod., 26g carb. (16g sugars, 2g fiber), 3g pro.

HOLIDAY HELPER

Dutch-processed cocoa has been treated to reduce acidity and thus it has a mellow flavor. In recipes, it's often paired with baking powder, which supplies the acid needed for leavening. It's best to use the cocoa called for.

CHOCOLATE MARSHMALLOW COOKIES

What fun—these double-chocolaty delights have a surprise bit of marshmallow. Kids love them!
—*June Formanek, Belle Plaine, IA*

Prep: 25 min. • **Bake:** 10 min./batch + cooling • **Makes:** 3 dozen

- ½ cup butter, softened
- 1 cup sugar
- 1 large egg, room temperature
- ¼ cup 2% milk
- 1 tsp. vanilla extract
- 1¾ cups all-purpose flour
- ⅓ cup baking cocoa
- ½ tsp. baking soda
- ½ tsp. salt
- 18 large marshmallows

ICING

- 6 Tbsp. butter, softened
- 2 Tbsp. baking cocoa
- ¼ cup 2% milk
- 1¾ cups confectioners' sugar
- ½ tsp. vanilla extract
   Pecan halves

1. Preheat oven to 350°. Cream butter and sugar until light and fluffy, 5-7 minutes. Add egg, milk and vanilla; mix well. Combine flour, cocoa, baking soda and salt; beat into the creamed mixture.
2. Drop by tablespoonfuls onto ungreased baking sheets; bake for 8 minutes. Meanwhile, cut marshmallows in half. Press a marshmallow half, cut side down, onto each cookie. Return to the oven for 2 minutes. Cool completely on a wire rack.
3. For icing, in a small saucepan, combine butter, cocoa and milk. Bring to a boil; boil for 1 minute, stirring constantly. Cool slightly; transfer to a small bowl. Beat in confectioners' sugar and vanilla until smooth. Spread over the cooled cookies. Top each with a pecan half.
1 COOKIE: 125 cal., 5g fat (3g sat. fat), 17mg chol., 92mg sod., 20g carb. (14g sugars, 0 fiber), 1g pro.

FUDGE-TOPPED SHORTBREAD

This combination of buttery shortbread and sweet chocolate is wonderful. Whenever I make it, there's nothing but crumbs left. Be sure to cut it into small squares because it's very rich.
—*Valarie Wheeler, DeWitt, MI*

Prep: 15 min. + chilling • **Bake:** 20 min. • **Makes:** 4 dozen

- 1 cup butter, softened
- ½ cup confectioners' sugar
- ¼ tsp. salt
- 1¼ cups all-purpose flour
- 1 can (14 oz.) sweetened condensed milk
- 2 cups semisweet chocolate chips
- ½ tsp. almond extract
- ⅓ cup sliced almonds, toasted

1. Preheat oven to 350°. Cream butter, sugar and salt until light and fluffy, 5-7 minutes. Gradually beat in flour. Spread into a greased 13x9-in. baking pan. Bake until lightly browned, 16-20 minutes.
2. In a microwave-safe bowl, combine condensed milk and chocolate chips. Microwave, uncovered, on high until chips are melted, 30-60 seconds; stir until smooth. Stir in extract. Spread chocolate mixture over shortbread. Sprinkle with almonds and press down gently. Refrigerate until firm. Cut into squares.
1 PIECE: 115 cal., 7g fat (4g sat. fat), 13mg chol., 54mg sod., 13g carb. (10g sugars, 1g fiber), 1g pro.

CHOCOLATE-STRAWBERRY PRETZEL COOKIES

Every year I try to come up with a new recipe for my cookie tray, and this one has become a favorite. Who would ever guess how good pretzels are in cookies?
—*Isabel Minunni, Poughkeepsie, NY*

Prep: 30 min. + chilling
Bake: 10 min./batch + cooling
Makes: about 1 dozen

- 1 cup unsalted butter, softened
- ½ cup sugar
- 2 large eggs, room temperature
- 1½ cups finely ground pretzels (about 6 oz.)
- 1 cup all-purpose flour
- 1 tsp. baking powder
- ⅔ cup semisweet chocolate chips, melted
- ⅓ cup seedless strawberry jam
  Confectioners' sugar

1. In a large bowl, cream butter and sugar until light and fluffy, 5-7 minutes. Add eggs, 1 at a time, beating well after each addition. In another bowl, mix ground pretzels, flour and baking powder; gradually beat into the creamed mixture. Divide dough in half. Shape each into a disk. Cover and refrigerate until firm enough to roll, about 1 hour.
2. Preheat oven to 350°. On a lightly floured surface, roll each portion of dough to ¼-in. thickness. Cut with a floured 3½-in. tree-shaped cookie cutter. Using a floured 1¾-in. tree-shaped cookie cutter, cut out the centers of half of the cookies. Place solid and window cookies 1 in. apart on ungreased baking sheets.
3. Bake until edges are light brown, 8-10 minutes. Remove from pans to wire racks to cool completely.
4. Spread melted chocolate onto bottoms of solid cookies; let stand until firm. Spread jam over cooled chocolate; top with window cookies. Dust lightly with confectioners' sugar.
FREEZE OPTION: Freeze baked but unassembled cookies in freezer containers. To use, thaw in covered containers and assemble as directed.
1 SANDWICH COOKIE: 245 cal., 15g fat (9g sat. fat), 54mg chol., 164mg sod., 28g carb. (14g sugars, 1g fiber), 3g pro.

DOUBLE DELIGHTS

You get the best of both worlds with these chocolate and vanilla cookies. They're an appealing addition to any cookie tray. I usually serve them at the holidays, when they're often the first cookies to disappear, but you can have them any time of year.
—*Ruth Ann Stelfox, Raymond, AB*

Prep: 30 min. + chilling
Bake: 10 min./batch
Makes: about 15 dozen

CHOCOLATE DOUGH

- 1 cup butter, softened
- 1½ cups sugar
- 2 large eggs, room temperature
- 2 tsp. vanilla extract
- 2 cups all-purpose flour
- ⅔ cup baking cocoa
- ¾ tsp. baking soda
- ½ tsp. salt
- 1 cup coarsely chopped pecans
- 5 oz. white baking chocolate, chopped

VANILLA DOUGH

- 1 cup butter, softened
- 1½ cups sugar
- 2 large eggs, room temperature
- 2 tsp. vanilla extract
- 2¾ cups all-purpose flour
- 2 tsp. cream of tartar
- 1 tsp. baking soda
- ½ tsp. salt
- 1 cup coarsely chopped pecans
- 4 oz. German sweet chocolate, chopped

1. For chocolate dough, in a large bowl, cream butter and sugar until light and fluffy, 5-7 minutes. Beat in eggs and vanilla. Combine the flour, cocoa, baking soda and salt; gradually add to creamed mixture and mix well. Stir in pecans and white chocolate.
2. For vanilla dough, in another large bowl, cream butter and sugar until light and fluffy, 5-7 minutes. Beat in eggs and vanilla. Combine the flour, cream of tartar, baking soda and salt; gradually add to the creamed mixture and mix well. Stir in pecans and German chocolate. Cover both doughs and refrigerate for 2 hours.
3. Divide both doughs in half. Shape each portion into a 12-in. roll; cover. Refrigerate until firm, about 3 hours.
4. Uncover dough and cut each roll in half lengthwise. Place a chocolate half and vanilla half together, pressing to form a log; repeat with the remaining dough. Cover and refrigerate until the dough holds together when cut, about 1 hour.
5. Preheat oven to 350°. Using a serrated knife, cut dough into ¼-in. slices. Place slices 2 in. apart on greased baking sheets. Bake until set, 8-10 minutes. Remove to wire racks to cool.
1 COOKIE: 62 cal., 4g fat (2g sat. fat), 10mg chol., 44mg sod., 7g carb. (4g sugars, 0 fiber), 1g pro.

GINGER THINS

I like to serve these special treats with lemon curd or lemon sherbet, either of which complements the ginger flavor.
—*Eleanor Senske, Rock Island, IL*

Prep: 15 min. + freezing • **Bake:** 10 min./batch + cooling
Makes: 4½ dozen

- 6   Tbsp. butter, softened
- ½   cup plus 2 Tbsp. sugar, divided
- 2   Tbsp. molasses
- 1   Tbsp. cold strong brewed coffee
- 1¼ cups all-purpose flour
- ¾   tsp. ground ginger
- ½   tsp. baking soda
- ½   tsp. ground cinnamon
- ¼   tsp. ground cloves
- ⅛   tsp. salt
      Optional: Melted semisweet chocolate and chopped crystallized ginger

1. In a large bowl, cream butter and ½ cup sugar until light and fluffy, 5-7 minutes. Beat molasses and coffee into creamed mixture. Combine the flour, ginger, baking soda, cinnamon, cloves and salt; add to the creamed mixture until well combined (dough will be soft). Cover and freeze for 15 minutes. Shape dough into a 7-in. roll; flatten to 1-in. thickness. Wrap and freeze for 8 hours or overnight.
2. Preheat oven to 350°. Unwrap dough and cut into ⅛-in. slices; place slices 2 in. apart on parchment-lined baking sheets. Sprinkle with remaining 2 Tbsp. sugar. Bake 8-10 minutes or until firm. Remove from pans to wire racks to cool. If desired, dip cookies in melted chocolate and sprinkle with ginger.
1 COOKIE: 33 cal., 1g fat (1g sat. fat), 3mg chol., 28mg sod., 5g carb. (3g sugars, 0 fiber), 0 pro.

FUDGE BONBON COOKIES

These fudgy favorites are double delights—the cookies are flavored with both chocolate chips and chocolate kisses. Drizzled with white chocolate on top, they're fancy enough for a buffet table.
—*Janice Smith, Cynthiana, KY*

Prep: 25 min. • **Bake:** 10 min./batch + cooling • **Makes:** 4 dozen

- 2   cups all-purpose flour
- ½   cup finely chopped pecans
- 2   cups semisweet chocolate chips
- ¼   cup butter, cubed
- 1   can (14 oz.) sweetened condensed milk
- 1   tsp. vanilla extract
- 1   pkg. (12 oz.) milk chocolate kisses
- 2   oz. white baking chocolate
- 1   tsp. canola oil

1. In a large bowl, combine flour and pecans; set aside.
2. In a microwave-safe bowl, melt chocolate chips and butter; stir until smooth. Stir in condensed milk and vanilla until blended. Add to flour mixture and mix well.
3. Preheat oven to 350°. When dough is cool enough to handle, shape 1 tablespoon around each chocolate kiss. Place 1 in. apart on ungreased baking sheets. Bake until tops begin to crack, 7-9 minutes. Cool on wire racks.
4. In a microwave, melt white chocolate and oil; stir until smooth. Drizzle over cookies.
1 BONBON: 132 cal., 7g fat (4g sat. fat), 7mg chol., 24mg sod., 17g carb. (13g sugars, 1g fiber), 2g pro.

CHOCOLATE MACADAMIA MACAROONS

This perfect macaroon contains dark chocolate, chewy coconut and macadamia nuts and is dipped in even more chocolate—sinful and delicious!
—*Darlene Brenden, Salem, OR*

Prep: 20 min. • **Bake:** 15 min. + cooling
Makes: 1½ dozen

- 2 cups sweetened shredded coconut
- ½ cup finely chopped macadamia nuts
- ⅓ cup sugar
- 3 Tbsp. baking cocoa
- 2 Tbsp. all-purpose flour
  Pinch salt
- 2 large egg whites, lightly beaten
- 1 Tbsp. light corn syrup
- 1 tsp. vanilla extract
- 4 oz. semisweet chocolate, melted

1. Preheat oven to 325°. In a large bowl, mix the first 6 ingredients. Stir in egg whites, corn syrup and vanilla until blended.
2. Drop by tablespoonfuls 2 in. apart onto greased baking sheets. Bake until set and dry to the touch, 15-20 minutes. Cool on pans 5 minutes. Remove to wire racks to cool completely.

3. Dip half of each cookie into melted chocolate, allowing excess to drip off. Place on waxed paper; let stand until set.
1 COOKIE: 136 cal., 9g fat (5g sat. fat), 0 chol., 52mg sod., 15g carb. (11g sugars, 1g fiber), 2g pro.

MELTING CHOCOLATE

The quickest way to melt chocolate is in the microwave, Use 70% power and heat in short 30-second intervals, stirring frequently. The safest way to melt chocolate is in a double boiler over just barely simmering water.

MAYAN CHOCOLATE BISCOTTI

Those who enjoy Mexican hot chocolate will also like the subtle sweetness and slight heat found in every bite of these perked-up biscotti.
—*Chris Michalowski, Dallas, TX*

Prep: 35 min. • **Bake:** 40 min. + cooling
Makes: 2 dozen

- ½ cup butter, softened
- ¾ cup sugar
- 2 large eggs, room temperature
- 1½ tsp. coffee liqueur
- 1½ tsp. vanilla extract
- 2 cups all-purpose flour
- 1½ tsp. ground ancho chile pepper
- ½ tsp. baking soda
- ½ tsp. baking powder
- ½ tsp. ground cinnamon
- ⅛ tsp. salt
- 1½ cups chopped pecans
- 1 cup semisweet chocolate chips
- 1 oz. 53% cacao dark baking chocolate, grated

1. Preheat oven to 350°. In a large bowl, cream the butter and sugar until light and fluffy, 5-7 minutes. Add eggs, 1 at a time, beating well after each addition. Stir in coffee liqueur and vanilla. In a second bowl, combine the flour, ground chile, baking soda, baking powder, cinnamon and salt; gradually add to the creamed mixture and mix well. Stir in the pecans, chocolate chips and grated chocolate.
2. Divide dough in half. On an ungreased baking sheet, shape each half into a 10x2-in. rectangle. Bake until set and lightly browned, 20-25 minutes.
3. Place pans on wire racks. When baked rectangles are cool enough to handle, transfer to a cutting board; cut diagonally with a serrated knife into ¾-in. slices. Place slices cut side down on ungreased baking sheets.
4. Bake until golden brown, 8-10 minutes on each side. Remove to wire racks to cool completely. Store in an airtight container.
1 COOKIE: 191 cal., 12g fat (4g sat. fat), 28mg chol., 81mg sod., 21g carb. (11g sugars, 1g fiber), 3g pro.

FOR THE
LOVE OF RUM

As cocktail, appetizer, entree or dessert, rum has
a place throughout the holiday menu—whether you're
creating a cozy, comforting fireside feel or dreaming of
a tropical escape from the cold winter weather.

HOT BUTTERED RUM

I received this recipe from a friend over 30 years ago, and I think of her every winter when I stir up a batch of this delightful mix. It keeps well in the freezer.
—Joyce Moynihan, Lakeville, MN

Takes: 15 min.
Makes: 7 servings (3½ cups mix)

- 1   cup butter, softened
- ½   cup confectioners' sugar
- ½   cup packed brown sugar
- 2   cups vanilla ice cream, softened
- 1   tsp. ground cinnamon
- 1   tsp. ground nutmeg

EACH SERVING

- ½   cup boiling water
- 1   to 3 Tbsp. rum

1. In a large bowl, cream butter and sugars until light and fluffy, 5-7 minutes. Beat in ice cream, cinnamon and nutmeg. Cover and store in the freezer.
2. For each serving, place ½ cup butter mixture in a mug, add boiling water and stir to dissolve. Stir in rum.
1 CUP: 428 cal., 30g fat (19g sat. fat), 85mg chol., 221mg sod., 33g carb. (30g sugars, 0 fiber), 2g pro.

HOLIDAY HELPER ✳☆★

This is a truly sweet holiday-time indulgence, but you can adjust it by using reduced-fat ice cream or frozen yogurt for the mix. Depending on your taste preferences, you can also use less mix per drink as well.

PUMPKIN RUM CREAM PUFFS

With their creamy rum and pumpkin filling, these yummy puffs will disappear quickly! You can just spoon the filling rather than using a bag to pipe. Maximize your time by making both the unfilled puffs and the filling in advance—the puffs can be frozen for three weeks and the filling can be kept, covered, in the fridge for two days.
—Trisha Kruse, Eagle, ID

Prep: 30 min. • **Bake:** 30 min. + cooling
Makes: 10 servings

- 1   cup water
- ½   cup butter, cubed
- 1   cup all-purpose flour
- ¼   tsp. salt
- 4   large eggs, room temperature

FILLING

- 1   pkg. (8 oz.) cream cheese, softened
- 1   cup confectioners' sugar
- 1   cup canned pumpkin
- ¼   cup rum
- ½   tsp. pumpkin pie spice
- 2   cups heavy whipping cream, whipped
- ½   lb. white candy coating, chopped and melted

1. Preheat oven to 400°. In a small saucepan, bring water and butter to a rolling boil. Add flour and salt all at once and beat until blended. Cook over medium heat, stirring vigorously until mixture pulls away from sides of pan and forms a ball. Remove from heat; let stand 5 minutes.
2. Add eggs, 1 at a time, beating well after each addition until smooth. Continue beating until mixture is smooth and shiny.
3. Drop dough by scant ¼ cupfuls 3 in. apart onto ungreased baking sheets. Bake until puffed, very firm and golden brown, 30-35 minutes. Pierce side of each puff with tip of a knife. Cool on wire racks. Split puffs open; pull out and discard soft dough from inside tops and bottoms.
4. For filling, beat cream cheese, confectioners' sugar, pumpkin, rum and pie spice until blended. Gently fold in whipped cream. Fill cream puffs just before serving; replace tops. Drizzle with candy coating; refrigerate until set.
1 CREAM PUFF: 587 cal., 43g fat (28g sat. fat), 176mg chol., 246mg sod., 42g carb. (30g sugars, 1g fiber), 7g pro.

TYPES OF RUM

All rum is made from a sugar-based product (sugar cane or molasses), but there's little standardization. If your recipe calls for just "rum," you may be confounded by the varieties on the shelves. Which to choose?

Light rum (aka clear or silver rum) is colorless with a mild flavor. It is aged up to a year and is filtered to remove color.

Some **gold rums** get their color from being aged in oak barrels; some simply have caramel and color added. **Dark** and **black rums** are aged longer in oak, so they have a stronger flavor. (Black rum retains much of the molasses flavor.)

Premium aged rums are darker with rich tones; these are best sipped neat or on the rocks.

Flavored and **spiced rums** can be either clear or dark; flavors such as ginger, cinnamon, cloves or orange are added.

For cooking and baking, opt for a rum with flavors that complement your dish. When in doubt, gold rum is a safe choice; dark or black rum is a solid option for baked goods as well.

HONEY CAKE WITH APPLES

Our family used to have this delicious cake every year at Christmas—but it can be used for Rosh Hashana, the Jewish new year, too, as apples and honey are a traditional way to wish someone a sweet year. At serving time, you could add a dusting of confectioners' sugar.
—*Tatiana Klein, North Miami Beach, FL*

Prep: 30 min. • **Bake:** 55 min. + cooling
Makes: 16 servings

- 1½ cups packed brown sugar
- 1 cup sugar
- 1 cup butter, cubed
- 1 cup 2% milk
- 4 large eggs, room temperature
- 1 cup honey
- 1 tsp. vanilla extract
- 4 cups all-purpose flour
- 2½ tsp. baking powder
- 1 tsp. baking soda
- 1 tsp. each ground cinnamon, nutmeg and cloves

SYRUP
- 2 medium apples, peeled and sliced
- 1 cup water
- ½ cup sugar
- 1 Tbsp. rum or unsweetened apple juice
  Additional honey, warmed

1. Preheat oven to 350°. Grease and flour a 10-in. fluted tube pan.
2. In a large saucepan, combine sugars, butter and milk; cook and stir over medium heat until sugar is dissolved, 3-5 minutes. Cool slightly. In a large bowl, beat eggs, honey and vanilla. Beat in the sugar mixture. In a small bowl, combine flour, baking powder, baking soda and spices; gradually add to egg mixture.
3. Transfer batter to prepared pan; place on a rimmed baking sheet. Bake until golden brown and a toothpick inserted in center comes out clean, 55-60 minutes.
4. Meanwhile, for syrup, in a small saucepan, combine apples, water, sugar and rum. Bring to a boil; reduce heat. Simmer, uncovered, until apples are tender, 8-10 minutes. Using a slotted spoon, remove apples to a bowl; set aside. Poke holes in warm cake using a fork or wooden skewer. Slowly spoon cooking juices over cake. Cool 15 minutes before removing from pan to a wire rack; cool completely.
5. To serve, brush warmed honey over cake; top with reserved apples. Sprinkle with additional cinnamon.
1 PIECE: 467 cal., 13g fat (8g sat. fat), 78mg chol., 278mg sod., 84g carb. (59g sugars, 1g fiber), 6g pro.

COQUITO

An all-time family favorite, this creamy frozen adult beverage features cream of coconut blended with cloves, cinnamon, vanilla and rum.

—Evelyn Robles, Oak Creek, WI

Prep: 15 min. + chilling • **Makes:** 8 servings

- 1 can (15 oz.) cream of coconut
- 1 can (14 oz.) sweetened condensed milk
- 1 can (12 oz.) evaporated milk
- ½ cup water
- 1 tsp. vanilla extract
- ½ tsp. ground cinnamon
- ¼ tsp. ground cloves
- 1 cup rum

Place the first 7 ingredients in a blender; cover and process until blended. Refrigerate until chilled. Stir in rum before serving.

¾ CUP: 488 cal., 17g fat (12g sat. fat), 30mg chol., 132mg sod., 63g carb. (63g sugars, 0 fiber), 7g pro.

HOLIDAY HELPER

Make sure you use cream of coconut instead of coconut milk. Cream of coconut is a very thick, sweet, smooth liquid commonly used in beverages and desserts. It is sold in cans and is most often found in the international foods or baking aisle or in liquor stores.

FRUIT & ALMOND-STUFFED BRIE

Our friends enjoy this special appetizer as part of all our Christmas celebrations. An apricot filling and a raspberry topping make it more special than the usual Brie cheese spread.

—Douglas Wasdyke, Effort, PA

Prep: 30 min. • **Bake:** 30 min.
Makes: 8 servings

- ⅔ cup sliced almonds
- ⅓ cup chopped dried apricots
- ¼ cup rum or brandy
- 1 sheet frozen puff pastry, thawed
- 1 round (8 oz.) Brie cheese, rind removed
- 1 large egg, lightly beaten

RASPBERRY SAUCE

- ½ cup sugar
- 1 Tbsp. cornstarch
- ½ cup cold water
- 2 cups fresh or frozen raspberries
  Assorted crackers

1. In a small saucepan with high sides, combine the almonds, apricots and liquor. Cook and stir over medium-low heat until liquid is almost evaporated. Remove from the heat; set aside. Preheat oven to 375°.

2. On a lightly floured surface, roll puff pastry into an 11x9-in. rectangle. Cut cheese in half horizontally; place bottom half in the center of pastry. Spread with half of the almond mixture. Top with the remaining cheese and almond mixture.

3. Fold pastry around the cheese; trim excess dough. Pinch edges to seal. Place seam side down on an ungreased baking sheet. Brush with egg.

4. Bake until puffed and golden brown, 30-35 minutes.

5. Meanwhile, for the sauce, in a small saucepan, combine sugar, cornstarch and water until smooth; add raspberries. Bring to a boil over medium heat, stirring constantly. Cook and stir until slightly thickened, 1 minute. Strain and discard seeds. Transfer the sauce to a small pitcher or bowl; serve with stuffed Brie and crackers.

1 SERVING: 397 cal., 21g fat (7g sat. fat), 55mg chol., 292mg sod., 40g carb. (17g sugars, 6g fiber), 11g pro.

MANGO TIRAMISU

Because I love tiramisu, I wanted to make one that was a little different. I substituted Grand Marnier and Malibu rum for the usual coffee liqueur, giving the traditional dessert a tropical twist.
—*Carla Mendres, Winnipeg, MB*

Prep: 30 min. • **Cook:** 5 min. + chilling
Makes: 12 servings

- 2 large egg yolks
- 1 cup confectioners' sugar, divided
- 2 cups heavy whipping cream, divided
- 1 carton (8 oz.) mascarpone cheese
- 2 large navel oranges
- ½ cup coconut rum
- ½ cup orange liqueur
- 1 tsp. vanilla extract
- 1 pkg. (7 oz.) crisp ladyfinger cookies
- 2 medium ripe mangoes, peeled and thinly sliced

1. In the top of a double boiler or a metal bowl over simmering water, combine egg yolks, ½ cup confectioners' sugar and ½ cup cream. Whisking constantly, heat mixture until thick and a thermometer reads 160°. Remove from heat; whisk in mascarpone cheese until almost smooth. In another bowl, beat remaining 1½ cups cream until it begins to thicken. Add remaining ½ cup confectioners' sugar; beat until soft peaks form. Fold whipped cream into mascarpone mixture.
2. Cut oranges crosswise in half; squeeze juice into a shallow bowl. Stir in the rum, orange liqueur and vanilla.
3. Quickly dip half the ladyfingers into rum mixture and place in the bottom of a 9-in. springform pan. Top with half the mascarpone mixture and half the mango slices. Repeat layers. Refrigerate, covered, at least 8 hours or overnight. To serve, loosen and remove rim.
1 PIECE: 413 cal., 25g fat (14g sat. fat), 117mg chol., 48mg sod., 38g carb. (31g sugars, 2g fiber), 5g pro.

HOLIDAY HELPER

If you want to make this recipe without alcohol, substitute additional orange juice for the orange liqueur, and orange juice plus ½ tsp. coconut extract for the coconut rum.

GRANDMA'S PECAN RUM BARS

My grandmother handed down the recipe for these gooey bars, which we all love. The candied cherries are a must.
—*Deborah Pennington, Falkville, AL*

Prep: 20 min. • **Bake:** 1 hour + cooling
Makes: 2 dozen

- 4 cups chopped pecans, divided
- 1 cup butter, softened
- 2¼ cups packed brown sugar
- 4 large eggs, room temperature
- 2 Tbsp. vanilla extract
- 1 cup all-purpose flour
- 2¼ cups red candied cherries
- 1½ cups chopped candied pineapple
- ½ cup chopped candied citron
- ⅓ cup rum

1. Sprinkle 3 cups pecans over a greased 15x10x1-in. baking pan; set aside.
2. Preheat oven to 350°. In a large bowl, cream butter and brown sugar until light and fluffy, 5-7 minutes. Add eggs, 1 at a time, beating well after each addition. Beat in vanilla. Gradually add flour to the creamed mixture, beating well.
3. Spread batter into prepared pan. Combine candied fruit and the remaining 1 cup pecans. Spread fruit mixture evenly over batter; press gently to help the layers adhere. Bake until a toothpick inserted in center comes out clean, about 1 hour.
4. Sprinkle rum over the top; cool completely in pan on a wire rack. Cut into bars. Store in an airtight container.
1 BAR: 401 cal., 22g fat (6g sat. fat), 51mg chol., 123mg sod., 49g carb. (40g sugars, 2g fiber), 4g pro.

RUM-RAISIN SWEET POTATOES

My family and I have traded in classic baked potatoes for these sweet potatoes with a spicy twist. The Chinese five-spice powder gives them an added tasty kick.
—*Pamela Weatherford, San Antonio, TX*

Prep: 20 min. • **Cook:** 1 hour + cooling
Makes: 16 servings (¾ cup each)

　8　large sweet potatoes (about 6½ lbs.)
　1　cup raisins
　⅔　cup dark rum
　1　cup half-and-half cream
　½　cup butter, cubed
　3　Tbsp. brown sugar
　1　Tbsp. Chinese five-spice powder
1¼　tsp. salt
　½　tsp. pepper
　½　cup chopped walnuts, toasted

1. Place potatoes in a stockpot; add water to cover. Bring to a boil. Reduce heat; cook, uncovered, until tender, 40-45 minutes. Drain potatoes. When cool enough to handle, peel potatoes; return to pan.
2. Meanwhile, in a microwave-safe bowl, combine raisins and rum. Microwave, uncovered, on high for 30 seconds; set aside. In a small saucepan, heat cream and butter until butter is melted.
3. Mash potatoes, gradually adding brown sugar, five-spice powder, salt, pepper and butter mixture. Stir in raisin mixture. If necessary, warm potatoes over low heat, stirring occasionally. Transfer to a serving bowl. Sprinkle with walnuts.
¾ CUP: 330 cal., 10g fat (5g sat. fat), 23mg chol., 257mg sod., 52g carb. (26g sugars, 6g fiber), 4g pro.

SLOW-COOKER BANANAS FOSTER

The flavors of caramel, rum and walnut naturally complement fresh bananas in this version of a dessert classic. It's my go-to choice for any family get-together.
—*Crystal Jo Bruns, Iliff, CO*

Prep: 10 min. • **Cook:** 2 hours
Makes: 5 servings

　5　medium firm bananas
　1　cup packed brown sugar
　¼　cup butter, melted
　¼　cup rum
　1　tsp. vanilla extract
　½　tsp. ground cinnamon
　⅓　cup chopped walnuts
　⅓　cup sweetened shredded coconut
　　　Optional: Vanilla ice cream or sliced pound cake

1. Cut bananas in half lengthwise, then widthwise; layer in the bottom of a 1½-qt. slow cooker. Combine the brown sugar, butter, rum, vanilla and cinnamon; pour over bananas. Cover and cook on low until heated through, about 1½ hours.
2. Sprinkle with walnuts and coconut; cook 30 minutes longer. Serve with ice cream or pound cake if desired.
1 SERVING: 462 cal., 17g fat (8g sat. fat), 24mg chol., 99mg sod., 74g carb. (59g sugars, 4g fiber), 3g pro.

COCONUT RUM BALLS

My mom has made rum balls for as long as I can remember. They look beautiful on a dessert spread and can be packaged in a decorative tin as a gift. I swapped in coconut rum for the traditional rum and added shredded coconut.
—*Jana Walker, Macomb, MI*

Prep: 25 min. + standing
Makes: about 4½ dozen

　1　pkg. (12 oz.) vanilla wafers, finely crushed
　1　cup confectioners' sugar
　2　Tbsp. baking cocoa
　1　cup sweetened shredded coconut
　1　cup chopped pecans
　½　cup light corn syrup
　¼　cup coconut rum
　　　Additional confectioners' sugar

1. Whisk crushed wafers, confectioners' sugar and cocoa. Stir in coconut and pecans. In a separate bowl, whisk corn syrup and rum; stir into wafer mixture. Shape into 1-in. balls; let stand 1 hour.
2. Roll in additional confectioners' sugar. Store in an airtight container.
1 COOKIE: 73 cal., 3g fat (1g sat. fat), 1mg chol., 31mg sod., 10g carb. (8g sugars, 1g fiber), 0 pro.

PORK TENDERLOIN WITH DRIED CHERRIES

Cherries pair beautifully with pork, and this wonderful dish takes only minutes to cook. It's fabulous both for weeknights and serving to special dinner guests.
—*Kathy Fox, Goodyear, AZ*

Prep: 20 min. • **Cook:** 15 min. • **Makes:** 4 servings

- ¾ cup chicken broth
- ⅓ cup dried tart cherries
- ¼ cup brandy or rum
- 1 tsp. minced fresh thyme or ¼ tsp. dried thyme
- ⅛ tsp. ground allspice
- 1 pork tenderloin (1 lb.), cut into 1-in. slices
- ½ tsp. salt, divided
- ½ tsp. pepper, divided
- 1 Tbsp. butter
- 1 shallot, minced
- ¼ cup heavy whipping cream

1. In a small saucepan, combine the first 5 ingredients. Bring to a boil; cook until liquid is reduced to ½ cup. Set aside and keep warm.
2. Flatten pork to ½-in. thickness; sprinkle with ¼ tsp. salt and ¼ tsp. pepper. In a large skillet, brown pork in butter; remove and keep warm.
3. In the same skillet, saute shallot in drippings until tender. Add cream, warm cherry mixture, and the remaining ¼ tsp. salt and ¼ tsp. pepper, stirring to loosen browned bits from pan. Bring to a boil; cook until liquid is reduced to sauce consistency. Return pork to the pan; cook until a thermometer reads 145°. Let stand 5 minutes before serving.
3 OZ. COOKED PORK WITH 1 TBSP. SAUCE: 269 cal., 12g fat (7g sat. fat), 92mg chol., 551mg sod., 11g carb. (6g sugars, 1g fiber), 24g pro.

RUM-GLAZED PUMPKIN CAKE

For years, my co-workers were taste testers as I worked on a recipe for pumpkin cake. This version wins, hands down.
—*Gilda Smith, Santee, CA*

Prep: 20 min. • **Bake:** 55 min. + cooling • **Makes:** 12 servings

- ½ cup chopped pecans
- 1 can (15 oz.) solid-pack pumpkin
- ½ cup sugar
- ½ cup canola oil
- 4 large eggs
- ¼ cup water
- 1 pkg. yellow cake mix (regular size)
- 1½ tsp. ground cinnamon
- ½ tsp. ground nutmeg
- ⅛ tsp. ground cloves

GLAZE
- 1 cup sugar
- ½ cup butter, cubed
- ¼ tsp. ground cinnamon
  Dash ground cloves
- ½ cup rum

1. Preheat oven to 350°. Grease and flour a 10-in. fluted tube pan; sprinkle pecans onto bottom of pan.
2. In a large bowl, beat pumpkin, sugar, oil, eggs and water until well blended. In another bowl, whisk cake mix and spices; gradually beat into pumpkin mixture. Transfer to prepared pan.
3. Bake until a toothpick inserted in center comes out clean, 55-60 minutes. Cool in pan for 10 minutes before removing to a wire rack.
4. In a small saucepan, combine sugar, butter, cinnamon and cloves; cook and stir over medium heat until butter is melted. Remove from heat. Stir in rum; cook and stir until sugar is dissolved, 2-3 minutes longer.
5. Gradually brush glaze onto warm cake, about ¼ cup at a time, allowing glaze to soak into cake before adding more. Cool completely.
1 PIECE: 352 cal., 22g fat (7g sat. fat), 82mg chol., 113mg sod., 32g carb. (28g sugars, 2g fiber), 3g pro.

BEEF TENDERLOIN WITH POMEGRANATE CHUTNEY

When I want to show family and friends some culinary love, I roast a tenderloin and serve it with a sweet-tart pomegranate and apple chutney.

—*Devon Delaney, Westport, CT*

Prep: 20 min. • **Bake:** 40 min. + standing
Makes: 8 servings

- 2 Tbsp. minced fresh thyme
- 1 Tbsp. minced fresh rosemary
- 1 Tbsp. brown sugar
- 1 tsp. sea salt
- 1 tsp. freshly ground pepper
- 1 beef tenderloin roast (3 lbs.)
- 2 Tbsp. Dijon mustard

CHUTNEY
- 1 pomegranate
- 2 Tbsp. olive oil
- 1 medium tart apple, peeled and chopped
- 4 shallots, coarsely chopped
- 2 Tbsp. minced fresh gingerroot
- 1 garlic clove, minced
- ¼ cup sugar
- ¼ cup rum or brandy
- ¼ cup cider vinegar
- ¼ tsp. sea salt
- ¼ tsp. coarsely ground pepper

1. Preheat oven to 425°. Mix thyme, rosemary, brown sugar, salt and pepper. Place tenderloin on a rack in a shallow roasting pan. Brush mustard over roast; sprinkle with herb mixture. Roast until meat reaches the desired doneness (for medium-rare, a thermometer should read 135°; medium, 140°; medium-well, 145°), 40-45 minutes. Remove roast from oven; tent with foil. Let stand 10 minutes before slicing.
2. Meanwhile, for chutney, cut the pomegranate in half. Working over a small bowl and using a small spoon, separate pomegranate seeds from membranes, placing seeds in bowl and discarding membranes. In a large skillet, heat oil over medium heat. Add apple and shallots; cook and stir until tender, 8-10 minutes. Add ginger and garlic; cook 1 minute longer. Remove from heat. Add sugar, liquor, vinegar, salt and pepper. Bring to a boil. Reduce heat; simmer, uncovered, until slightly thickened. Stir in pomegranate seeds; heat through. Serve with roast.
5 OZ. COOKED MEAT WITH ¼ CUP CHUTNEY: 381 cal., 14g fat (4g sat. fat), 74mg chol., 395mg sod., 21g carb. (15g sugars, 2g fiber), 37g pro.

ORANGE SHRIMP MOJO

With jalapeno, orange and avocado, this enticing entree is spicy, tangy and fresh with every bite.

—*Don Thompson, Houston, OH*

Prep: 25 min. • **Cook:** 45 min.
Makes: 8 servings

- 1 Tbsp. cumin seeds
- 1 Tbsp. whole peppercorns
- 1 Tbsp. grated orange or tangerine zest
- ½ tsp. dried oregano
- ½ tsp. salt
- 1 lb. uncooked jumbo shrimp, peeled and deveined
- 4 tsp. olive oil
- 3 cups orange juice
- 3 Tbsp. rum or chicken broth
- 1 garlic clove, minced
- 1 large navel orange, peeled, sectioned and chopped
- ½ cup chopped sweet onion
- 1 cup cubed avocado
- ½ cup minced fresh cilantro, divided
- 1 tsp. chopped seeded jalapeno pepper

1. In a small dry skillet over medium heat, toast cumin seeds and peppercorns until aromatic, 1-2 minutes. Remove from skillet. Crush seeds using a spice grinder or mortar and pestle.
2. In a small bowl, combine the orange zest, oregano, salt and crushed spices. Sprinkle 1 Tbsp. spice mixture over the shrimp.
3. In a large skillet, cook shrimp in oil over medium-high heat 1 minute; turn shrimp. Add orange juice, rum, garlic and 1 Tbsp. spice mixture. Cook and stir until shrimp turn pink, 1-2 minutes longer; remove and keep warm.
4. Bring liquid in skillet to a boil. Cook until reduced to ⅔ cup, about 35 minutes. Meanwhile, for salsa, combine orange, onion, avocado, ¼ cup cilantro, jalapeno and the remaining spice mixture in a small bowl.
5. Stir shrimp and remaining cilantro into sauce; heat through. Serve with salsa.
NOTE: Wear disposable gloves when cutting hot peppers; the oils can burn skin. Avoid touching your face.
1 SERVING: 172 cal., 6g fat (1g sat. fat), 69mg chol., 218mg sod., 16g carb. (11g sugars, 2g fiber), 11g pro. **DIABETIC EXCHANGES:** 1 starch, 1 lean meat, 1 fat.

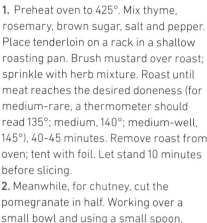

PINEAPPLE CIDER WASSAIL

Pineapple juice prevents this hot drink from becoming overly sweet. You can skip the rum for a beverage that's appropriate for guests of all ages.
—*Lori Schmeling, Hartland, WI*

Takes: 30 min. • **Makes:** 14 servings (about 2½ qt.)

- 1 cinnamon stick (3 in.)
- 1 tsp. whole cloves
- 2 cardamom pods, crushed
- 4 cups apple cider or juice
- 4 cups unsweetened pineapple juice
- 1½ cups apricot nectar
- 1 cup orange juice
- ½ cup rum, optional

1. Place the cinnamon stick, cloves and cardamom on a double thickness of cheesecloth; bring up corners of cloth and tie with string to form a bag.
2. In a large saucepan, combine the apple cider, pineapple juice, apricot nectar and orange juice. Add spice bag. Bring to a boil. Reduce heat; simmer, uncovered, until the flavors are blended, 15-20 minutes. Discard the spice bag. If desired, stir in rum. Serve warm.
¾ CUP: 95 cal., 0 fat (0 sat. fat), 0 chol., 9mg sod., 24g carb. (20g sugars, 0 fiber), 0 pro.

HOLIDAY HELPER

Wassail comes from an Anglo-Saxon phrase meaning "be in good health!" Wassail is often served from a large bowl; long-ago carolers carrying wassail offered drinks to residents of houses they visited, in exchange for gifts.

WARM CABBAGE, FENNEL & PEAR SALAD

This crunchy salad makes an elegant first course or side dish, but it's hearty enough to be an entree when paired with a crusty artisan bread. We love it served warm.
—*Grace Voltolina, Westport, CT*

Takes: 25 min. • **Makes:** 4 servings

- 2 firm medium pears
- ¼ cup rum, brandy or Cognac, optional
- 3 Tbsp. olive oil
- 1 large fennel bulb, halved, cored and thinly sliced
- 4 cups shredded or thinly sliced cabbage
- ¼ cup water
- 3 Tbsp. lemon juice
- 2 tsp. honey or agave nectar
- 1 tsp. kosher salt
- ½ tsp. pepper
- ¾ cup crumbled or sliced Gorgonzola cheese
- ½ cup chopped walnuts, toasted

1. Peel and core pears; cut into ½-in. slices. If desired, toss with liquor. Set pears aside.
2. In a large skillet, heat oil over medium-high heat. Add fennel; saute until crisp-tender, 2-3 minutes. Add cabbage; toss with fennel. Cook until both are tender, 2-3 minutes longer. Add pears, water, lemon juice, honey, salt and pepper to skillet, gently combining ingredients. Cook until liquid is evaporated, 6-8 minutes.
3. Transfer to a serving bowl. Top with Gorgonzola cheese and toasted walnuts. Serve warm or at room temperature.
NOTE: To toast nuts, bake in a shallow pan in a 350° oven for 5-10 minutes or cook in a skillet over low heat until lightly browned, stirring occasionally.
1 CUP: 391 cal., 26g fat (7g sat. fat), 19mg chol., 810mg sod., 28g carb. (14g sugars, 8g fiber), 9g pro.

NIGHT OF PIES

Pies can be large or small, sweet or savory—making them
just right for appetizers, sides and main courses as well as desserts.
So why not celebrate the season with a whole menu full of pies?

MINI SCALLOP POTPIES

Tiny and tender bay scallops take center stage in these miniature dishes. They're creamy, comforting and packed with flavorful veggies in every bite.
—*Vivian Manary, Nepean, ON*

Prep: 30 min. • **Bake:** 20 min. • **Makes:** 4 servings

- 3 celery ribs, chopped
- 1 cup sliced fresh mushrooms
- 1 medium green pepper, chopped
- 1 small onion, chopped
- 2 Tbsp. butter
- ⅓ cup all-purpose flour
- ¼ tsp. salt
- ¼ tsp. pepper
- 2 cups fat-free milk
- 1 lb. bay scallops

TOPPING
- 1 cup soft bread crumbs
- 1 Tbsp. butter, melted
- ¼ cup shredded cheddar cheese

1. Preheat oven to 350°. In a large skillet, saute celery, mushrooms, green pepper and onion in butter until tender. Stir in flour, salt and pepper until blended; gradually add milk. Bring to a boil; cook and stir until thickened, about 2 minutes.
2. Reduce heat; add scallops. Cook, stirring occasionally, until scallops are firm and opaque, 3-4 minutes.
3. Divide mixture among four 10-oz. ramekins or custard cups. In a small bowl, combine crumbs and butter; sprinkle over scallop mixture.
4. Bake, uncovered, 15-20 minutes or until bubbly. Sprinkle with cheese; bake 5 minutes longer or until cheese is melted.
1 POTPIE: 332 cal., 12g fat (7g sat. fat), 70mg chol., 588mg sod., 27g carb. (9g sugars, 2g fiber), 28g pro.

MINI CHICKEN EMPANADAS

Refrigerated pie crust makes quick work of assembling these bite-sized appetizers loaded with chicken and cheese. I've made them several times since receiving the recipe from a friend.
—*Betty Fulks, Onia, AR*

Prep: 30 min. • **Bake:** 15 min./batch • **Makes:** about 2½ dozen

- 1 cup finely chopped cooked chicken
- ⅔ cup shredded Colby-Monterey Jack cheese
- 3 Tbsp. cream cheese, softened
- 4 tsp. chopped sweet red pepper
- 2 tsp. chopped seeded jalapeno pepper
- 1 tsp. ground cumin
- ½ tsp. salt
- ⅛ tsp. pepper
- 2 sheets refrigerated pie crust
  Optional: Egg wash and salsa verde

1. Preheat oven to 400°. In a small bowl, combine the first 8 ingredients. On a lightly floured surface, roll each crust into a 15-in. circle. Cut with a floured 3-in. round biscuit cutter.
2. Place about 1 tsp. filling on 1 half of each circle. Moisten edges with water. Fold crust over filling. Press edges with a fork to seal.
3. Transfer to greased baking sheets. If desired, brush with egg wash. Bake until golden brown, 12-15 minutes. Remove to wire racks. Serve warm, with salsa if desired.
NOTE: Wear disposable gloves when cutting hot peppers; the oils can burn skin. Avoid touching your face.
1 EMPANADA: 81 cal., 5g fat (2g sat. fat), 10mg chol., 108mg sod., 7g carb. (1g sugars, 0 fiber), 2g pro. **DIABETIC EXCHANGES:** 1 fat, ½ starch.

MIDNIGHT MOON PIES

I absolutely love chocolate, and this recipe satisfies my craving for it. A rich, buttery filling is sandwiched between moist chocolate cookies.
—Roz Keimig, Guymon, OK

Prep: 20 min.
Bake: 10 min./batch + cooling
Makes: 2 dozen

- ⅔ cup dark chocolate chips
- ½ cup butter, cubed
- 2 cups all-purpose flour
- ⅔ cup sugar
- ⅓ cup packed brown sugar
- ¼ cup baking cocoa
- ½ tsp. baking soda
- ¼ tsp. salt
- 1 large egg, room temperature, beaten
- ½ cup buttermilk
- 1 tsp. vanilla extract
- ¼ tsp. almond extract

FILLING

- ⅔ cup dark chocolate chips
- ¼ cup butter, cubed
- 4 oz. cream cheese, softened
- 1 jar (7 oz.) marshmallow creme
- ¼ tsp. almond extract
- 1 cup miniature semisweet chocolate chips

1. Preheat oven to 350°. In a microwave, melt chocolate chips and butter; stir until smooth. Cool.
2. In a large bowl, combine flour, sugars, cocoa, baking soda and salt. Combine egg, buttermilk, extracts and the cooled chocolate mixture; add to dry ingredients and beat just until moistened (batter will be very thick).
3. Drop by tablespoonfuls or with a small scoop 2 in. apart onto parchment-lined baking sheets.
4. Bake until edges are set, 8-10 minutes. Cool for 2 minutes before removing from pans to wire racks to cool completely.
5. For filling, melt chocolate chips and butter; stir until smooth. Cool. In a small bowl, beat cream cheese, marshmallow creme and almond extract until smooth. Beat in the cooled chocolate mixture. Spread 1 heaping tsp. filling on the bottoms of half the cookies; top with the remaining cookies.
6. Roll sides of cookies in miniature chocolate chips. Store in the refrigerator.
1 SANDWICH COOKIE: 279 cal., 14g fat (9g sat. fat), 29mg chol., 122mg sod., 37g carb. (25g sugars, 1g fiber), 3g pro.

FRENCH MEAT & VEGETABLE PIE

Some time ago, a co-worker brought a meat pie to lunch. The aroma was familiar—and after one taste, I was amazed to discover it was the same pie my grandmother used to serve when I was a youngster! My co-worker shared the recipe, and I have been enjoying it ever since.
—Rita Winterberger, Huson, MT

Prep: 20 min. • **Bake:** 30 min.
Makes: 8 servings

- 2 Tbsp. canola oil
- 1 large onion, thinly sliced
- 1 lb. ground beef
- 1 lb. ground pork
- 1 cup mashed potatoes (with added milk and butter)
- 1 can (8 oz.) mixed vegetables, drained
- 2 tsp. ground allspice
- 1 tsp. salt
- ¼ tsp. pepper
  Dough for double-crust pie
- 1 large egg, lightly beaten, optional

1. Preheat oven to 375°. In a skillet, heat oil over medium heat. Saute onion until tender, 1-2 minutes. Remove and set aside. In the same skillet, brown beef and pork together until no longer pink, breaking meat into crumbles. Drain. Combine onion, meat, potatoes, vegetables and seasonings.
2. On a lightly floured surface, roll half the dough to a ⅛-in.-thick circle; transfer to a 9-in. pie plate. Trim even with rim. Roll the remaining dough to a ⅛-in.-thick circle. Fill bottom crust with the meat mixture. Place top crust over filling; trim, seal and flute edge. Cut slits in top. If desired, brush with egg.
3. Bake 30-35 minutes or until crust is golden brown.
DOUGH FOR DOUBLE-CRUST PIE (9 IN.):
Combine 2½ cups all-purpose flour and ½ tsp. salt; cut in 1 cup cold butter until crumbly. Gradually add ⅓-⅔ cup ice water, tossing with a fork until dough holds together when pressed. Divide dough in half. Shape each into a disk; wrap and refrigerate 1 hour.
1 SERVING: 531 cal., 32g fat (12g sat. fat), 103mg chol., 724mg sod., 35g carb. (4g sugars, 1g fiber), 25g pro.

BRANDY PEAR PIE

I tapped into my French heritage for this recipe by incorporating Calvados, an apple brandy from the Normandy region of France. A buttery crust balances out the sweet filling, making for an indulgent treat.
—*Nicole Jackson, Beverly, MA*

Prep: 1 hour 20 min.
Bake: 45 min. + cooling
Makes: 8 servings

2½ cups all-purpose flour
½ tsp. salt
1 cup cold butter
½ cup ice water
FILLING
1 cup raisins
½ cup apple brandy
½ cup sugar
¼ cup all-purpose flour
½ tsp. ground cinnamon
¼ tsp. salt
¼ tsp. ground nutmeg
4 cups cubed peeled fresh pears
2 Tbsp. lemon juice
2 Tbsp. butter

1. In a large bowl, combine flour and salt; cut in butter until crumbly. Gradually add water, tossing with a fork until a ball forms. Divide dough in half so that 1 portion is slightly larger than the other; wrap each and refrigerate for at least 1 hour or until easy to handle.
2. Meanwhile, preheat oven to 400°. In a small saucepan over low heat, cook raisins in brandy until raisins are plump, 13-15 minutes. Strain, reserving liquid. Set raisins aside.
3. In a large bowl, combine the sugar, flour, cinnamon, salt and nutmeg. Add pears, lemon juice, raisins and ½ tsp. reserved liquid.
4. On a lightly floured surface, roll out larger portion of dough to a ⅛-in.-thick circle; transfer to a 9-in. pie plate. Trim even with rim. Add filling; dot with butter. Roll out remaining dough to a ⅛-in.-thick circle. Place over filling. Trim, seal and flute edge. Cut slits in top. Cover edge loosely with foil.
5. Bake until bubbly, 45-55 minutes. Cool on a wire rack at least 30 minutes.
1 PIECE: 542 cal., 26g fat (16g sat. fat), 68mg chol., 406mg sod., 73g carb. (32g sugars, 4g fiber), 6g pro.

BACON-CHEESE APPETIZER PIE

I first made this crowd-pleasing pie for an open house several years ago. Cheesecake is popular in these parts—and this recipe makes it fun to serve as a savory appetizer instead of the typical dessert.
—*Joanie Elbourn, Gardner, MA*

Prep: 25 min. • **Bake:** 40 min. + cooling
Makes: 20 servings

Dough for single-crust pie
3 pkg. (8 oz. each) cream cheese, softened
4 large eggs, room temperature, lightly beaten
¼ cup 2% milk
1 cup shredded Swiss cheese
½ cup sliced green onions
6 bacon strips, cooked and crumbled
½ tsp. salt
⅛ tsp. pepper
⅛ tsp. cayenne pepper
Assorted crackers

1. Preheat oven to 450°. Roll the dough into a 13½-in. circle. Fit into the bottom and up the sides of an ungreased 9-in. springform pan. Lightly prick the bottom. Bake until lightly browned, 8-10 minutes. Cool slightly. Reduce oven temperature to 350°.
2. In a large bowl, beat cream cheese until fluffy. Add eggs and milk; beat until smooth. Add cheese, onions, bacon, salt, pepper and cayenne; mix well. Pour into the crust.
3. Bake until set and a knife inserted in center comes out clean, 40-45 minutes. Cool 20 minutes. Remove side of pan. Cut into thin slices; serve warm with crackers.
DOUGH FOR SINGLE-CRUST PIE (9 IN.): Combine 1¼ cups all-purpose flour and ¼ tsp. salt; cut in ½ cup cold butter until crumbly. Gradually add 3-5 Tbsp. ice water, tossing with a fork until dough holds together when pressed. Shape into a disk; wrap and refrigerate 1 hour.
1 SERVING: 136 cal., 10g fat (5g sat. fat), 64mg chol., 191mg sod., 6g carb. (1g sugars, 0 fiber), 5g pro.

COCONUT EGGNOG PIE

This easy recipe became a family favorite by happy accident. I was trying to use up extra eggnog and coconut from other holiday baking—and they are so good together.
—*Fay Moreland, Wichita Falls, TX*

Prep: 10 min. • **Bake:** 55 min. + cooling • **Makes:** 10 servings

    2   large eggs
    1¼ cups packed brown sugar
    ¾   cup eggnog
    ½   cup butter, melted
    2   Tbsp. all-purpose flour
    1   tsp. ground cinnamon
        Dash salt
    2½ cups sweetened shredded coconut, divided
    1   graham cracker crust (10 in.)
    ¼   cup chopped walnuts or pecans
        Heavy whipping cream, whipped, optional

1. Preheat oven to 425°. In a large bowl, beat first 7 ingredients until blended; stir in 2 cups coconut. Pour into crust; sprinkle with walnuts and the remaining ½ cup coconut. Bake on a lower oven rack 10 minutes.
2. Reduce oven setting to 325°. Cover top loosely with foil. Bake until filling is set, 45-50 minutes longer. Cool on a wire rack. If desired, top with whipped cream. Refrigerate leftovers.
GRAHAM CRACKER CRUST (10 IN.): Combine 2 cups crushed graham cracker crumbs (32 squares), ⅓ sugar and ½ cup melted butter. Press onto the bottom and up the sides of an ungreased 10-in. pie plate. Bake at 375° until lightly browned, 8-10 minutes. Cool on a wire rack before filling.
1 PIECE: 485 cal., 27g fat (15g sat. fat), 73mg chol., 327mg sod., 58g carb. (51g sugars, 2g fiber), 5g pro.

MINIATURE SHEPHERD'S PIES

These mini pies are ideal for nibbling at holiday parties. If ground beef isn't your preference, change up the flavor with ground lamb and a teaspoon of dried rosemary instead.
—*Suzanne Banfield, Basking Ridge, NJ*

Prep: 40 min. • **Bake:** 15 min. • **Makes:** 4 dozen

    ½   lb. ground beef
    ⅓   cup finely chopped onion
    ¼   cup finely chopped celery
    3   Tbsp. finely chopped carrot
    1½   tsp. all-purpose flour
    1   tsp. dried thyme
    ¼   tsp. salt
    ⅛   tsp. ground nutmeg
    ⅛   tsp. pepper
    ⅔   cup beef broth
    ⅓   cup frozen petite peas
    2   pkg. (17.3 oz. each) frozen puff pastry, thawed
    3   cups mashed potatoes

1. Preheat oven to 400°. In a large skillet, cook beef, onion, celery and carrot over medium heat until beef is no longer pink and vegetables are tender, 5-7 minutes, breaking up into crumbles. Drain. Stir in flour, thyme, salt, nutmeg and pepper until blended; gradually add broth. Bring to a boil; cook and stir until sauce is thickened, 2 minutes. Stir in peas; heat through. Set aside.
2. Unfold puff pastry. Using a floured 2¼-in. round cutter, cut 12 circles from each sheet (save scraps for another use). Press circles onto the bottoms and up the sides of ungreased miniature muffin cups.
3. Fill each with 1½ tsp. beef mixture; top or pipe with 1 Tbsp. mashed potatoes. Bake until heated through and potatoes are lightly browned, 13-16 minutes. Serve warm.
1 APPETIZER: 86 cal., 4g fat (1g sat. fat), 4mg chol., 112mg sod., 10g carb. (0 sugars, 1g fiber), 2g pro.

MINCE PIES

Most people use canned mincemeat, but this is the old-fashioned way to make a mince pie. It's a sweet holiday dish that will satisfy you and your loved ones.
—*Diane Selich, Vassar, MI*

Prep: 20 min. + chilling
Bake: 20 min./batch • **Makes:** 20 mini pies

- 4   cups all-purpose flour
- 2   tsp. salt
- 1⅓ cups shortening
- ½   cup plus 2 Tbsp. ice water

FILLING

- ¼   lb. ground beef
- 3   medium apples, peeled and chopped
- 1   medium apricot, peeled and chopped
- ¾   cup packed light brown sugar
- ½   cup golden raisins
- ½   cup unsweetened apple juice
- 1   Tbsp. cider vinegar
- 1½ tsp. grated orange zest
- 1½ tsp. ground cinnamon
- ½   tsp. salt
- ½   tsp. ground cloves
- ¼   cup rum
- 1   large egg, beaten
- 1   to 2 Tbsp. coarse sugar

1. In a large bowl, mix flour and salt; cut in shortening until crumbly. Gradually add ice water, tossing with a fork until dough forms a ball. Divide dough in half. Shape each into a disk; wrap and refrigerate 1 hour or overnight.
2. For filling, in a large skillet or Dutch oven, cook beef over medium heat until no longer pink, 3-5 minutes, crumbling beef. Drain. Add apples, apricot, brown sugar, raisins, apple juice, vinegar, orange zest and seasonings. Bring to a boil; reduce heat. Simmer until apples are tender, 15-17 minutes. Stir in rum. Remove from heat; cool slightly.
3. Preheat oven to 375°. On a lightly floured surface, roll half the dough to ⅛-in. thickness. Cut 20 circles with a floured 2¾-in. round biscuit cutter. Top half the circles with 1 Tbsp. filling. Top with remaining circles; press edges with a fork to seal. Cut slits in top. Brush tops with egg; sprinkle with coarse sugar. Repeat with remaining dough and filling.
4. Bake until crust is golden brown and filling is bubbly, 20-25 minutes. Cool on a wire rack.
1 MINI PIE: 280 cal., 14g fat (4g sat. fat), 4mg chol., 302mg sod., 34g carb. (14g sugars, 1g fiber), 4g pro.

EASY SPINACH & CHEDDAR CRUSTLESS PIE

I first tried this recipe the year I was married, over 37 years ago. I've tweaked it a bit over the years, and now I have it just the way I like it. You can bake it in a pie plate or an 8x8-in. pan—or easily double the recipe for a 13x9-in. pan. I love cheddar in this pie, but pepper jack makes a nice change with a kick. Sometimes I'll add chopped ham. You can do the first steps ahead of time, and finish with the egg mixture when ready to bake. Bonus: It reheats nicely.
—*Kallee Krong-McCreery, Escondido, CA*

Prep: 10 min. • **Bake:** 40 min. + standing
Makes: 6 servings

- 1   pkg. (10 oz.) frozen chopped spinach, thawed and squeezed dry
- 1⅓ cups plus ¼ cup shredded cheddar cheese, divided
- 1   small onion, chopped
- 1½ cups 2% milk
- 3   large eggs, room temperature
- ¾   cup biscuit/baking mix
- 1   tsp. salt
- ¼   tsp. pepper
- 2   plum tomatoes, sliced

1. Preheat oven to 400°. In a greased 8-in. square baking dish, combine spinach, 1⅓ cups cheese and onion. In a blender, process milk, eggs, baking mix, salt and pepper until smooth. Pour over spinach mixture.
2. Bake on a lower oven rack for 30 minutes. Arrange tomatoes over top; sprinkle with remaining ¼ cup cheese. Bake until a knife inserted near the center comes out clean, 8-10 minutes longer. Let stand 10 minutes before cutting.
1 PIECE: 266 cal., 15g fat (8g sat. fat), 127mg chol., 833mg sod., 19g carb. (5g sugars, 2g fiber), 15g pro.

HAM & LEEK PIES

I've been making these pies for years, so lots of friends and family now have the recipe. If you can't find leeks, a sweet or mild onion works just as well.
—Bonny Tillman, Acworth, GA

Prep: 40 min. • **Bake:** 20 min.
Makes: 4 servings

- ¼ cup butter, cubed
- 4 cups sliced leeks (white portion only)
- ½ lb. sliced fresh mushrooms
- 3 medium carrots, sliced
- ½ cup all-purpose flour
- 1¼ cups 2% milk
- 1¼ cups vegetable broth
- 1¾ cups cubed fully cooked ham
- 2 Tbsp. minced fresh parsley
- ¼ to ½ tsp. ground nutmeg
  Dash pepper
- 1 sheet frozen puff pastry, thawed
- 1 large egg, lightly beaten

1. Preheat oven to 425°. In a large saucepan, heat butter over medium-high heat. Add leeks, mushrooms and carrots; cook and stir until tender.
2. Stir in flour until blended. Gradually stir in milk and broth. Bring to a boil over medium heat, stirring constantly; cook and stir or until thickened, about 2 minutes. Remove from heat; stir in ham, parsley, nutmeg and pepper.
3. On a lightly floured surface, unfold puff pastry; roll to ¼-in. thickness. Using a 10-oz. ramekin as a template, cut out 4 tops for pies. Fill 4 greased 10-oz. ramekins with leek mixture; top with pastry. Cut slits in pastry. Brush tops with egg.
4. Bake pies until golden brown, 18-22 minutes. Let stand 5 minutes before serving.
1 PIE: 713 cal., 37g fat (15g sat. fat), 123mg chol., 1,461mg sod., 72g carb., 9g fiber, 25g pro.

DILLED MUSHROOM TURNOVERS

My bite-sized mushroom pastries are hard to resist. For parties, I prep and freeze them, then pop them into the oven when guests are on the way.
—Isabella Michel-Clark, Sparks, NV

Prep: 1 hour + chilling
Bake: 15 min./batch
Makes: about 5 dozen

- 1 cup butter, softened
- 2 pkg. (8 oz. each) cream cheese, softened
- 3 cups all-purpose flour

FILLING
- 3 Tbsp. butter
- ½ lb. fresh mushrooms, finely chopped
- 1 large onion, finely chopped
- ¼ cup sour cream
- 2 Tbsp. all-purpose flour
- 1 tsp. salt
- 1 tsp. snipped fresh dill
- 1 large egg, beaten

1. Cream butter and cream cheese until smooth. Gradually beat in flour. Divide dough in half. Shape each half into a disk; wrap and refrigerate 1 hour or until firm enough to handle.
2. In a large skillet, heat butter over medium heat. Add mushrooms and onion; cook and stir until vegetables are tender, 6-8 minutes. Remove from heat; stir in sour cream, flour, salt and dill. Cool to room temperature.
3. Preheat oven to 400°. On a lightly floured surface, roll dough to ⅛-in. thickness. Cut circles with a floured 2½-in. round cookie cutter. Place about 1 tsp. filling on 1 side of each. Brush edges with egg; fold dough over filling. Press edges with a fork to seal.
4. Place on ungreased baking sheets; brush egg over tops. Bake until edges are golden brown, 12-14 minutes.
TO MAKE AHEAD: Dough can be made up to 2 days in advance.
FREEZE OPTION: Cover and freeze unbaked turnovers on waxed paper-lined baking sheets until firm. Transfer to freezer containers; cover and return to freezer. To use, bake as directed, increasing time by 2-3 minutes.
1 TURNOVER: 87 cal., 7g fat (4g sat. fat), 22mg chol., 98mg sod., 6g carb. (0 sugars, 0 fiber), 1g pro.

SWEET ONION PIE

Loaded with sweet onions, this creamy pie makes a scrumptious addition to a buffet. By using less butter to cook the onions and substituting lighter ingredients, I cut calories and fat.
—*Barbara Reese, Catawissa, PA*

Prep: 35 min. • **Bake:** 30 min.
Makes: 8 servings

- 2 sweet onions, halved and sliced
- 1 Tbsp. butter
- 1 frozen deep-dish pie crust (9 in.)
- 1 cup egg substitute
- 1 cup fat-free evaporated milk
- 1 tsp. salt
- ¼ tsp. pepper

1. In a large nonstick skillet, cook onions in butter over medium-low heat until very tender, 30 minutes.
2. Meanwhile, line unpricked pie crust with a double thickness of heavy-duty foil. Bake at 450° for 6 minutes. Remove foil; cool crust on a wire rack. Reduce oven setting to 425°.
3. Spoon onions into crust. In a small bowl, whisk the egg substitute, milk, salt and pepper; pour over onions. Bake until a knife inserted in the center comes out clean, 30-35 minutes. Let stand for 5-10 minutes before cutting.

1 PIECE: 169 cal., 7g fat (2g sat. fat), 5mg chol., 487mg sod., 21g carb. (8g sugars, 1g fiber), 7g pro. **DIABETIC EXCHANGES:** 1 starch, 1 lean meat, 1 fat.

HOLIDAY HELPER

This scrumptious pie makes a standout side dish for an evening meal, but it also makes a delicious addition to a brunch spread. If you like, top it with a little cheddar or Swiss cheese in the last 4 minutes of cooking time.

CRAN-RASPBERRY PIE

Jewel-toned fruits team up to pack this tempting holiday pie. If you like, create a cutout crust (shown on p. 180); the bright filling makes a lovely contrast.
—*Verona Koehlmoos, Pilger, NE*

Prep: 15 min. + chilling • **Bake:** 1¼ hours
Makes: 8 servings

- Dough for double-crust pie
- 2 cups chopped fresh or frozen cranberries
- 5 cups fresh or frozen unsweetened raspberries, thawed
- ½ tsp. almond extract
- 1 cup sugar
- ¼ cup quick-cooking tapioca
- ¼ tsp. salt
- Optional: Egg wash and coarse sugar

1. On a lightly floured surface, roll half the dough to a ⅛-in.-thick circle; transfer to a 9-in. pie plate. Trim even with rim of plate. Chill until filling is ready.
2. In a large bowl, combine cranberries, raspberries and extract. Combine sugar, tapioca and salt. Add to fruit mixture; toss gently to coat. Let stand for 15-20 minutes. Preheat oven to 375°.
3. Add filling to prepared bottom crust. Roll remaining dough to a ⅛-in.-thick circle. Make a lattice crust; place over filling. Trim, seal and flute edge. Chill 25 minutes or until crust is cold and firm. If desired, brush crust with egg wash and sprinkle with coarse sugar.
4. Bake on the bottom rack of oven until crust is golden brown and filling is bubbly, about 1¼ hours. Cover edge with foil if it begins to get too dark. Cool on a wire rack.

DOUGH FOR DOUBLE-CRUST PIE (9 IN.): Combine 2½ cups all-purpose flour and ½ tsp. salt; cut in 1 cup cold butter until crumbly. Gradually add ⅓-⅔ cup ice water, tossing with a fork until dough holds together when pressed. Divide dough in half. Shape each into a disk; wrap and refrigerate 1 hour.

1 PIECE: 391 cal., 14g fat (6g sat. fat), 10mg chol., 275mg sod., 64g carb. (31g sugars, 2g fiber), 3g pro.

GLUTEN-FREE PIE CRUST

Some recipes are tricky to convert, but taking gluten out of the equation actually makes pie crust easier. Without gluten—which can result in a tough crust if overworked—the dough is more forgiving. So, while still using a light touch, press it into the pie pan, and feel free to pinch the dough to repair any tears. If the dough is getting too soft, chill it for a few minutes to let the butter reharden.

NOTE: This recipe is for a 9-in. single-crust pie; for a double-crust pie, double the recipe and use 1 whole egg, beaten.

INGREDIENTS
- 1 cup gluten-free all-purpose baking flour
- ⅓ cup ground almonds
- 3 Tbsp. sugar
- ¼ tsp. salt
- ¼ tsp. xanthan gum (omit this if your gluten-free flour blend includes xanthan gum)
- 6 Tbsp. cold unsalted butter or margarine, cubed
- 2 Tbsp. beaten egg
- 1 to 2 Tbsp. ice water

INSTRUCTIONS
1. Whisk the first 5 ingredients until well combined.
2. Use a pastry cutter or 2 forks to cut the butter or margarine into the flour mixture until pea-sized crumbles form.
3. Stir in the beaten egg.
4. Using a fork, gradually stir in the ice water until the dough just comes together.
5. Form the dough into a small disk and wrap tightly; refrigerate 1 hour or overnight.

CANDIED SWEET POTATO PIES

My grandmother made the best candied sweet potatoes and incredible apricot fried pies. I think this recipe combines the best of both!
—*Angela Eshelman, Phoenix, AZ*

Prep: 1 hour 25 min. + chilling
Cook: 5 min./batch • **Makes:** 12 pies

- 6 cups all-purpose flour
- 2 tsp. salt
- 2 cups shortening
- ⅔ cup water
- 2 large eggs
- 2 Tbsp. white vinegar
- 1 large sweet potato, peeled and cut into 1-in. cubes
- ¾ cup sugar
- ¼ cup butter, cubed
- 1½ tsp. lemon juice
- ½ tsp. salt
- ¼ tsp. vanilla extract
  Oil for deep-fat frying
  Confectioners' sugar

1. In a large bowl, combine flour and salt; cut in shortening until mixture resembles coarse crumbs. Combine water, eggs and vinegar; gradually add to dry ingredients, tossing with a fork until a ball forms. Cover and chill until easy to handle, 1-1½ hours.

2. Meanwhile, place sweet potato in a small saucepan; cover with water. Bring to a boil. Reduce heat; cover and cook just until tender, 10-15 minutes. Drain.

3. In a large skillet, combine the sugar, butter and potatoes; cook and stir until syrup is golden brown, 15-20 minutes. Remove from the heat and mash. Stir in the lemon juice, salt and vanilla. Cool to room temperature.

4. Roll out dough to ¼-in. thickness. Cut 12 circles with a floured 5½-in. round cookie cutter. Spoon 2 Tbsp. filling onto half of each circle. Moisten edges with water; fold crust over filling and press edges with a fork to seal.

5. In a deep cast-iron or electric skillet, heat 1 in. oil to 375°. Fry pies in batches until golden brown, about 5 minutes, turning once. Drain on paper towels. Dust with confectioners' sugar.

1 PIE: 771 cal., 51g fat (12g sat. fat), 41mg chol., 538mg sod., 67g carb. (16g sugars, 3g fiber), 8g pro.

MERRY BIRTHDAY!

All too often, December-birthday babies can get overlooked during the holiday rush. Dip into this chapter to find recipes to celebrate every part of their day, from a decadent breakfast to a special dinner and cake—lots and lots of cake!

HONEY PECAN & GOAT CHEESE SALAD

I first made this salad for my wife and son while a pizza was baking. My son loves goat cheese—and one of my dreams is to own a herd of goats and make cheese!
—*Greg Fontenot, The Woodlands, TX*

Takes: 25 min. • **Makes:** 4 servings

- ½ cup chopped pecans
- 2 tsp. plus 1 Tbsp. honey, divided
- ⅓ cup plus 3 Tbsp. olive oil, divided
- 2 Tbsp. balsamic vinegar
- ½ tsp. salt
- ⅛ tsp. pepper
- ¼ cup all-purpose flour
- 1 large egg, beaten
- ¾ cup seasoned bread crumbs
- 8 oz. fresh goat cheese
- 4 cups spring mix salad greens

1. In a shallow microwave-safe dish, combine pecans and 2 tsp. honey; microwave, uncovered, on high until toasted, 1½-2 minutes, stirring twice. Immediately transfer to a waxed paper-lined baking sheet to cool.
2. For dressing, in a small bowl, whisk ⅓ cup oil, vinegar, remaining 1 Tbsp. honey, and the salt and pepper; set aside.
3. Place flour, egg and bread crumbs in separate shallow bowls. Shape cheese into 8 balls; flatten slightly. Coat cheese with flour, then dip in egg and coat with bread crumbs.
4. Heat remaining oil in a large skillet over medium-hight heat. Fry cheese until golden brown, 1-2 minutes on each side. Drain on paper towels.
5. Divide salad greens among 4 plates; top with cheese. Drizzle with dressing and sprinkle with honey pecans.
1 SERVING: 570 cal., 47g fat (10g sat. fat), 64mg chol., 763mg sod., 29g carb. (11g sugars, 3g fiber), 11g pro.

RUSTIC BRAISED CHICKEN

This is the complete and total package for comfort food. It's an elbows-on-the-table kind of meal that is sure to please. It reminds me of my youth and the happiest of memories of cooking in the kitchen with my mother.
—*Katie O'Keeffe, Derry, NH*

Prep: 45 min. • **Bake:** 45 min. • **Makes:** 6 servings

- ¼ cup olive oil
- 5 garlic cloves, peeled
- 5 fresh dill sprigs
- 3½ lbs. bone-in chicken breast halves
- 2 tsp. minced fresh thyme or ¾ tsp. dried thyme
- 2 tsp. minced fresh rosemary or
  ¾ tsp. dried rosemary, crushed
- 1 tsp. salt
- ½ tsp. pepper
- 2 large turnips, peeled and chopped
- 3 medium carrots, chopped
- 4 celery ribs, chopped
- 8 fingerling potatoes, chopped
- 1 medium onion, chopped
- 2 cups chicken stock
- 2 medium apples, quartered
- 1 can (14½ oz.) whole tomatoes, undrained

1. Preheat oven to 300°. In an ovenproof Dutch oven, heat oil over medium heat. Add garlic and dill; cook and stir until fragrant, 30-60 seconds. Sprinkle chicken with thyme, rosemary, salt and pepper. Brown chicken in batches; remove from pot.
2. Add turnips, carrots, celery, potatoes and onion; cook and stir until crisp-tender. Add stock, apples and tomatoes; return chicken to pot. Bake, uncovered, until a thermometer inserted in chicken reads 170° and vegetables are tender, 45-60 minutes. If desired, top with additional fresh dill just before serving.
1 SERVING: 424 cal., 14g fat (3g sat. fat), 106mg chol., 850mg sod., 31g carb. (13g sugars, 6g fiber), 43g pro.

CARAMEL CASHEW CHEESECAKE

When a friend served this luscious cheesecake at a birthday party, I left with the recipe. Every time I make it, rave reviews and recipe requests come my way.
—*Pat Price, Bucyrus, OH*

Prep: 30 min. • **Bake:** 65 min. + chilling
Makes: 16 servings

- ¼ cup cold butter
- ½ cup all-purpose flour
- ¾ cup chopped unsalted cashews, toasted
- 2 Tbsp. confectioners' sugar
- ⅛ tsp. salt

FILLING
- 4 pkg. (8 oz. each) cream cheese, softened
- 1¼ cups sugar
- 1 Tbsp. vanilla extract
- 5 large eggs, room temperature, lightly beaten
- 2 Tbsp. heavy whipping cream

TOPPING
- 1 cup sugar
- 3 Tbsp. water
- ¾ cup heavy whipping cream
- 1 cup unsalted cashews, toasted

1. Preheat the oven to 350°. Place a greased 9-in. springform pan on a double thickness of heavy-duty foil (about 18 in. square). Wrap foil securely around pan. Place on a baking sheet.
2. In a small bowl, cut butter into flour until mixture resembles coarse crumbs. Stir in cashews, confectioners' sugar and salt. Press onto the bottom and ½ in. up the sides of prepared pan. Bake for 15 minutes. Cool on a wire rack. Reduce heat to 325°.
3. Beat cream cheese, sugar and vanilla until smooth. Add eggs and cream; beat on low just until blended. Pour over crust. Place springform pan in a larger baking pan; add 1 in. hot water to larger pan.
4. Bake until center is just set and top appears dull, 65-75 minutes. Remove springform pan from water bath.

Cool on a wire rack 10 minutes. Carefully run a knife around edge of pan to loosen. Cool 1 hour longer. Refrigerate overnight, covering when completely cooled.
5. For topping, combine sugar and water in saucepan. Cook over medium-low heat until sugar is dissolved. Bring to a boil over medium-high heat; cover and boil 2 minutes. Uncover; boil until mixture is golden brown and a candy thermometer reads 300° (hard-crack stage), about 8 minutes.
6. Remove from heat. Stir in cream until smooth, about 5 minutes (mixture will appear lumpy at first). Add cashews; cool to lukewarm.
7. Remove cheesecake from pan to a serving platter. Spoon cooled caramel over cheesecake. Refrigerate leftovers.
1 PIECE: 507 cal., 36g fat (18g sat. fat), 138mg chol., 248mg sod., 41g carb. (33g sugars, 1g fiber), 9g pro.

DOLLAR STORE GIFT BAG STAND

Simple magazine holders from a dollar store make a budget-friendly way of organizing gift bags and sorting them into various types and sizes. It'll help you keep birthday bags separate from Christmas bags so you can snag what you need. You can easily fold them to fit nicely, and they'll all be visible for quick and easy picks.

CINDY'S SEAFOOD CHOWDER

My grandmother-in-law used to make a fish stew with shellfish, but I hated being elbow deep in sauce and shells, so I created this version. It was a huge hit with the family, even my grandmother-in-law. I'm now a grandmother and my grandchildren love this chowder too. There's never a drop left.
—*Cynthia Adams, Tracy, CA*

Prep: 30 min. • **Cook:** 1 hour 20 min.
Makes: 12 servings (4 qt.)

- 1   Tbsp. canola oil
- 1   large onion, chopped
- 2   celery ribs, chopped
- 1   medium sweet red pepper, chopped
- ½   cup shredded carrot
- 8   garlic cloves, minced
- 1   carton (32 oz.) chicken broth
- 1   can (28 oz.) crushed tomatoes
- 1   bottle (12 oz.) beer
- 1   can (11½ oz.) spicy tomato juice
- ¼   cup Worcestershire sauce
- 4   bay leaves
- 1   tsp. salt
- 1   tsp. dried oregano
- 1   tsp. pepper
- ½   tsp. crushed red pepper flakes
- 1   lb. tilapia fillets, cut into 1-in. pieces
- 1   lb. sea scallops, quartered
- 1   lb. uncooked medium shrimp, peeled and deveined
- 2   cans (6½ oz. each) chopped clams, undrained
- 2   cups hot cooked rice
- 4   green onions, chopped

1. In a Dutch oven, heat oil over medium heat. Add onion, celery, red pepper, carrot and garlic; cook and stir until tender, about 5 minutes. Stir in the broth, tomatoes, beer, tomato juice, Worcestershire sauce and seasonings. Bring to a boil. Reduce heat; simmer, covered, 1 hour.
2. Stir in seafood; return just to a boil. Reduce heat; simmer, uncovered, until fish just begins to flake easily with a fork and scallops are firm and opaque, 5-7 minutes. Remove bay leaves. Ladle soup into bowls; top individual servings with rice and green onions.

1⅓ CUPS: 217 cal., 3g fat (0 sat. fat), 84mg chol., 998mg sod., 22g carb. (4g sugars, 2g fiber), 25g pro.

BIRTHDAY CAKE WAFFLES

These super fun waffles—soft on the inside, crisp on the outside—taste just like cake batter! They are quick to whip up anytime but would make birthday mornings feel even more special.
—*Andrea Fetting, Franklin, WI*

Prep: 20 min. • **Cook:** 25 min.
Makes: 6 waffles

- 1   cup all-purpose flour
- 1   cup (about 5 oz.) confetti cake mix or flavor of choice
- 2   Tbsp. cornstarch
- 3   tsp. baking powder
- ¼   tsp. salt
- 2   Tbsp. rainbow sprinkles, optional
- 2   large eggs, room temperature
- 1¾ cups 2% milk
- ¾   to 1 cup plain Greek yogurt
- ½   tsp. vanilla extract
- ½   tsp. almond extract

CREAM CHEESE FROSTING

- 4   oz. softened cream cheese or reduced-fat cream cheese
- ¼   cup butter, softened
- 1½ to 2 cups confectioners' sugar
- ½   tsp. vanilla extract
- 1   to 3 Tbsp. 2% milk

1. Preheat oven to 300°. Combine the first 5 ingredients and, if desired, rainbow sprinkles. In another bowl, whisk eggs, milk, yogurt and extracts. Add yogurt mixture to flour mixture; mix until smooth.
2. Preheat waffle maker coated with cooking spray. Bake waffles according to manufacturer's directions until golden brown. Transfer cooked waffles to oven until ready to serve.
3. For frosting, beat cream cheese and butter on high until light and fluffy, 2-3 minutes. Gradually beat in confectioners' sugar, ½ cup at a time, until smooth. Beat in vanilla. Add enough milk to reach desired consistency. Spread over warm waffles.

1 WAFFLE: 528 cal., 22g fat (13g sat. fat), 115mg chol., 695mg sod., 72g carb. (45g sugars, 1g fiber), 10g pro.

HOLIDAY HELPER

For a cakelike look, cut waffles into fourths and stack them; decorate with birthday candles.

CARAMELIZED KALE & APPLES SAUTE

My garden and my vegetarian daughter inspired me to create this quick, easy and nutritious side. No one would ever guess that this restaurant-quality dish was prepared in less than 30 minutes! If you're not vegetarian, a teaspoon of bacon drippings makes a wonderful addition to the saute step.
—*Cindy Beberman, Orland Park, IL*

Takes: 30 min. • **Makes:** 4 servings

- 2 Tbsp. olive oil
- 1 large sweet onion, halved and thinly sliced
- 1 large Gala or Honeycrisp apple, peeled and sliced
- 6 cups chopped fresh kale, stems removed and lightly packed
- ½ cup vegetable broth
- 2 Tbsp. cider vinegar
- 1 Tbsp. honey
- 1 Tbsp. lemon juice
- 1 cup diced fresh tomatoes with juice
- ½ tsp. salt

1. In a large skillet, heat oil over medium heat. Add onion and apple; saute, stirring frequently, until tender and starting to brown, 8-10 minutes.
2. Add kale to skillet. In a small bowl, stir together broth, vinegar, honey and lemon juice; pour over kale. Bring to a boil. Reduce heat; cook, covered, stirring occasionally, until kale is wilted, about 10 minutes longer.
3. Stir in tomatoes and salt. Cook, covered, just until tomatoes are heated through, about 2 minutes longer. Remove from heat; serve with cooking juices.
1 SERVING: 146 cal., 7g fat (1g sat. fat), 0 chol., 396mg sod., 21g carb. (14g sugars, 2g fiber), 2g pro.

EASY POACHED SALMON

In 46 years of marriage, we had never tasted salmon until a friend told me about poaching it in a slow cooker. I tried it and got flaky, moist results with little fuss. I added some soy sauce for extra flavor.
—*Johnna Johnson, Scottsdale, AZ*

Prep: 45 min. • **Cook:** 1 hour • **Makes:** 8 servings

- 6 cups water
- 1 medium onion, chopped
- 2 celery ribs, chopped
- 4 sprigs fresh parsley
- ½ cup dry white wine
- 1 Tbsp. soy sauce
- 8 whole peppercorns
- 1 bay leaf
- 1 salmon fillet (3 lbs.)
  Lemon slices and fresh dill

1. In a large saucepan, combine the first 8 ingredients. Bring to a boil; reduce heat. Simmer, covered, 30 minutes. Strain, discarding vegetables and spices.
2. Cut three 20x3-in. strips of heavy-duty foil; crisscross so they resemble spokes of a wheel. Place strips on bottom and up sides of a 7-qt. oval slow cooker. Pour poaching liquid into slow cooker. Carefully add salmon.
3. Cook, covered, on high 60-70 minutes or just until fish flakes easily with a fork (a thermometer inserted in fish should read at least 145°). Using foil strips as handles, remove salmon from cooking liquid. Serve warm or cold, with lemon and dill.
6 OZ. COOKED SALMON: 266 cal., 16g fat (3g sat. fat), 85mg chol., 97mg sod., 0 carb. (0 sugars, 0 fiber), 29g pro. **DIABETIC EXCHANGES:** 4 lean meat.

BANANA CAKE WITH CHOCOLATE FROSTING

Banana and chocolate—what could be better? Make sure the cream cheese is at room temperature before you use it, or it will chill the softened butter and make for lumpy frosting.
—Jeanne Ambrose, Des Moines, IA

Prep: 45 min. • **Bake:** 45 min. + cooling
Makes: 16 servings

- ¾ cup unsalted butter, softened
- 2 cups sugar
- 3 large eggs, room temperature
- 1½ cups mashed ripe bananas (2 to 3 large)
- 1½ tsp. vanilla extract
- 3 cups all-purpose flour
- 1½ tsp. baking powder
- 1½ tsp. baking soda
- 1 tsp. salt
- ¾ cup buttermilk
- ¾ cup chopped unsalted pistachios, toasted

CREAM CHEESE FROSTING

- 2 containers (8 oz. each) whipped cream cheese, room temperature
- ½ cup butter, softened
- ½ cup baking cocoa
- 4½ cups confectioners' sugar
- 2 tsp. vanilla extract

1. Preheat oven to 350°. In a large bowl, cream butter and sugar until light and fluffy, 5-7 minutes. Add eggs, 1 at a time, beating well after each addition. Beat in bananas and vanilla. Combine flour, baking powder, baking soda and salt; add to creamed mixture alternately with buttermilk, beating well after each addition. Fold in chopped pistachios.
2. Transfer batter to 2 greased and floured 8-in. round baking pans. Bake until a toothpick inserted in center comes out clean, 45-55 minutes. Cool 10 minutes before removing from pans to wire racks to cool completely.
3. For frosting, in a large bowl, beat cream cheese and butter until smooth. Add cocoa; mix until blended. Add confectioners' sugar and vanilla; beat until creamy.
4. Place 1 cake layer on a serving plate; spread top with 1 cup frosting. Top with remaining cake. Spread top and sides with 2 cups frosting.
5. Decorate cake as desired with remaining frosting. Refrigerate for at least 1 hour or until frosting is set.
1 PIECE: 606 cal., 28g fat (16g sat. fat), 111mg chol., 510mg sod., 85g carb. (62g sugars, 2g fiber), 7g pro.

CREAMY SOURDOUGH SNACK

This snack was a big hit at my mom's 50th birthday party!
—Darelyn Payes, Hayward, CA

Takes: 20 min. • **Makes:** 3½ cups

- 1½ cups sour cream
- 6 oz. cream cheese, softened
- ½ cup chopped green onions
- 1 tsp. Worcestershire sauce
- 2 cups shredded sharp cheddar cheese
- 1½ cups cubed fully cooked ham
- 1 round loaf (1 lb.) sourdough bread
  Chopped fresh parsley, optional

1. In a saucepan, combine the sour cream, cream cheese, onions and Worcestershire sauce; cook and stir over low heat until blended. Add cheese and ham; cook and stir until cheese is melted and ham is heated through.
2. Cut off top of loaf; carefully hollow out top and bottom, leaving a ½-in. shell. Cut removed bread into cubes. Pour dip into shell; if desired, sprinkle with parsley. Serve with bread cubes.
2 TBSP. WITH ABOUT ½ OZ. BREAD: 177 cal., 12g fat (7g sat. fat), 39mg chol., 321mg sod., 10g carb. (2g sugars, 0 fiber), 8g pro.

HOLIDAY HELPER

Sourdough goes nicely with the tangy cream cheese and sour cream plus the salty ham, but you can use a different bread if you prefer. Try a crusty rustic Italian loaf, or a French boule instead.

BEST EVER VANILLA ICE CREAM

This ice cream is technically a custard since it contains eggs. I've found that eggs are the key to making a smooth and creamy treat that rivals what you can get at a premium ice cream shop.
—*Peggy Woodward, Shullsburg, WI*

Prep: 15 min. + chilling
Process: 25 min./batch + freezing
Makes: 4½ cups

- 2 cups heavy whipping cream
- 2 cups 2% milk
- ¾ cup sugar
- ⅛ tsp. salt
- 1 vanilla bean
- 6 large egg yolks

1. In a large heavy saucepan, combine cream, milk, sugar and salt. Split vanilla bean in half lengthwise. With a sharp knife, scrape seeds into pan; add bean. Heat cream mixture over medium heat until bubbles form around sides of pan, stirring to dissolve sugar.

2. In a small bowl, whisk a small amount of the hot mixture into the egg yolks; return all to the pan, whisking constantly. Cook over low heat until the mixture is just thick enough to coat a metal spoon and temperature reaches 180°, stirring constantly. Do not allow to boil. Immediately transfer to a bowl.

3. Place bowl in a pan of ice water. Stir gently and occasionally for 2 minutes; discard vanilla bean. Press waxed paper onto surface of mixture. Refrigerate for several hours or overnight.

4. Fill cylinder of ice cream maker two-thirds full; freeze according to the manufacturer's directions. (Refrigerate remaining mixture until ready to freeze.) Transfer ice cream to a freezer container; freeze until firm, 4-6 hours. Repeat with remaining mixture.

½ CUP: 310 cal., 23g fat (14g sat. fat), 188mg chol., 78mg sod., 21g carb. (21g sugars, 0 fiber), 5g pro.

COOKIES & CREAM ICE CREAM: After freezing in an ice cream maker, layer 1 cup crushed Oreo cookies with ice cream in a freezer container; freeze until firm.

CHOCOLATE ICE CREAM: Melt 2 cups semisweet chocolate; cool to room temperature. Whisk melted chocolate into egg yolks before whisking a small amount of hot cream mixture into yolks. Proceed with recipe as directed.

STRAWBERRY ICE CREAM: In a small bowl, crush 2 cups sliced fresh strawberries with ¼ cup sugar. Stir into cooked custard as it cools in the pan of ice water. Proceed with recipe as directed.

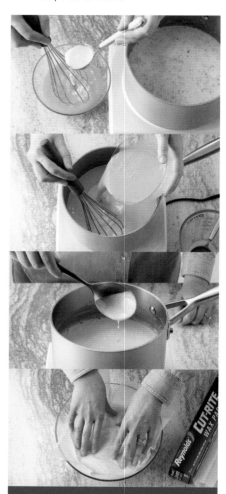

GENTLY DOES IT

This homemade ice cream is simple, but does require some attention. Adding a bit of the cream mixture to the eggs before adding all the eggs to the pan keeps the eggs from cooking. Watch for the mixture to coat the back of a metal spoon to test for doneness and avoid boiling it. And pressing waxed paper to the top of the mixture will prevent the forming of a rubbery film.

TURKEY CREPES

This savory crepe recipe has been passed down through many generations in my family. You can also use the turkey filling to make a potpie.
—Andrea Price, Grafton, WI

Prep: 30 min. + chilling • **Cook:** 50 min.
Makes: 6 servings

- 3 large eggs, room temperature
- 3¼ cups 2% milk
- 2 cups all-purpose flour
- 1 tsp. salt
- 1 tsp. baking powder

FILLING
- 3 Tbsp. butter, divided
- 1 cup frozen peas and carrots (about 5 oz.), thawed
- ½ cup chopped onion
- 3 Tbsp. all-purpose flour
- 1 cup 2% milk
- 1 cup chicken broth
- 2 cups chopped cooked turkey
- ½ tsp. minced fresh thyme or ¼ tsp. dried thyme
- ½ tsp. salt
- ⅛ tsp. pepper

1. In a large bowl, whisk eggs and milk. In another bowl, mix flour, salt and baking powder; add to egg mixture and mix well. Refrigerate, covered, 1 hour.

2. Heat a lightly greased 8-in. nonstick skillet over medium heat. Stir batter. Fill a ¼-cup measure with batter; pour into center of pan. Quickly lift and tilt pan to coat bottom evenly. Cook until top appears dry; turn crepe over and cook until bottom is cooked, 15-20 seconds longer. Remove to a wire rack. Repeat with remaining batter, greasing pan as needed. When cool, stack crepes between pieces of waxed paper or paper towels.

3. For filling, in a large saucepan, heat 2 Tbsp. butter over medium heat. Add peas and carrots and onion; cook and stir until onion is tender, 8-10 minutes. Stir in flour until blended; gradually whisk in milk and broth. Bring to a boil, stirring constantly; cook and stir until thickened, 5-8 minutes. Stir in turkey, thyme, salt and pepper; heat through.

4. Spread ¼ cup filling down the center of each crepe; fold sides and ends over filling and roll up. Wipe out skillet. In batches, heat remaining 1 Tbsp. butter over medium heat. Cook crepes until golden brown, 2-4 minutes on each side.
2 FILLED CREPES: 434 cal., 14g fat (7g sat. fat), 170mg chol., 1063mg sod., 47g carb. (9g sugars, 2g fiber), 28g pro.

HOLIDAY HELPER

If you have one, use a crepe pan to cook these. The difference between a crepe pan and a regular skillet is the height of the sides: A crepe pan has very short sides, making it easier to flip the tender crepes. But a regular skillet will do nicely as well!

LASAGNA CASSEROLE

While growing up, I always wanted this meal on my birthday. Mother made the sauce from scratch, but now I use store-bought spaghetti sauce to save time. Replace the ground beef with Italian sausage if you want more spice.
—*Deb Morrison, Skiatook, OK*

Prep: 15 min. • **Bake:** 1 hour + standing
Makes: 8 servings

- 1 lb. ground beef
- ¼ cup chopped onion
- ½ tsp. salt
- ½ tsp. pepper, divided
- 1 lb. medium pasta shells, cooked and drained
- 4 cups shredded part-skim mozzarella cheese, divided
- 3 cups 4% cottage cheese
- 2 large eggs, lightly beaten
- ⅓ cup grated Parmesan cheese
- 2 Tbsp. dried parsley flakes
- 1 jar (24 oz.) pasta sauce

1. Preheat oven to 350°. In a large skillet, cook beef and onion over medium heat until meat is no longer pink, breaking meat into crumbles; drain. Sprinkle with salt and ¼ tsp. pepper; set aside.
2. In a large bowl, combine pasta, 3 cups mozzarella cheese, cottage cheese, eggs, Parmesan cheese, parsley and the remaining ¼ tsp. pepper. Transfer to a greased shallow 3-qt. or 13x9-in. baking dish. Top with beef mixture and spaghetti sauce (dish will be full).
3. Bake, covered, for 45 minutes. Sprinkle with remaining 1 cup mozzarella cheese. Bake, uncovered, until bubbly and cheese is melted, 15 minutes longer. Let stand 10 minutes before serving.
FREEZE OPTION: Sprinkle unbaked casserole with remaining mozzarella cheese. Cover and freeze unbaked casserole. To use, partially thaw in refrigerator overnight. Remove from refrigerator 30 minutes before baking. Bake casserole at 350° as directed, increasing time as necessary until heated through and a thermometer inserted in center reads 165°.
1 SERVING: 667 cal., 30g fat (14g sat. fat), 157mg chol., 1209mg sod., 56g carb. (12g sugars, 4g fiber), 44g pro.

BLUE-RIBBON RED VELVET CAKE

This two-layer beauty features a striking red interior. It calls for more baking cocoa than most red velvet cakes, making it extra chocolaty. I'm proud to say that this recipe won a blue ribbon in the holiday cake division at the 2006 Alaska State Fair. I think this award-winning red velvet cake recipe will be a winner in your house, too!
—*Cindi DeClue, Anchorage, AK*

Prep: 35 min. • **Bake:** 25 min. + cooling
Makes: 16 servings

- 1½ cups canola oil
- 1 cup buttermilk
- 2 large eggs, room temperature
- 2 Tbsp. red food coloring
- 1 tsp. white vinegar
- 2½ cups all-purpose flour
- 1½ cups sugar
- 3 Tbsp. baking cocoa
- 1 tsp. baking soda

FROSTING
- 1 pkg. (8 oz.) cream cheese, softened
- ½ cup butter, softened
- 2 tsp. vanilla extract
- 3¾ cups confectioners' sugar

1. Preheat oven to 350°. Line bottoms of 2 greased 9-in. round pans with parchment; grease parchment. Beat the first 5 ingredients until well blended. In another bowl, whisk together flour, sugar, baking cocoa and baking soda; gradually beat into oil mixture.
2. Transfer batter to the prepared pans. Bake until a toothpick inserted in center comes out clean, 25-30 minutes. Cool in pans for 10 minutes before removing to wire racks; remove parchment. Let cool completely.
3. For frosting, beat cream cheese, butter and vanilla until blended. Gradually beat in confectioners' sugar until smooth. Using a long serrated knife, trim tops of cakes; set tops aside. Place 1 cake layer on a serving plate. Spread with ¾ cup frosting. Top with remaining cake layer, bottom side up. Frost top and sides with remaining frosting.
4. Break cake tops into pieces. Pulse in a food processor until fine crumbs form. Decorate cake with crumbs as desired.
1 PIECE: 559 cal., 33g fat (8g sat. fat), 53mg chol., 208mg sod., 64g carb. (48g sugars, 1g fiber), 4g pro.

BOURBON CHOCOLATE PUMPKIN LATTE

I created this by adapting two of my favorite recipes. It's the perfect beverage to warm you up at a special occasion or a weekend breakfast.
—*Ellen Riley, Murfreesboro, TN*

Takes: 15 min. • **Makes:** 8 servings

- 3   cups 2% milk
- ¾   cup canned pumpkin
- ½   cup baking cocoa
- ⅓   cup packed brown sugar
- 1½ tsp. pumpkin pie spice
- 1½ cups hot brewed espresso or
      strong brewed dark roast coffee
- ½   cup bourbon or whiskey
      Whipped cream, optional

Place the first 5 ingredients in a large saucepan. Cook and stir over medium heat until heated through. Remove from heat; stir in hot espresso and bourbon. Pour into warm mugs. If desired, top with whipped cream and additional pie spice.
¾ CUP: 141 cal., 3g fat (1g sat. fat), 7mg chol., 53mg sod., 19g carb. (14g sugars, 2g fiber), 4g pro.

HOLIDAY HELPER

If you like, you can keep this beverage warm in a slow cooker set on low for a party buffet. Let the guests add their own whipped cream as they please!

WARM CRAB & SPINACH DIP

On a visit to Maryland, we stayed at a hotel that sent guests home with a crab dip recipe and a spice pouch. Now I've made my own dip that rekindles memories of that trip.
—*Kristina Wenner, Jamison, PA*

Prep: 20 min. • **Cook:** 15 min. • **Makes:** 4½ cups

- 2   Tbsp. olive oil
- ⅓   cup finely chopped sweet onion
- 2   garlic cloves, minced
- 1   pkg. (8 oz.) softened cream cheese, cubed
- 1   pkg. (5.2 oz.) Boursin garlic and fine herbs cheese
- ¼   cup 2% milk
- ¼   cup half-and-half cream
- ¼   cup white wine or chicken broth
- 1   Tbsp. seafood seasoning
- 2   tsp. Worcestershire sauce
- 1   tsp. Louisiana-style hot sauce
- ⅛   tsp. crushed red pepper flakes, optional
- 2   cans (6 oz. each) lump crabmeat, drained and picked over
- 1   pkg. (10 oz.) frozen chopped spinach, thawed and squeezed dry
- 2   cups shredded cheddar cheese
      Blue tortilla chips

1. In a large nonstick skillet, heat oil over medium heat. Add onion and garlic; cook 3 minutes. Stir in cream cheese and Boursin until melted. Add milk, cream and wine, stirring constantly.
2. Add seafood seasoning, Worcestershire, hot sauce and, if desired, red pepper flakes. Stir in crab, spinach and cheddar cheese until cheese melts and mixture is bubbly. Serve warm with blue tortilla chips.
NOTE: Boursin garlic and fine herbs cheese, sold in a 5.2-oz. package, has a firmer texture than the spreadable cheese product.
¼ CUP: 170 cal., 14g fat (8g sat. fat), 55mg chol., 421mg sod., 2g carb. (1g sugars, 1g fiber), 9g pro.

CHRISTMAS SNACK EXCHANGE

Want a fun idea for a casual holiday party? Try a simple
get-together where the focus is on a smorgasbord of snacks.
These tempting nibbles are perfect as party fare or as gifts—
and with a snack exchange party, they can be both!

COCONUT ALMOND CANDY

The secret ingredient in this homemade candy is a true surprise—no one tasting these delicious morsels will guess what's in the sweet, creamy filling!
—*Katrina Smith, Lawrence, KS*

Prep: 45 min. + chilling • **Makes:** 2 dozen

2	cups sweetened shredded coconut
½	cup mashed potatoes (with added milk and butter)
¼	tsp. vanilla extract
⅛	tsp. salt, optional
2	cups confectioners' sugar
24	unblanched almonds, toasted
1	pkg. (11½ oz.) milk chocolate chips
1	Tbsp. butter

1. In a large bowl, mix coconut, potatoes, vanilla and, if desired, salt. Gradually beat in confectioners' sugar. Refrigerate, covered, until firm enough to shape, about 1 hour.

2. With hands dusted with confectioners' sugar, shape mixture into twenty-four 1-in. ovals. Flatten slightly, then wrap each around an almond. Place on waxed paper-lined baking sheets; freeze until firm, at least 30 minutes.

3. In a microwave, melt chocolate chips and butter; stir until smooth. Using a fork, dip candies into chocolate mixture; allow excess to drip off. Return to baking sheets; refrigerate until set. Store between layers of waxed paper in an airtight container in the refrigerator.

1 CANDY: 167 cal., 8g fat (5g sat. fat), 5mg chol., 61mg sod., 23g carb. (20g sugars, 1g fiber), 2g pro.

THE SNACK EXCHANGE: PARTY TIPS

Consider these tips for a fun, festive and stress-free snack exchange!

1. INVITE EARLY!
Send invites out several weeks in advance. Whether sending digital invites or printed invitations, ask for a firm RSVP so you can provide numbers to your guests closer to the party day.

2. FOLLOW UP WITH CLEAR INSTRUCTIONS
Before the party, let guests know how much of their snack to bring, and how it will be distributed. Ask for one larger bowl or plate for sampling, then a set number of small bundles that guests can carry away. Think of a bowl of popcorn, accompanied by 12 small bags, or a platter of candies with 12 bags containing 2 or 3 candies each.

3. SET OUT THE TREATS
Choose a central spot with good access. As guests arrive, have them place their snacks on the table and fill out a card to set in front of them. This card should contain not just the name of the snack, but any ingredients that might trigger allergies.

4. SET THE RULES
An exchange is not meant to be an all-you-can-scoop-up buffet. The large plates are so everyone can get a taste! You may need to set a limit on how many bags your guests can choose. If so, consider a random pull to assign numbers, then go in order and let each guest choose one snack bundle in turn, repeating until all the snacks are chosen.

EASY PUPPY CHOW

This easy version of everyone's favorite sweet-salty snack mix uses a whole box of cereal, so there's less measuring. And there's enough to feed a hungry crowd.
—Taste of Home *Test Kitchen*

Takes: 15 min. • **Makes:** 13 cups

- 1 box (12 oz.) Corn Chex
- 2 cups semisweet chocolate chips
- ¾ cup creamy peanut butter
- ⅓ cup butter, cubed
- 3 cups confectioners' sugar

1. Pour cereal into a very large bowl. In a large microwave-safe bowl, combine chocolate chips, peanut butter and butter. Microwave on high for 30 seconds. Stir gently. Continue microwaving on high, stirring every 30 seconds, until melted and blended. Pour over cereal; gently stir to coat.
2. In batches, place confectioners' sugar in a large airtight container, add cereal mixture, close container and shake until well coated. Spread cereal on a baking sheet. Let stand until set. Store in airtight containers.
½ CUP: 229 cal., 10g fat (5g sat. fat), 6mg chol., 146mg sod., 35g carb. (23g sugars, 2g fiber), 3g pro.

HOLIDAY HELPER

You can play with this recipe if you like—try using Cinnamon or Honey Nut Chex instead, or swapping bittersweet or milk chocolate for the semisweet, depending on your taste preferences.

DOUBLE CHOCOLATE WALNUT FUDGE

Anyone who's fond of chocolate will like this smooth, nutty fudge twice as much. I enjoy making several batches when Christmas rolls around. It doesn't last long at our house during the December festivities!
—Florence Hasty, Louisiana, MO

Prep: 10 min. • **Cook:** 20 min. + chilling
Makes: about 2½ lbs. (81 pieces)

- 1 tsp. butter
- 1 pkg. (12 oz.) semisweet chocolate chips
- 1 can (14 oz.) sweetened condensed milk, divided
- 1 cup chopped walnuts, divided
- 2 tsp. vanilla extract, divided
- 1 pkg. (11½ oz.) milk chocolate chips

1. Line a 9-in. square pan with foil, letting ends extend over sides by 1 in.; grease foil with butter. In a large heavy saucepan, combine semisweet chocolate chips and ¾ cup milk over low heat. Remove from heat; stir in ½ cup walnuts and 1 tsp. vanilla. Spread into prepared pan.
2. In another saucepan, combine milk chocolate chips and remaining milk. Remove from heat; stir in remaining ½ cup walnuts and 1 tsp. vanilla. Spread over first layer. Refrigerate, covered, until firm, about 2 hours.
3. Lift fudge out of pan. Remove foil; cut fudge into 1-in. squares. Store between layers of waxed paper in an airtight container.
1 PIECE: 69 cal., 4g fat (2g sat. fat), 3mg chol., 10mg sod., 8g carb. (7g sugars, 0 fiber), 1g pro.

TERIYAKI BEEF JERKY

Jerky is a portable, chewy snack—and you can make your own with our recipe. The meat has a savory flavor and a bit of heat.
—Taste of Home *Test Kitchen*

Prep: 40 min. + marinating
Bake: 3 hours + cooling
Makes: 8 servings

  1   beef flank steak (1½ to 2 lbs.)
  ⅔   cup reduced-sodium soy sauce
  ⅔   cup Worcestershire sauce
  ¼   cup honey
  3   tsp. coarsely ground pepper
  2   tsp. onion powder
  2   tsp. garlic powder
1½   tsp. crushed red pepper flakes
  1   tsp. liquid smoke

1. Trim all visible fat from steak. Freeze, covered, until firm, about 30 minutes. Slice steak along the grain into long ⅛-in.-thick strips.
2. Transfer to a large resealable container. In a small bowl, whisk remaining ingredients; add to beef. Seal container and turn to coat. Refrigerate 2 hours or overnight, turning occasionally.
3. Preheat oven to 170°. Transfer beef and marinade to a large saucepan; bring to a boil. Reduce heat; simmer 5 minutes. Using tongs, remove beef from marinade. Drain on paper towels; pat dry. Discard marinade.
4. Arrange beef strips in single layer on wire racks placed on 15x10x1-in. baking pans. Dry in oven until beef becomes dry and leathery, 3-4 hours, rotating pans occasionally. (Or use a commercial dehydrator or smoker, following the manufacturer's directions.)
5. Remove from oven; cool completely. Using paper towels, blot any beads of oil on jerky. Store jerky, covered, in refrigerator or freezer.
DEHYDRATE IN A SMOKER: To make in a smoker, follow steps 1-3 then proceed with the recipe following manufacturer's directions for temperature and time. We cooked ours at 170° for 2 hours.
1 OZ.: 132 cal., 6g fat (3g sat. fat), 40mg chol., 139mg sod., 2g carb. (1g sugars, 0 fiber), 17g pro. **DIABETIC EXCHANGES:** 2 lean meat.

SUGAR & SPICE POPCORN

Our family can't get enough of this light cinnamon-sweet popcorn. The baked kernels are wonderfully crunchy and coated just right. Try mixing some to have on hand as an anytime nibble.
—*Naomi Yoder, Leeseburg, IN*

Takes: 20 min. • **Makes:** 4 qt.

  4   qt. air-popped popcorn
  3   Tbsp. butter
  ¼   cup sugar
  1   Tbsp. water
  1   tsp. ground cinnamon
  ¼   tsp. salt

1. Place popcorn in a large roasting pan coated with cooking spray. In a small saucepan, melt butter over low heat. Add the sugar, water, cinnamon and salt; cook and stir over low heat until sugar is dissolved.
2. Pour over popcorn; toss to coat. Bake, uncovered, at 300° for 10-15 minutes. Serve immediately.
1 CUP: 62 cal., 2g fat (1g sat. fat), 6mg chol., 59mg sod., 9g carb. (0 sugars, 1g fiber), 1g pro. **DIABETIC EXCHANGES:** ½ starch.

HOLIDAY HELPER
If you don't own an air popper, add the kernels to a paper bag, fold the top over and microwave it on high for 2-3 minutes.

BANANAS FOSTER CRUNCH MIX

Bananas Foster is one of my favorite desserts, so I thought that a crunchy, snackable version would be a hit. It is heated in the microwave and takes just a few minutes to make.
—*David Dahlman, Chatsworth, CA*

Prep: 10 min. • **Cook:** 5 min. + cooling
Makes: 2½ qt.

  3   cups Honey Nut Chex
  3   cups Cinnamon Chex
2¼   cups pecan halves
1½   cups dried banana chips
  ⅓   cup butter, cubed
  ⅓   cup packed brown sugar
  ½   tsp. ground cinnamon
  ½   tsp. banana extract
  ½   tsp. rum extract

1. Place the first 4 ingredients in a large microwave-safe bowl; set aside. Place butter, brown sugar and cinnamon in a small microwave-safe bowl; microwave on high for 2 minutes, stirring once. Stir in extracts. Pour over cereal mixture; toss to coat.
2. Microwave cereal mixture on high for 3 minutes, stirring every 1 minute. Spread onto baking sheets to cool. Store in an airtight container.
¾ CUP: 358 cal., 24g fat (9g sat. fat), 14mg chol., 170mg sod., 36g carb. (18g sugars, 4g fiber), 4g pro.

MINE RUN CANDY

This candy always brings back memories of my childhood in mining country. It's so easy to make, and you can choose whether you want the pieces coated in chocolate.
—*Lisa Henshall, Wichita, KS*

Prep: 20 min. • **Cook:** 20 min. + cooling
Makes: 2 lbs.

- 2 tsp. butter
- 1 cup sugar
- 1 cup dark corn syrup
- 1 Tbsp. vinegar
- 1 Tbsp. baking soda
- 1 pkg. (11½ oz.) milk chocolate chips
- 1 Tbsp. shortening

1. Line a 13x9-in. pan with foil and grease the foil with butter; set aside. In a large heavy saucepan, combine the sugar, corn syrup and vinegar. Cook and stir over medium heat until sugar is dissolved. Bring to a boil. Cook, without stirring, until a candy thermometer reads 300° (hard-crack stage).
2. Remove from the heat; stir in baking soda. Immediately pour into prepared pan. Do not spread candy. Cool. Using foil, lift candy out of pan. Gently peel off foil; break candy into pieces.
3. In a microwave-safe bowl, melt chips and shortening; stir until smooth. Dip candies into the chocolate mixture, allowing excess to drip off. Place on waxed paper; let stand until set. Store in an airtight container.
2 OZ.: 223 cal., 7g fat (3g sat. fat), 5mg chol., 284mg sod., 41g carb. (28g sugars, 1g fiber), 2g pro.

HOLIDAY HELPER

The easiest way to dip candies into chocolate is to use a fork: Lay the candy on the fork, dip it into the chocolate, then let the excess chocolate drain off through the tines of the fork. Another quick and easy method (depending on your dexterity!) is to use chopsticks.

PEPPERMINT PRETZEL DIPPERS

A friend made these treats and gave them away in pretty canning jars. The combination of sweet, salty and peppermint is just right. For variety, try dipping them in white candy coating and rolling them in crushed candy canes.
—*Michelle Krzmarzick, Torrance, CA*

Prep: 15 min. + chilling
Makes: about 4 dozen

- 2 cups semisweet chocolate chips
- 1 Tbsp. shortening
- 1 pkg. (10 oz.) pretzel rods
- 40 red and/or green hard mint candies, crushed

In a microwave-safe bowl, melt chocolate chips and shortening; stir until smooth. Break each pretzel rod in half. Dip the broken end about halfway into melted chocolate; allow excess to drip off. Roll in crushed candies. Place on a waxed paper-lined baking sheet. Chill until set.
1 PRETZEL PIECE: 75 cal., 3g fat (1g sat. fat), 0 chol., 80mg sod., 13g carb. (7g sugars, 1g fiber), 1g pro.

CHERRY SWIRL FUDGE

For Christmas fudge with a new twist, give this confection a whirl! We used vanilla chips instead of the traditional chocolate and added fruit flavoring.
—Taste of Home *Test Kitchen*

Prep: 15 min. + chilling • **Makes:** 5 dozen

- 1½ tsp. butter
- 1 pkg. (10 to 12 oz.) white baking chips
- 1 can (16 oz.) or 2 cups vanilla frosting
- 1 tsp. cherry or almond extract
- 4 drops red liquid food coloring

1. Line an 8-in. square pan with foil; butter the foil. In a microwave-safe bowl, melt chips; stir until smooth. Beat in frosting and extract until smooth. Pour into prepared pan.
2. Randomly place drops of food coloring over the fudge; cut through fudge with a knife to swirl. Cover and refrigerate until firm, about 4 hours, before cutting into squares.
1 PIECE: 60 cal., 3g fat (1g sat. fat), 1mg chol., 21mg sod., 8g carb. (5g sugars, 0 fiber), 0 pro.

MINTY SNOWMEN

Each year I choose a different decorating theme for my holiday kickoff party—last time it was snowmen and snowflakes. These cute little snowman mints were fun to make and drew lots of smiles from guests.

—*Shelly Rynearson, Oconomowoc, WI*

Prep: 50 min. • **Makes:** 9 snowmen

- 1   Tbsp. butter, softened
- 1   Tbsp. light corn syrup
- ½   tsp. mint extract
- ⅛   tsp. salt
- 1   cup confectioners' sugar
      Red, green, blue and/or purple liquid or gel food coloring
      Colored sprinkles, nonpareils and cake decorator candies

1. Combine butter, corn syrup, extract and salt. Gradually stir in confectioners' sugar. Knead by hand until mixture becomes pliable, 1-2 minutes.

2. For each color of dough, combine 1 Tbsp. dough and food coloring (tint to desired shade); knead until blended. Leave remaining dough white. Roll white dough into a log; remove a fourth of the log and set aside.

3. For the snowmen's bodies, divide the main log into 9 pieces; roll each into a ball. For the snowmen's heads, divide the reserved white dough into 9 pieces and roll each into a ball. Stack 1 smaller ball on top of each larger ball.

4. Use the colored dough to form hats, scarves and earmuffs as desired. Use candies to make eyes, noses and buttons.

1 SNOWMAN: 80 cal., 1g fat (1g sat. fat), 4mg chol., 55mg sod., 17g carb. (15g sugars, 0 fiber), 0 pro.

SALTED PEANUT ROLLS

A Christmas gift of homemade candy is always a hit. I dip the bottoms of these peanut rolls in chocolate, but they're yummy plain too.

—*Elizabeth Hokanson, Arborg, MB*

Prep: 1 hour + freezing
Makes: about 5 dozen

- 1   jar (7 oz.) marshmallow creme
- 2   to 2¼ cups confectioners' sugar, divided
- 1   pkg. (14 oz.) caramels
- 2   Tbsp. water
- 4   cups salted peanuts, chopped
- 2   cups semisweet chocolate chips
- 2   tsp. shortening

1. Line two 15x10x1-in. pans with waxed paper. In a large bowl, beat marshmallow creme and 1 cup confectioners' sugar until blended. Knead in enough remaining confectioners' sugar until mixture is smooth and easy to handle.

2. Divide mixture into 4 portions. Roll each portion into a ½-in.-thick log. Cut each log crosswise into 1½-in. pieces; place pieces on 1 prepared pan. Freeze until firm, about 15 minutes. Meanwhile, heat the caramels and water over low heat until melted, stirring occasionally. Working with one-fourth of the pieces at a time, dip in melted caramel; roll in peanuts. Place on remaining prepared pan. Repeat with remaining pieces; freeze all until set.

3. In the top of a double boiler or a metal bowl over barely simmering water, melt chocolate chips and shortening; stir until smooth. Dip bottom of rolls into melted chocolate; allow excess to drip off. Return to prepared pans. Refrigerate until set. Store candies between layers of waxed paper in an airtight container at room temperature.

1 PIECE: 154 cal., 9g fat (3g sat. fat), 0 chol., 48mg sod., 18g carb. (15g sugars, 2g fiber), 3g pro.

CHOCOLATE-COVERED CHERRIES

Not only is this my family's favorite festive dessert, it also makes a delicious gift. The candy gets better as it's stored, with the centers becoming even juicier.
—*Linda Hammerich, Bonanza, OR*

Prep: 25 min. + chilling • **Makes:** 3 dozen

2½ cups confectioners' sugar
¼   cup butter, softened
1   Tbsp. 2% milk
½   tsp. almond extract
2   jars (8 oz. each) maraschino cherries
     with stems, well drained
2   cups semisweet chocolate chips
2   Tbsp. shortening

1. In a small bowl, combine the sugar, butter, milk and extract. Knead until smooth and pliable. Shape into 1-in. balls and flatten each into a 2-in. circle.
2. Wrap 1 circle around each cherry and lightly roll in hands. Place with stems up on a waxed paper-lined baking sheet. Cover loosely and refrigerate 4 hours or overnight.
3. In a microwave-safe bowl, melt chocolate and shortening; stir until smooth. Holding by the stems, dip cherries into chocolate; allow excess to drip off. Place on waxed paper until set. Store in a covered container. Refrigerate 1-2 weeks before serving.
2 CANDIES: 206 cal., 10g fat (5g sat. fat), 7mg chol., 28mg sod., 33g carb. (31g sugars, 1g fiber), 1g pro.

SPICY ALMONDS

We like to venture out into the Selkirk mountain range surrounding our family cabin. These nuts never tasted better than when we enjoyed them together at the peak at the end of an amazing hike. Almonds are extremely nutritious, and, when dressed up with a wonderful blend of spices, they go from ordinary to awesome!
—*Gina Myers, Spokane, WA*

Prep: 10 min. • **Bake:** 30 min. + cooling • **Makes:** 2½ cups

1   Tbsp. sugar
1½ tsp. kosher salt
1   tsp. paprika
½   tsp. ground cinnamon
½   tsp. ground cumin
½   tsp. ground coriander
¼   tsp. cayenne pepper
1   large egg white, room temperature
2½ cups unblanched almonds

Preheat oven to 325°. In a small bowl, combine the first 7 ingredients. In another bowl, whisk egg white until foamy. Add almonds; toss to coat. Sprinkle with spice mixture; toss to coat. Spread in a single layer in a greased 15x10x1-in. baking pan. Bake 30 minutes, stirring every 10 minutes. Spread on waxed paper to cool completely. Store in an airtight container.
¼ CUP: 230 cal., 20g fat (2g sat. fat), 0 chol., 293mg sod., 9g carb. (3g sugars, 4g fiber), 8g pro.

HOLIDAY HELPER

If you like, you can use this recipe with other kinds of nuts too. Try it with cashews, hazelnuts or macadamia nuts for a different look and taste.

CHRISTMAS IN AN INSTANT POT®

With all the bustle of the season, this ultra convenient gadget helps keep things on track by cutting down on cooking time and freeing up oven space. Whether you're planning for the feast or feeding a household during the holiday week, make the most of your Instant Pot!

EGGS IN PURGATORY

Tomatoes and red pepper flakes add spicy zing to these saucy eggs. Serve them with toasted bread or warm polenta rounds for an unforgettable morning meal.
—*Nick Iverson, Denver, CO*

Prep: 30 min. • **Cook:** 5 min. • **Makes:** 4 servings

- 2 cans (14½ oz. each) fire-roasted diced tomatoes, undrained
- 1 medium onion, chopped
- ½ cup water
- 2 Tbsp. canola oil
- 2 garlic cloves, minced
- 2 tsp. smoked paprika
- ½ tsp. sugar
- ½ tsp. crushed red pepper flakes
- ¼ cup tomato paste
- 4 large eggs
- ¼ cup shredded Manchego or Monterey Jack cheese
- 2 Tbsp. minced fresh parsley
- 1 tube (18 oz.) polenta, sliced and warmed, optional

1. Place the first 8 ingredients in a 6-qt. electric pressure cooker. Lock lid; close pressure-release valve. Adjust to pressure-cook on high for 4 minutes. Quick-release pressure.
2. Select saute setting and adjust for low heat. Add tomato paste; simmer, uncovered, until mixture is slightly thickened, about 10 minutes, stirring occasionally.
3. With the back of a spoon, make 4 wells in sauce. Break an egg into each well; sprinkle with cheese. Cover (do not lock lid). Simmer until the egg whites are completely set and yolks begin to thicken but are not hard, 8-10 minutes. Sprinkle with parsley. If desired, serve with polenta.
1 SERVING: 255 cal., 14g fat (4g sat. fat), 193mg chol., 676mg sod., 20g carb. (9g sugars, 3g fiber), 11g pro. **DIABETIC EXCHANGES:** 1½ fat, 1 starch, 1 medium-fat meat.

FRENCH ONION SOUP

I love French onion soup on a cold night, but I don't love the time it takes. This is my shortcut version for when we're pressed for time.
—*Teri Rasey, Cadillac, MI*

Prep: 20 min. • **Cook:** 15 min. • **Makes:** 16 servings (4 qt.)

- ⅓ cup butter
- 3 lbs. onions, thinly sliced (10 cups)
- 2 garlic cloves, minced
- 2 Tbsp. sugar
- 4 cups beef stock
- 4 cups chicken stock
- ¾ cup white wine
- 1 tsp. salt
  Optional: Salad croutons and grated Parmesan cheese

1. Select saute setting on a 6-qt. electric pressure cooker and adjust for medium heat; add butter. Add onion; cook and stir until tender, 6-8 minutes. Add garlic and sugar; cook 6 minutes longer. Stir in stocks, wine and salt. Press cancel. Lock lid; close pressure-release valve. Adjust to pressure-cook on high for 8 minutes.
2. Let pressure release naturally for 3 minutes; quick-release any remaining pressure. If desired, serve with croutons and Parmesan cheese.
1 CUP: 87 cal., 4g fat (2g sat. fat), 10mg chol., 724mg sod., 9g carb. (6g sugars, 1g fiber), 2g pro.

PRESSURE-COOKER CAPONATA

This Italian eggplant dip preps quickly and actually gets better as it stands. Serve it warm or at room temperature. Try adding a little leftover caponata to scrambled eggs for a savory breakfast.
—Nancy Beckman, Helena, MT

Prep: 20 min. • **Cook:** 5 min. • **Makes:** 6 cups

- 2 medium eggplants, cut into ½-in. pieces
- 1 can (14½ oz.) diced tomatoes, undrained
- 1 medium onion, chopped
- ½ cup dry red wine
- 12 garlic cloves, sliced
- 3 Tbsp. extra virgin olive oil
- 2 Tbsp. red wine vinegar
- 4 tsp. capers, undrained
- 5 bay leaves
- 1½ tsp. salt
- ¼ tsp. coarsely ground pepper
   French bread baguette slices, toasted
   Optional: Fresh basil leaves, toasted pine nuts and additional olive oil

1. Place the first 11 ingredients in a 6-qt. electric pressure cooker (do not stir). Lock lid; close pressure-release valve. Adjust to pressure-cook on high for 3 minutes. Quick-release pressure.

2. Cool slightly; discard bay leaves. Serve with toasted baguette slices and, if desired, fresh basil, toasted pine nuts and a drizzle of extra virgin olive oil.

¼ CUP: 34 cal., 2g fat (0 sat. fat), 0 chol., 189mg sod., 5g carb. (2g sugars, 2g fiber), 1g pro.

CELEBRATION BRUSSELS SPROUTS

This recipe hits all the flavor points for a fantastic side. Plus, you have to love a dish that requires minimal effort and doesn't take up oven space. You can always omit the bacon if you need a vegetarian option.
—Lauren McAnelly, Des Moines, IA

Prep: 20 min. • **Cook:** 5 min. • **Makes:** 10 servings

- 2 lbs. fresh Brussels sprouts, sliced
- 2 large apples (Fuji or Braeburn), chopped
- ⅓ cup dried cranberries
- 8 bacon strips, cooked and crumbled, divided
- ⅓ cup cider vinegar
- ¼ cup maple syrup
- 2 Tbsp. olive oil
- 1 tsp. salt
- ½ tsp. coarsely ground pepper
- ¾ cup chopped hazelnuts or pecans, toasted

Combine Brussels sprouts, apples, cranberries and half the crumbled bacon. In a small bowl, whisk vinegar, syrup, oil, salt and pepper; pour over Brussels sprouts mixture, tossing to coat. Transfer to a 6-qt. electric pressure cooker. Lock lid; close pressure-release valve. Adjust to pressure-cook on high for 3 minutes. Quick-release pressure. To serve, sprinkle with hazelnuts and remaining bacon.

1 SERVING: 204 cal., 11g fat (2g sat. fat), 7mg chol., 375mg sod., 24g carb. (15g sugars, 5g fiber), 6g pro.

HOLIDAY HELPER

To shave Brussels sprouts, first trim off the ends. Then put them in a food processor, slice with a mandoline, or halve and slice finely using a very sharp knife.

MARINATED MUSHROOMS

Here's a terrific healthy addition to any buffet spread. Mushrooms and pearl onions seasoned with herbs, balsamic vinegar and red wine are fantastic on their own or alongside a tenderloin roast.
—*Courtney Wilson, Fresno, CA*

Prep: 15 min. • **Cook:** 5 min. • **Makes:** 5 cups

- 2   lbs. medium fresh mushrooms
- 1   pkg. (14.4 oz.) frozen pearl onions
- 4   garlic cloves, minced
- ¾   cup reduced-sodium beef broth
- ¼   cup dry red wine
- 3   Tbsp. balsamic vinegar
- 3   Tbsp. olive oil
- 1   tsp. salt
- 1   tsp. dried basil
- ½   tsp. dried thyme
- ½   tsp. pepper
- ¼   tsp. crushed red pepper flakes

Place mushrooms, onions and garlic in a 6-qt. electric pressure cooker. In a small bowl, whisk remaining ingredients; pour over mushrooms. Lock lid; close pressure-release valve. Adjust to pressure-cook on high for 4 minutes. Quick-release pressure.

1 SERVING: 43 cal., 2g fat (0 sat. fat), 0 chol., 138mg sod., 4g carb. (2g sugars, 0 fiber), 1g pro.

HOLIDAY HELPER

To make these in a slow cooker, increase the broth to 2 cups and the wine to 1/2 cup; cook on low for 6-8 hours.

CURRIED PUMPKIN RISOTTO

This easy pumpkin risotto tastes like harvest season and gets a flavor boost from the curry.
—*Andrea Reaves, Stephens City, VA*

Prep: 15 min. • **Cook:** 15 min.
Makes: 6 servings

- 1   Tbsp. olive oil
- 1   small onion, chopped
- 1   cup uncooked arborio rice
- 2   garlic cloves, minced
- 2   cups chicken stock
- ½   cup canned pumpkin
- 1   Tbsp. curry powder
- 1½ tsp. minced fresh rosemary or
      ¾ tsp. dried rosemary, crushed
- ½   tsp. salt
- ¼   tsp. pepper

1. Select saute setting on a 6-qt. electric pressure cooker. Adjust for medium heat; add oil. When oil is hot, cook and stir onion until crisp-tender, 5-7 minutes. Add rice and garlic; cook and stir until rice is coated, 1-2 minutes. Add stock; cook 1 minute, stirring to loosen any browned bits from pan. Press cancel.
2. Stir in pumpkin, curry powder, rosemary, salt and pepper. Lock lid; close pressure-release valve. Adjust to pressure-cook on high for 7 minutes. Quick-release pressure. If desired, serve with additional minced rosemary.

SLOW-COOKER OPTION: Heat oil in a 3- or 4-qt. slow cooker on high until hot. Add rice; stir to coat. Stir in the remaining ingredients. Cook, covered, on low until rice is tender, 3-4 hours, stirring halfway through cooking.

½ CUP: 163 cal., 3g fat (0 sat. fat), 0 chol., 369mg sod., 30g carb. (2g sugars, 2g fiber), 4g pro. **DIABETIC EXCHANGES:** 2 starch, ½ fat.

BEEF SHORT RIBS WITH CHUTNEY

Slow-roasted tender meats can happen in half the time if you have the right equipment. I like to serve these savory beef short ribs over mashed potatoes, egg noodles or rice.
—*Caitlin Marcellino, Apopka, FL*

Prep: 30 min. • **Cook:** 35 min. + releasing
Makes: 4 servings

- 1   tsp. olive oil
- 3   bacon strips, chopped
- 1   lb. boneless beef short ribs
- ½   tsp. salt
- ¼   tsp. pepper
- 1   lb. grape tomatoes
- 1   medium onion, chopped
- 3   garlic cloves, minced
- 2   cups water
- 1   cup Marsala wine or beef broth
- ¼   cup fig preserves
- 3   Tbsp. minced fresh rosemary or
      1 Tbsp. dried rosemary, crushed

1. Select saute setting on a 6-qt. electric pressure cooker. Adjust for medium heat; add oil. When oil is hot, cook and stir bacon until crisp. Remove with a slotted spoon; drain on paper towels. Sprinkle ribs with salt and pepper. Brown on all sides in the drippings. Remove from pressure cooker.

2. Add tomatoes, onion and garlic to drippings; cook and stir until crisp-tender, 3-5 minutes, mashing tomatoes lightly. Stir in water, Marsala, preserves and rosemary. Cook for 1 minute, stirring to loosen browned bits. Press cancel.

3. Return ribs and bacon to pressure cooker. Lock lid; close pressure-release valve. Adjust to pressure-cook on high for 35 minutes. Let pressure release naturally. Remove ribs; shred with 2 forks and serve with tomato chutney and cooking liquid.

SLOW-COOKER OPTION: In a large skillet, heat oil over medium heat; cook and stir bacon until crisp. Remove with a slotted spoon; drain on paper towels. Sprinkle ribs with salt and pepper. Brown on all sides in drippings. Transfer to a 4-qt. slow cooker. In same skillet, add tomatoes, onion and garlic to drippings; cook and stir until crisp-tender, 3-5 minutes, mashing tomatoes lightly. Add tomato mixture to slow cooker; stir in water, Marsala, preserves and rosemary. Cook, covered, on low 6-8 hours or until ribs are tender. Remove ribs; shred with 2 forks and serve with tomato chutney and cooking liquid.

1 SERVING: 368 cal., 19g fat (7g sat. fat), 60mg chol., 472mg sod., 25g carb. (18g sugars, 2g fiber), 19g pro.

CONVERTING INSTANT POT® RECIPES

Many home cooks swear by this super timesaving gadget, but if you don't have an Instant Pot, you can still use the same recipes with a few adjustments.

For cooking on the stovetop or in the oven, anything that is cooked on the saute setting in the Instant Pot can be sauteed in a pan on the stovetop instead. Then, for oven cooking, increase the cook time by a factor of 3, and set the oven temperature to 375°. You may need to add more liquid to your recipe, as liquid will not evaporate from the pressure cooker as it will from a traditional cooking pot.

Converting Instant Pot recipes to the slow cooker isn't a one-size-fits-all conversion. Again, any sauteing should be done on the stovetop before being transferred to the slow cooker. As a general rule, 30 minutes of cook time in an Instant Pot is roughly equal to 4 hours on high or 8 hours on low in the slow cooker. Remember to add any dairy ingredients late in the cooking time.

HERBED TURKEY BREASTS

An array of flavorful herbs enhance tender turkey breasts in this juicy, comforting dish.
—*Laurie Mace, Los Osos, CA*

Prep: 25 min. + marinating
Cook: 20 min. + releasing
Makes: 12 servings

- 1   can (14½ oz.) chicken broth
- ½   cup lemon juice
- ¼   cup packed brown sugar
- ¼   cup fresh sage
- ¼   cup fresh thyme leaves
- ¼   cup lime juice
- ¼   cup cider vinegar
- ¼   cup olive oil
- 1   envelope onion soup mix
- 2   Tbsp. Dijon mustard
- 1   Tbsp. minced fresh marjoram
- 1½ tsp. paprika
- 1   tsp. garlic powder
- 1   tsp. pepper
- ½   tsp. salt
- 2   boneless skinless turkey breast halves (2 lbs. each)
      Optional: Additional fresh thyme, marjoram and lemon wedges

1. In a blender, process the first 15 ingredients until blended. Place turkey in a bowl or shallow dish; pour marinade over turkey and turn to coat. Refrigerate, covered, 8 hours or overnight, turning occasionally.
2. Transfer turkey and marinade to a 6-qt. electric pressure cooker. Lock lid; close pressure-release valve. Adjust to pressure-cook on high for 20 minutes.
3. Let pressure release naturally for 10 minutes; quick-release any remaining pressure. A thermometer inserted in turkey breasts should read at least 165°.
4. Remove turkey from pressure cooker; tent with foil. Let stand 10 minutes before slicing. If desired, top with additional fresh thyme and marjoram and serve with lemon wedges.

5 OZ. COOKED TURKEY: 219 cal., 5g fat (1g sat. fat), 87mg chol., 484mg sod., 5g carb. (3g sugars, 0 fiber), 36g pro. **DIABETIC EXCHANGES:** 5 lean meat.

STEAMED MUSSELS WITH PEPPERS

Here's a worthy way to use your one-pot cooker! Serve French bread along with the mussels to soak up the deliciously seasoned broth. If you like your food spicy, add the jalapeno seeds.
—*Taste of Home Test Kitchen*

Prep: 30 min. • **Cook:** 5 min.
Makes: 4 servings

- 2   lbs. fresh mussels, scrubbed and beards removed
- 2   Tbsp. olive oil
- 1   jalapeno pepper, seeded and chopped
- 3   garlic cloves, minced
- 1   bottle (8 oz.) clam juice
- ½   cup white wine or additional clam juice
- ⅓   cup chopped sweet red pepper
- 3   green onions, sliced
- ½   tsp. dried oregano
- 1   bay leaf
- 2   Tbsp. minced fresh parsley
- ¼   tsp. salt
- ¼   tsp. pepper
      French bread baguette, sliced, optional

1. Tap mussels; discard any that do not close. Set aside. Select saute setting on a 6-qt. electric pressure cooker. Adjust for medium heat; add oil. When oil is hot, cook and stir jalapeno until crisp-tender, 2-3 minutes. Add garlic; cook 1 minute longer. Press cancel.
2. Stir in mussels, clam juice, wine, red pepper, green onions, oregano and bay leaf. Lock lid; close pressure-release valve. Adjust to pressure-cook on high 2 minutes. Quick-release pressure.
3. Discard bay leaf and any unopened mussels. Sprinkle with parsley, salt and pepper. If desired, serve with baguette slices.
NOTE: Wear disposable gloves when cutting hot peppers; the oils can burn skin. Avoid touching your face.
12 MUSSELS: 293 cal., 12g fat (2g sat. fat), 65mg chol., 931mg sod., 12g carb. (1g sugars, 1g fiber), 28g pro.

HOLIDAY HELPER

Before cooking mussels, always clean them. Rinse them with cold water in a colander, shaking gently. Use a sharp knife to remove any beards (furry patches) still attached to the mussels. Discard any mussel that isn't closed, or doesn't close when you tap it.

TOMATO-POACHED HALIBUT

Simple halibut with a burst of lemon comes together easily. Serve it with bread or—even better—try it with polenta or angel hair pasta.

—*Danna Rogers, Westport, CT*

Prep: 15 min. • **Cook:** 5 min.
Makes: 4 servings

- 1   Tbsp. olive oil
- 2   poblano peppers, finely chopped
- 1   small onion, finely chopped
- 1   can (14½ oz.) fire-roasted diced tomatoes, undrained
- 1   can (14½ oz.) no-salt-added diced tomatoes, undrained
- ½   cup water
- ¼   cup chopped pitted green olives
- 3   garlic cloves, minced
- ¼   tsp. pepper
- ⅛   tsp. salt
- 4   halibut fillets (4 oz. each)
- ⅓   cup chopped fresh cilantro
- 4   lemon wedges
     Crusty whole grain bread, optional

1. Select saute setting on a 6-qt. electric pressure cooker. Adjust for medium heat; add oil. When oil is hot, cook and stir poblano peppers and onion until crisp-tender, 2-3 minutes. Press cancel.

2. Stir in tomatoes, water, olives, garlic, pepper and salt. Top with fillets. Lock lid; close pressure-release valve. Adjust to pressure-cook on high for 3 minutes. Quick-release pressure.
A thermometer inserted in fish should read at least 145°.

3. Sprinkle with cilantro. Serve with lemon wedges and, if desired, bread.

NOTE: Wear disposable gloves when cutting hot peppers; the oils can burn skin. Avoid touching your face.

1 FILLET WITH 1 CUP SAUCE: 215 cal., 7g fat (1g sat. fat), 56mg chol., 614mg sod., 16g carb. (7g sugars, 3g fiber), 23g pro.
DIABETIC EXCHANGES: 3 lean meat, 1 starch, ½ fat.

MOLTEN MOCHA CAKE

When I first made my decadent chocolate cake, my husband's and daughter's expressions said it all. Later, I took one of these to our next-door neighbors. Their teenage son, who answered the door, ate the whole thing without telling anyone else about it!

—*Aimee Fortney, Fairview, TN*

Prep: 10 min. • **Cook:** 25 min. + releasing
Makes: 6 servings

- 4   large eggs, room temperature
- 1½ cups sugar
- ½   cup butter, melted
- 1   Tbsp. vanilla extract
- 1   cup all-purpose flour
- ½   cup baking cocoa
- 1   Tbsp. instant coffee granules
- ¼   tsp. salt
     Optional: Fresh raspberries or sliced fresh strawberries and vanilla ice cream

1. Place trivet insert and 1 cup water in a 6-qt. electric pressure cooker. In a large bowl, beat eggs, sugar, butter and vanilla until blended. In another bowl, whisk flour, cocoa, coffee granules and salt; gradually beat into the egg mixture.

2. Transfer to a greased 1½-qt. baking dish. Cover loosely with foil to prevent moisture from getting into dish. Fold an 18x12-in. piece of foil lengthwise into thirds, making a sling. Use the sling to lower the dish onto the trivet. Lock lid; close pressure-release valve. Adjust to pressure-cook on high for 25 minutes.

3. Allow pressure to naturally release for 10 minutes, then quick-release any remaining pressure. A toothpick should come out with moist crumbs. Using foil sling, carefully remove baking dish. If desired, serve warm cake with berries and ice cream.

1 SERVING: 482 cal., 19g fat (11g sat. fat), 165mg chol., 269mg sod., 71g carb. (51g sugars, 2g fiber), 8g pro.
TURTLE FLAVOR MOLTEN MOCHA CAKE: Top with caramel and chopped nuts.

CRANBERRY APPLE RED CABBAGE

When I was looking for something new, I started playing with flavors and came up with this very tasty dish. My German grandmother would be impressed, I think! The colorful side is just right with pork.
—Ann Sheehy, Lawrence, MA

Prep: 15 min. • **Cook:** 5 min.
Makes: 8 servings

 1 medium head red cabbage, coarsely chopped
 1 can (14 oz.) whole-berry cranberry sauce
 2 medium Granny Smith apples, peeled and coarsely chopped
 1 medium onion, chopped
 ½ cup cider vinegar
 ¼ cup sweet vermouth, white wine or unsweetened apple juice, optional
 1 tsp. kosher salt
 ¾ tsp. caraway seeds
 ½ tsp. coarsely ground pepper

Combine all ingredients including vermouth if desired; transfer to a 6-qt. electric pressure cooker. Lock lid; close pressure-release valve. Adjust to pressure-cook on high for 3 minutes. Allow pressure to naturally release for 5 minutes. Quick-release any remaining pressure. Serve with a slotted spoon.
¾ CUP: 144 cal., 0 fat (0 sat. fat), 0 chol., 296mg sod., 34g carb. (21g sugars, 4g fiber), 2g pro.

MIXED FRUIT & PISTACHIO CAKE

This cake is a guaranteed-delicious dessert for several days, if you can make it last that long. It's a wonderful treat for the holidays.
—Nancy Heishman, Las Vegas, NV

Prep: 20 min. • **Cook:** 50 min. + cooling
Makes: 8 servings

 1½ cups all-purpose flour
 1½ tsp. ground cinnamon
 ½ tsp. baking soda
 ½ tsp. baking powder
 ½ tsp. ground allspice
 ¼ tsp. salt
 1 can (8 oz.) jellied cranberry sauce
 ⅓ cup packed brown sugar
 ⅓ cup buttermilk
 ¼ cup butter, melted
 2 tsp. grated orange zest
 ½ tsp. orange extract
 1 large egg, room temperature
 1 cup mixed dried fruit bits
 1 cup pistachios, chopped
   Optional: Whipped cream and additional chopped pistachios

1. Place trivet insert and 1 cup water in a 6-qt. electric pressure cooker.
2. In a bowl, whisk together the dry ingredients. In another bowl, combine the next 7 ingredients. Add the cranberry mixture to the flour mixture; stir until smooth. Add dried fruit and pistachios.
3. Pour batter into a greased 1½-qt. baking dish. Cover dish with aluminum foil. Fold an 18x12-in. piece of foil lengthwise into thirds, making a sling. Use sling to lower dish onto trivet. Lock lid; close pressure-release valve. Adjust to pressure-cook on high for 50 minutes.
4. Allow pressure to naturally release for 15 minutes, then quick-release any remaining pressure. A toothpick inserted in center of cake should come out clean. Using foil sling, carefully remove baking dish to a wire rack. Cool 30 minutes before inverting onto a serving platter.
5. Cut into wedges with a serrated knife; if desired, serve with whipped cream and additional pistachios.
1 PIECE: 385 cal., 14g fat (5g sat. fat), 39mg chol., 364mg sod., 59g carb. (32g sugars, 4g fiber), 7g pro.

PORK WITH APPLES & DRIED PLUMS

The classic flavors of herbes de Provence, apples and dried plums make this easy pork dish taste like a hearty meal at a French country cafe. For a traditional pairing, serve with braised lentils.
—*Suzanne Banfield, Basking Ridge, NJ*

Prep: 20 min.
Cook: 35 min. + releasing
Makes: 10 servings

1   boneless pork loin roast (3 to 4 lbs.)
2   Tbsp. all-purpose flour
1   Tbsp. herbes de Provence
1½   tsp. salt
¾   tsp. pepper
2   Tbsp. olive oil
1   cup apple cider or unsweetened apple juice
2   medium onions, halved and thinly sliced
1   cup beef stock
2   bay leaves
2   large tart apples, peeled and chopped
1   cup pitted dried plums (prunes)

1. Halve roast. Mix flour, herbes de Provence, salt and pepper; rub over pork. Select saute or browning setting on a 6-qt. electric pressure cooker. Adjust for medium heat; add 1 Tbsp. oil. When oil is hot, brown a roast half on all sides. Remove; repeat with remaining pork and oil.
2. Add cider to pressure cooker. Cook 1 minute, stirring to loosen browned bits. Press cancel. Add the onions, stock, bay leaves and roast.
3. Lock lid; close pressure-release valve. Adjust to pressure-cook on high for 25 minutes. Let pressure release naturally for 10 minutes; quick-release any remaining pressure. A thermometer inserted in pork should read at least 145°. Remove roast and onions to a serving platter, discarding the bay leaves; tent with foil.
4. Select saute setting and adjust for low heat. Add apples and plums; simmer, uncovered, until apples are tender, 6-8 minutes, stirring occasionally. Serve with roast.

4 OZ. COOKED PORK WITH ¾ CUP FRUIT MIXTURE: 286 cal., 9g fat (3g sat. fat), 68mg chol., 449mg sod., 22g carb. (13g sugars, 2g fiber), 28g pro.

WINTER FRUIT COMPOTE

You can make this vibrant and easy fruit relish up to a week in advance. It's an outstanding accompaniment to all kinds of holiday menus.
—*Esther Chesney, Carthage, MO*

Prep: 5 min. • **Cook:** 5 min.
Makes: 2½ cups

1   pkg. (12 oz.) fresh or 3 cups frozen cranberries
⅔   cup packed brown sugar
¼   cup thawed orange juice concentrate
2   Tbsp. raspberry vinegar
½   cup chopped dried apricots
½   cup golden raisins
½   cup chopped walnuts, toasted

1. In a 6-qt. electric pressure cooker, combine cranberries, brown sugar, orange juice concentrate and vinegar. Lock lid; close pressure-release valve. Adjust to pressure-cook on high for 3 minutes. Let pressure release naturally for 5 minutes; quick-release any remaining pressure.
2. Stir in apricots, raisins and walnuts. Refrigerate leftovers.

2 TBSP.: 161 cal., 4g fat (0 sat. fat), 0 chol., 32mg sod., 32g carb. (28g sugars, 3g fiber), 2g pro.

HOLIDAY HELPER

Serve this compote over waffles, pancakes or French toast and sprinkle with powdered sugar. It also goes well with savory meat dishes. Try it as a sauce for pork, chicken or turkey.

Getting Ready for the Holidays

PARTY TIMELINE

This useful checklist will help you budget your time wisely and keep your party on schedule.

1 MONTH PRIOR:

❑ Choose date and time.

❑ Set budget.

❑ Determine guest list.

3 WEEKS PRIOR:

❑ Send out invitations (ask about any food allergies).

❑ Check to make sure you have enough chairs, linens, serving dishes and utensils. Rent or buy more if needed.

❑ Arrange for a helper (this would be a good thing to ask an older child or teenager to do).

2 WEEKS PRIOR:

❑ Plan the menu; create a master shopping list.

❑ Make a large grocery shopping trip to buy nonperishables and ingredients for freezer-friendly dishes. Prepare and freeze any dishes that can be made in advance.

1 WEEK PRIOR:

❑ Follow up with any guests who haven't responded.

❑ Clean the house thoroughly; put away breakable items.

❑ Stock the bar.

❑ Choose the music.

2 TO 3 DAYS PRIOR:

❑ Notify neighbors if cars will be parked on the street.

❑ Clean glassware, china and silverware. Wash and iron table linens.

❑ Think about the party space: Where will coats go? Where are the trash cans? How will people move around your house? Move furniture if necessary. Set up cleanup stations (salt, stain remover, club soda, clean cloths) to have at the ready.

❑ Put up decorations.

❑ Finish grocery shopping.

1 DAY PRIOR:

❑ Buy flowers.

❑ Finish as much of the cooking and prep work as possible.

❑ Do a quick cleanup of the house. Check the guest bathroom—empty trash and set out fresh hand towels.

DAY OF:

❑ Chill wine, set up the bar, and slice lemons and any other garnishes.

❑ Set the table and/or buffet.

❑ Finish any cooking.

❑ Set aside space for dirty dishes.

❑ Take out trash; have trash cans and extra garbage bags ready.

HOW TO SET THE TABLE

- The dinner plate is the center of the place setting; everything else is positioned around it. Arrange the flatware in the order in which it will be used.

- Forks go to the left of the plate. If you're serving a salad, place a small salad fork to the left of the dinner fork. Place the napkin under the forks or on the plate.

- The knife and spoons go to the right of the plate. Place the knife with the sharp edge toward the plate. The soupspoon goes outside of the teaspoon. If soup is to be served, set the bowl on the plate.

- The dessert utensil—whether a fork or a spoon—can either be placed horizontally above the plate or be brought out when dessert is served.

- Smaller plates for salad or bread go above and to the left of the forks. Position the butter plate with the butter spreader across the plate.

- Cup and saucer go above the spoons with the handle to the right.

- Water and wine glasses go to the left of the coffee cup; the water glass goes on the left.

HOW MUCH FOOD & DRINK TO SERVE

Take the stress out of planning with our guide for how many drinks and how much food to stock, course by course. A good rule of thumb is to round up from these and err on the side of having too much—better to end up with a few leftovers than to leave your guests hungry.

APPETIZERS

On average, each guest will have about six appetizers (this number may double if you're having a cocktail-style event). Stock up on bulk items like nuts, pretzels and olives, both to supplement prepared appetizers and to set out before guests arrive.

Guests	Appetizers
5	30 appetizers
10	60 appetizers
20	120 appetizers

ENTREES AND SIDES

- Poultry, fish or meat: 6 oz. per serving
- Grains: 1½ oz. as a side dish, 2 oz. as a main dish casserole
- Potatoes: 5 oz.
- Vegetables: 4 oz.
- Beans: 2 oz.
- Pasta: 4 oz. (main dish)
- Bread such as buns, rolls or cornbread: 1 to 2 pieces

DESSERTS

Guests	Cake/Tart/Pastry	Creamy Dessert	Ice Cream
5	5 pieces	20 oz.	25 oz.
10	10 pieces	40 oz.	50 oz.
20	20 pieces	80 oz.	100 oz.

DRINKS

These guidelines are for parties that last two hours, if serving one type of alcohol—if you're offering more, reduce the amount of each type. Figure on 1 lb. of ice per guest.

Guests	Wine/Champagne	Beer	Spirits	Liqueurs	Nonalcoholic
5	3 bottles	15 bottles	1 bottle	1 bottle	5 *(if serving alcohol as well)* / 15 *(if not)*
10	5 bottles	30 bottles	2 bottles	1 bottle	10/30
20	10 bottles	60 bottles	4 bottles	2 bottles	20/60

Holiday Menus

Use these menu cards to record what you served at Christmas dinner and other seasonal gatherings. Make note of beverage pairings, ingredient substitutions or anything else you want to remember about your holiday menu.

OCCASION: _____

GUESTS: _____

_____

_____

_____

_____

FOOD: _____

_____

_____

_____

_____

_____

_____

_____

_____

DRINKS: _____

_____

_____

NOTES: _____

_____

_____

_____

OCCASION: _____

GUESTS: _____

_____

_____

_____

_____

FOOD: _____

_____

_____

_____

_____

_____

_____

_____

_____

DRINKS: _____

_____

_____

NOTES: _____

_____

_____

_____

OCCASION: _____

GUESTS: _____

_____

_____

_____

_____

FOOD: _____

_____

_____

_____

_____

_____

_____

_____

DRINKS: _____

_____

_____

NOTES: _____

_____

_____

_____

_____

_____

OCCASION: _____

GUESTS: _____

_____

_____

_____

_____

FOOD: _____

_____

_____

_____

_____

_____

_____

_____

DRINKS: _____

_____

_____

NOTES: _____

_____

_____

_____

_____

_____

Holiday Memories

FAMILY MILESTONES

What major events happened in your family this year? Births, weddings, graduations, a new home or job, or a particularly memorable vacation?

_____

_____

_____

_____

_____

_____

_____

_____

_____

_____

_____

_____

_____

_____

_____

_____

MEMORIES OF THE FEAST

What was most memorable about the time spent around the holiday table? What things did your loved ones say or do that you want to remember? Ask your family a question—what are they most thankful for, or which dish was their favorite— and record their answers!

_____

_____

_____

_____

_____

_____

_____

_____

_____

_____

_____

_____

_____

_____

SPECIAL PEOPLE

Whom did you see this year that you hadn't seen in a while? Who came to visit, or hosted you? Who sent a particularly lovely card, or a favorite gift?

_____

_____

_____

_____

ALL ABOUT THE COOKIES!

What cookies did you make this year, and which were your favorites?
Who is on your list for getting a cookie platter or box?

_____

_____

_____

_____

RECIPE NOTES

What other recipes did you try this year? Any changes you want to make the next time around?

_____

_____

_____

_____

For Next Year

GIFTS & STOCKING STUFFERS

Have a great idea for a gift for next Christmas? Make a note of it so you remember it when Christmas-shopping season rolls around.

CHRISTMAS CARD LIST

Keep track of everyone who should be on your list to get a holiday card!

RECIPES TO TRY

If there are recipes you wanted to try but just didn't have time for, jot them down here so you can include them in future celebrations.

_____

_____

_____

_____

_____

_____

_____

_____

_____

_____

_____

_____

_____

DECORATION IDEAS

Don't let your brainstorms be forgotten—record your ideas for festive decor here to get a jump on next year.

_____

_____

_____

_____

_____

_____

_____

RESTOCK!

What did you use the last of that you'll need next December? Wrapping paper? Ribbon? Shipping boxes? Make a list and check back next fall.

_____

_____

_____

_____

_____

INDEX

This index lists every recipe in the book in alphabetical order.
Just search for the titles when you want to find your favorites.
On page 240, you'll find an index of all the special bonus content—
including homemade gifts and decor, tips, how-tos and more!

P. 159

P. 42

P. 157

BONUS CONTENT